Technical Services Today
and Tomorrow

Technical Services Today
and
Tomorrow

MICHAEL GORMAN
and associates

1990
LIBRARIES UNLIMITED, INC.
Englewood, Colorado

LIBRARIES UNLIMITED, INC.
P.O. Box 3988
Englewood, CO 80155-3988

Library of Congress Cataloging-in-Publication Data

Technical services today and tomorrow / Michael Gorman [compiler].
   xvi, 207p. 17x25cm
   Includes bibliographical references.
   ISBN 0-87287-608-X
   1. Processing (Libraries)   I. Gorman, Michael, 1941- .
Z688.5.T43   1990
025'.02--dc20

          90-34856
          CIP

CONTENTS

Acknowledgments xi

Contributors xiii

Introduction xv

Technical Services Today, *Michael Gorman* 1
    Notes 5

ACQUISITIONS

The Ordering, Claiming, and Receipt of Materials,
    Karen A. Schmidt 7
    Procedures 7
    Organization 10
    Staffing 11
    Future Trends 12
    Notes 13

A Perspective on Library Book Gathering Plans,
    Edward J. Lockman, with Edna Laughrey and
    Kevin Coyle 15
    The Approval Plan 15
    The Blanket Order Plan 18
    A New Gathering Plan Proposal 19
    Further Readings 22

Gifts and Exchanges, *Joseph W. Barker*.................................23
    Exchanges...23
    Gifts...26
    Trends and Likely Futures.................................29
        Organizational Trends.............................29
        Automation Trends................................30
        Trends in Policy: Costs/Benefits, Assessing and Supporting
          Real Needs....................................31
        Other Factors Affecting Trends in Gifts and Exchanges...........34
    General Observations......................................35
    Notes..35
    Further Readings..37

Serial Acquisitions: Trends and Prospects, *Betsy Kruger*...................38
    Trends in Journal Publishing and Pricing.......................39
    Serial Vendor Selection, Services, and Evaluation.....................41
    Serials Automation..44
    Trends in Serials Automation................................45
    Notes..47

Monitoring the Information Resources Budget: Acquisitions
    Accounting, *Jennifer Cargill*.................................50
    Importance of Monitoring...................................51
    From the Materials Budget to the Information Resources
      Budget...51
    Accounting within the Library...............................52
        Acquisitions Accounting...........................52
        Location..53
        Accountability...................................54
        Access to Accounting Information....................54
        What to Monitor?................................54
        Work Flow......................................55
        Staffing..56
        System Planning.................................57
        Statistics and Reports.............................58
        Other Issues of Concern...........................58
    Summary and Prospects....................................60
    Further Readings..61

BIBLIOGRAPHIC CONTROL

Descriptive Cataloguing: Its Past, Present, and Future,
    Michael Gorman..63
    Bibliographic Description...................................64
    Access Points..67
    Authority Files...69
    MARC and the Future of Descriptive Cataloguing...................70
    Notes..72
    Further Readings..73

Subject Cataloguing and Classification: The Late 1980s
and Beyond, *Lois Mai Chan and Theodora Hodges* 74
Subject Cataloguing 76
    Keyword Searching 77
    Boolean Operations 78
    Limiting 78
    Automatic Switching (Synonym Operation) 78
    Subject Browsing 79
    Improvements 79
Classification 80
    Classification Schemes as Enhanced Vocabulary 80
    Classification in Online Subject Browsing 81
    Class Number or Call Number Searching 82
Conclusion 82
Notes 83
Further Readings 84

Authority Work, Authority Records, and Authority Files,
Arnold S. Wajenberg 86
The Need for Authority Work 86
Cooperative Authority Work 88
Authority Work in Online Catalogues 88
The Use of References in Online Catalogues 89
Catalogue Maintenance 91
Notes 92
Further Readings 94

Copy Cataloguing and the Bibliographic Networks,
Leslie A. Bleil and Charlene Renner 95
Historical Perspective 96
Networks 96
Quality Control 98
Economic Realities 99
Role of the Library of Congress 100
Future Trends 101
Notes 103
Further Readings 103

SPECIAL TOPICS

Preservation in the Research Library: Its Past, Present
Status, and Encouraging Future, *Norman B. Brown* 105
Preservation's American Past 106
The Reorganization of Research Libraries 106
The Paper Problem: Its Nature, Dimensions, and
    Resolution 108
    The Reformatting of Embrittled Materials 109
    Mass Deacidification Systems 110
The Search for a National Preservation Strategy 112

Special Topics — *continued*
Preservation Today and Tomorrow......................114
The Institutional Preservation Program........................114
Selection.........................116
Prevention.........................117
Preservation Microfilming.........................118
Mass Deacidification.........................120
Preservation Priorities.........................120
Notes.........................122

Slavic Technical Services, *Robert H. Burger*.........................130
Acquisitions.........................131
Organization and Administration.........................131
Blanket Orders.........................132
Exchange Agreements.........................132
Recordkeeping.........................133
Financial Aspects.........................134
Preservation.........................134
Cataloguing.........................135
Organization and Administration.........................135
Personnel.........................135
Special Problems.........................136
Future of Slavic Technical Services.........................139
Notes.........................140
Further Readings.........................141

AUTOMATION AND TECHNICAL SERVICES

Circulation Services, *Marsha J. Stevenson and*
Paul M. Anderson.........................143
Manual Files.........................145
Keypunch Cards.........................146
Online Systems.........................146
Problems.........................151
Conclusion.........................155
Notes.........................155

The Evolving Online Catalogue in Academic Libraries,
William Gray Potter.........................157
The Generic Online Catalogue.........................157
Changing Traditional Technical Services Functions.........................158
Collection Development and Selection.........................158
Acquisitions.........................158
Cataloguing.........................159
Catalogue Maintenance.........................160
Summary.........................161
New Technical Services Functions.........................161
Retrospective Conversion.........................161
Enhanced Access.........................162

Remote Access..163
Transaction Monitoring..................................163
Intelligent Workstations................................163
Additional Files...164
Gateway...164
Hierarchy of Databases..................................165
Evolution to Full Text...................................166
The Online Catalogue and Electronic Publishing.............166
Changes in Staffing and Organization......................167
Conclusion 167
Notes 168

ADMINISTRATION OF TECHNICAL SERVICES

**Technical Services Organization: Where We Have Been
and Where We Are Going,** *Jennifer A. Younger
and D. Kaye Gapen*..171
Historical Background...171
Contemporary Influences......................................172
Specialized Knowledge and New Departments....................173
Economies of Scale and New Departments.......................173
Coordination of Work Flow and New Departments.................173
Coordination, Not Direction, of Technical Services.............174
Criticisms of the Technical Services Division Concept...............175
Brief Review of Advantages and Disadvantages..................176
A Second Paradigm Shift Is on the Way..........................176
Social Psychology and Group Dynamics.........................176
Changing Paradigms of Library Services........................177
Technical Services in the Year 2001.............................178
Original Cataloguing Becomes Part of Public Services............179
Technical Services in a User- or Subject-Oriented
        Department..179
Decentralized Technical Services..............................180
Technical Services Coordinators...............................180
Conclusion 181
Notes 181

Technical Services Budgeting and Finance, *Susan F. Rhee*.................184
The Purpose of, and Need for, a Budget.........................185
Types of Budgets and Budgeting Systems.........................186
The Budget Cycle...188
Implementing a Participatory Budgetary Process.................189
Trends in Technical Services Budgeting.........................190
Conclusion 192
Further Readings...192

POSTSCRIPTUM

Technical Services Tomorrow, *Michael Gorman*. 195

Index 199

ACKNOWLEDGMENTS

My thanks are due, firstly and most obviously, to my associates—the authors of the chapters in this book, many of whom were colleagues of mine at the Library of the University of Illinois at Urbana-Champaign in happier times. The quality of their contributions will become evident as you read. I also wish to thank them for their superhuman forbearance during the very long time it has taken me to assemble the book. My sincere thanks for their assistance are also due to Janet Bancroft, Lisa Boise, Jennifer Osborne, and especially Anne Phillips. I am grateful to Karen Schmidt for her advice and assistance throughout the project. Lastly, I wish to thank Bohdan Wynar and the staff of Libraries Unlimited for their patience and encouragement.

Michael Gorman

CONTRIBUTORS

Paul M. Anderson

Head of Access Services
University of Delaware

Joseph W. Barker

Acquisitions Librarian
University of California at Berkeley

Leslie A. Bleil

Cataloguer
Western Michigan University

Norman B. Brown

Assistant Director for Special Collections
    and Preservation
University of Illinois at Urbana-Champaign

Robert H. Burger

Head, Slavic and East European Library
University of Illinois at Urbana-Champaign

Jennifer Cargill

Associate University Librarian
Rice University

Lois Mai Chan

Professor, College of Library and Information
    Science
University of Kentucky

Kevin Coyle

Midwestern Regional Sales Manager
The Blackwell Group

D. Kaye Gapen	Dean, General Library System University of Wisconsin, Madison
Michael Gorman	Dean of Library Services California State University, Fresno
Theodora Hodges	formerly on the faculty of the School of Library and Information Studies University of California at Berkeley
Betsy Kruger	Assistant Acquisitions & Binding Librarian University of Illinois at Urbana-Champaign
Edna Laughrey	Manager, Continuation Services Faxon
Edward J. Lockman	Director, Continuation Services Faxon
William Gray Potter	University Librarian University of Georgia
Charlene Renner	University Librarian Western Michigan University
Susan F. Rhee	Associate Director, Technical Services University of California at Berkeley
Karen A. Schmidt	Acquisitions Librarian University of Illinois at Urbana-Champaign
Marsha J. Stevenson	Head of Reference University of Notre Dame
Arnold S. Wajenberg	Principal Cataloguer University of Illinois at Urbana-Champaign
Jennifer A. Younger	Assistant Director, Central Technical Services University of Wisconsin, Madison

INTRODUCTION

The purpose of this book is to examine the present state of each of the major areas of technical services in libraries, to provide individual views on the future of those areas and of technical services in general, and to furnish the reader with further readings on the topic in question. We hope that the book will be useful to students and teachers of librarianship and to practicing librarians of all kinds who wish to know more about technical services topics. Though the chapters in this book are, by and large, not for the absolute beginner, the topics should have been rendered accessible to the general reader who is a librarian or library school student.

It should be noted that the majority of contributors to this book have an academic/research library background. In one or two instances, notably in the chapter on preservation, the discussion is largely or wholly devoted to academic/research library concerns. In the other chapters, a conscious effort has been made to generalize the topic and, thus, make it interesting and relevant to the reader no matter what her or his library background may be.

In 1954, Maurice Tauber gave his important book on technical services the subtitle "Acquisitions, cataloging, classification, binding, photographic reproduction, and circulation operations."[1] One of the purposes of the present book is to be, if one can say this without immodesty, a modern version of the classic Tauber work. Although there is broad agreement about the centrality of acquisitions (defined narrowly) and cataloguing and classification to anyone's definition of technical services, the definition of the rest of the technical services task varies from one period to another and from one library to another. The definition of technical services that informs this book is discussed in the first chapter, "Technical Services Today." This book seeks to address technical services tasks, to chronicle the manner in which they have developed, and to predict their future.

To summarize, the chapters in this book seek to examine the present state of each of a number of aspects of technical services work, to provide some further readings in each of those aspects, and to give each author's view of the prospects for the area that she or he addresses. It is, unlike the Tauber book, the product of a number of authors working individually and, therefore, the contributions are as different in tone and style as are their authors. We hope that this diversity will be stimulating to the reader and that the total effect of this book will be a comprehensive picture of the present and future of one of the two most important facets of librarianship.

NOTES

[1]Tauber, Maurice. Technical services in libraries / by Maurice F. Tauber and associates. New York: Columbia University Press, 1954

TECHNICAL SERVICES TODAY

MICHAEL GORMAN

The many and different definitions of the term *technical services* have been, as this book will show, complicated by the many and far-reaching changes in the nature of librarianship in the past decade or so. Changes in technology, in ideas about the organization of libraries, and in ideas about the very nature of libraries themselves have combined to confuse an already thorny problem of definition. The main purpose of this introduction is to set a working definition of modern technical services activities in the context of a definition of what librarianship is, and is not, about.

The dictionary nearest to hand defines a library as a place set apart to contain books for reading, study, and reference. If one broadens the definition to include library materials other than books, this somewhat old-fashioned definition has still a great deal of utility. In the real world of librarianship (as opposed to the dystopias of the "information scientists"), libraries are places in which library materials of all kinds are collected, preserved, made accessible, and used for pleasure, for study, and for reference. The fact that those materials now include those for which the use of a machine is required (microforms, videorecordings, computer software, etc.) does not alter the old definition materially, and neither does the fact that many libraries are linked electronically for the purposes of cooperation and the sharing of resources. These changes, important as they are, do not change the *nature* of libraries and the great purpose of libraries. From the beginning, librarians have gathered recorded knowledge in all the forms in which it was available and have sought in various ways to preserve and make accessible those carriers of knowledge. There is a golden thread that connects the earliest libraries of clay tablets or papyri or vellum manuscripts to the most up-to-date library and information center of today. Through all the ages, true librarians have known the true purposes of libraries and librarianship and have recognized their kinship with all the librarians that have gone before.

The greatest librarian of the 20th century, S. R. Ranganathan, set down his Laws of Library Science more than half a century ago. They have much to teach the student of technical services; indeed they have much to teach all librarians:

> Books are for use
> To every reader his [or her] book
> To every book its reader
> Save the time of the reader
> The library is a growing organism

If for *book* we substitute *carrier of knowledge*, and for *reader* we substitute *library user*, these laws are as relevant today as when they were first penned. To put it at its simplest, the task of the librarian is to ensure that relevant library materials are collected (or otherwise made available), that those materials be accessible to the users of the library (direct and indirect), and that the access be as speedy and efficient as possible. All of librarianship stems from those few uncomplicated duties. There is no aspect of even the most advanced modern library technology that goes beyond the historic mission of the librarian. It is in recognizing the common purpose of libraries in all times, of all types, and in all places, that we approach a real understanding of our profession.

In the modern era (i.e., for about the last century), it has been common for large and medium-sized libraries in the West to categorize the tasks carried on within their libraries as being divided between what are commonly called *technical* and *public* services. This distinction has become so entrenched in modern North American libraries (especially academic and public libraries of any size) that it is sometimes forgotten that the distinction is relatively recent and is largely confined to the kinds of library that I have mentioned. Not so long ago, it was considered quite heretical even to question the utility and validity of the distinction. That attitude has changed somewhat, but the fact remains that some such categorization is almost universal even today. The distinction between the two is so rooted in the practice of librarianship and in education for librarianship that it has spawned a kind of library parapsychology that postulates that the two "kinds" of librarian (technical and public service) have actually evolved different personality types. I mention this not to endorse an unlikely idea but to indicate the depth of feeling and the degree to which librarians are inured to the idea that technical services and public services are somehow different *in kind* and that difference is both ordained and immutable. The chapter by Younger and Gapen (p. 171) addresses the question of the way in which we organize the processes that go on in libraries. However, no matter how libraries are organized (and I support the view that a more rational organization is of great benefit), the fact remains that there are certain tasks that we group under the rubric of *technical services* that will go on in libraries for the foreseeable future.

The broad definition of technical services that informs this book is as follows: All the tasks carried on in a library that are concerned with the processing of library materials in order to make them accessible to the users of the library. Such processes include:

- ordering, claiming, and receipt of library materials

- cataloguing and classification

- serials control

- database and catalogue maintenance

- marking of processed materials

- shelving and retrieval

- circulation (charging and discharging)

- binding and preservation

- collection management

- budgeting and planning for these activities

It may be helpful for the purposes of definition to state briefly the tasks carried out by library professionals that are *not* comprehended by this definition. Broadly speaking they are:

- selection of library materials

- collection development

- reference and other user services

- instruction in the use of the library and its services

There are, it is evident, areas of overlap and there are individual libraries in which one department performs tasks that are separated by the categorization given here (e.g., many *acquisitions* departments are involved in materials selection *and* the ordering, claiming, and receipt of those materials). To give another example, there are many libraries that, for reasons that have always eluded me, regard circulation as a public service rather than a technical service function.

In addition, I have excluded the following for my categorization:

- creation and implementation of automated systems

- personnel work

- accounting (other than acquisition accounting)

- support services (mail room, photocopying, etc.)

- library administration

My reasons for excluding these important aspects of modern library work are various. The first (the creation and implementation of automated library systems) is excluded because I believe very strongly that it should be the task of all the library staff working cooperatively, and not the exclusive bailiwick of one part of the library. Successful automation programs have, almost invariably, been the result of cooperation between technical and public service librarians, systems people, and library administrators. Poor automation programs (of which there are regrettably many) are, almost invariably, the result of one of those groups having exclusive responsibility for their creation.

Library administration is the most complex of the matters under discussion. It is a job for which few are trained (and those who are trained to be administrators seem less able than the rest). Most administrators have learned their jobs through trial and error and the Peter Principle (which states that everyone is, eventually, promoted to a position above their level of competence) is visibly operating in libraries throughout the land. The best library administrator I have ever known defined library administrators as "mice training to be rats." The worst library administrator I have ever known told his staff that his favorite reading is "books on organization and management." I have no idea what the moral is; all I know is that administration is important and not often done well.

Personnel work, accounting, and support services fall into the category of nonlibrary jobs that are important to modern libraries. The debate as to whether they should be carried out by librarians or nonlibrarians is as yet unresolved and is probably unresolvable. In any event, the librarians that work in technical service areas are affected by systems work, administration, and the others listed above. These factors must be taken into account when one thinks about the tasks that are more directly relevant to technical services today.

This is a book written by librarians for librarians and those who study and teach librarianship. In discussing the definition of technical services work and, indeed any aspect of library work, one is led into a discussion of the nature of librarianship as a profession and the distinction between it and other kinds of work in libraries. It is my contention that much of the obfuscation that surrounds this topic is engendered by the notion that the discussion is about the relative *value* of professional work as opposed to other kinds of library work. It is about no such thing. To the user of a library, the work of the person who reshelves library materials may be of much more immediate importance than the work of the person who selects those materials. To say that the first task is obviously nonprofessional and the second is equally obviously professional is merely to state that they are *different* and not that one is of more value than the other. To turn to the dictionary again, one finds the following definition of a profession: A vocation requiring specialized training in a field of learning, art, or science. I believe that librarianship is a vocation; it is a fact that one is required to undergo specialized training (in the United States, training leading to an MLS) in order to be a librarian; whether librarianship is a branch of learning, an art or a science, or some combination of all three is a matter I leave to the semanticists. The only question that remains, in my view, is what constitutes appropriate education and training for librarians. In this question lies one of the main reasons that the question, Is librarianship a profession? still lingers in the air. There are other negative influences—the growing propensity for academic institutions to appoint nonlibrarian academics to head their libraries, the self-doubt of many librarians, the antiprofessionalism of some library administrators—but the relationship of library education to the practice of librarianship is the one issue above all that will determine the success or failure of librarianship today.

There can be few who would argue with the proposition that library education and library practice are too far apart and that this apartness is growing. The fault is, I would contend, more with library educators than with the profession as a whole, but there is enough blame to go around. The fact remains that students graduate from library schools (to use an, unfortunately, old-fashioned term) without knowing very much about some of the most important parts of being a librarian. Very much to the point, in the context of this book, they are ignorant of most of the processes that go on in technical services areas and of many of the theories and policies that underlie those processes. One excellent recent study has shown that library schools have taught acquisitions work only intermittently over the years and that the subject as such is almost never taught today.[1] Cataloguing fares better, not least because there are some very good teachers of cataloguing (two of whom — Lois Mai Chan and Arnold Wajenberg — are represented in this volume). It would be unrealistic, however, to claim that cataloguing is taught well in all library schools. It would be even more unrealistic to claim that each generation of students is fired with enthusiasm when faced with its first exposure to cataloguing and classification in library school. The problem is not that the library schools are turning out few persons with the desire and qualifications to be cataloguers (indeed, it is arguable that the world has a sufficiency of trained cataloguers), but that library schools are not teaching a basic discipline and *way of thinking as a librarian* to the librarians of tomorrow. Seduced by the barren illusions of "information science," library schools are forgetting their basic duty — the education of persons to work in libraries as professionals, including an understanding of the technical processes that underpin so much of librarianship.

Technical services today are as important to librarianship as they have ever been. The imaginative use of automation in the delivery of library service has, to a great extent, stemmed from innovations in technical services areas. The technical services librarian is uniquely placed to have a rewarding career in the service of humankind — the ultimate purpose of all librarianship.

NOTES

[1]Schmidt, Karen A. The education of the acquisition librarian: a survey of ARL acquisitions librarians. *Library resources and technical services* (in press); *see also* Schmidt, Karen A. University of Illinois Graduate School of Library and Information Science, 1988 (doctoral dissertation)

Acquisitions

THE ORDERING, CLAIMING, AND RECEIPT OF MATERIALS

KAREN A. SCHMIDT

PROCEDURES

Acquisitions is a fundamental process within libraries, and many other functions flow from it. Without the ordering, claiming, and receipt of materials — acquisitions — there would be little or no cataloguing, the process of book selection would be rather futile, and reference queries would remain largely unsatisfied. Despite this essential role, the acquisitions process receives relatively little attention in library literature, is for the most part only vaguely understood by educators and practitioners alike, and to some resembles a sort of library "black hole" to which orders are sent and from which materials mysteriously appear after some period of time.

The reasons for this situation arise from the nature of acquisitions procedures, which are largely clerical in content and more closely intertwined with the for-profit sector of the economy than any other aspect of librarianship. Successful acquisitions departments are dependent more upon business acumen than upon bibliographical skills and demand of their staff, as a prerequisite, knowledge of the publishing industry, wholesaling, budgeting, personnel, and general administrative principles. Since these skills are usually covered in only a cursory manner, if at all, in the library school curriculum and since acquisitions procedures are not well documented and vary from library to library, it is not surprising that acquisitions does not receive its share of interest and understanding from the library profession.

Originally, the term *acquisitions* included all the work which today is usually performed by bibliographers or selectors; collection development units; and ordering, claiming, and receipt units. At one time, treatises on acquisitions included discussions on the nature of acquisitions policies — collection development statements — and the skills necessary for appropriate book selection, as well as the procedures necessary for acquiring the material.[1] With the emergence and evolution of the collection development librarian and the proliferation of publishing of books and periodicals and materials in other formats, acquisitions today has become a process of its own, restricted to the ordering, claiming, and receipt of materials for the library. This development has brought with it various specific organizational structures and processes for acquisitions departments, as well as specific staffing needs which allow libraries to procure material in a timely and cost-effective fashion.

Acquisitions may encompass a wide variety of procedures, depending upon the overall structure of the library in which it operates. Included among these procedures are bibliographic searching; bibliographic or order preparation; order placement; file maintenance; correspondence, claiming, and cancellations; receipt; and billing. Each of these procedures has a specific purpose which supports the acquisitions process and without which acquisitions would not be successful. These procedures occur regardless of the type of material that is being acquired—monographic or serial in nature, database, audio-visual material, or microform. Unfortunately, few books or articles describe these processes in any detail, with the exception of Ford's *The Acquisition of Library Materials* and *Melcher on Acquisition*.[2] These two works, published in 1973 and 1971 respectively, are excellent introductions to the internal procedures upon which acquisitions departments operate, but they cannot reflect the wide array of practices which occur in acquisitions departments in libraries throughout the country today. The following synopsis of the basic components of acquisitions work updates Ford and Melcher and presents some of the issues which, though generally not documented in the literature, form the basis for discussion about the successful management of library acquisitions.

Bibliographic searching involves the correct identification of the piece to be ordered, including author, title, publisher, edition, price, ISBN or ISSN, and other relevant bibliographic information about the material in question (e.g., series information). This information is found in varying degrees of completeness in standard bibliographies such as *Books in Print*, national bibliographies, publishers' catalogues, automated bibliographic files such as OCLC or LIBRIS, and internal library files.[3] Bibliographic searching is performed for a variety of reasons: it assures that the publication information of requested material is in fact correct (as in the case of a patron who may inadvertently request a book by its subtitle); it establishes that the material is in-print or out-of-print before the ordering takes place; it provides the wholesaler with accurate information; it verifies the correct price; and it guards against libraries purchasing duplicate titles. The necessity of performing preorder searching depends upon the size of the library, the degree to which the library is automated, and, to a certain extent, upon the organizational structure of the library. Many libraries do preorder searching in the acquisitions department for every title. In fact, if the information which is collected during the selection process is transmitted accurately to the acquisitions department, there is little, if any, need for preorder bibliographic searching using the standard bibliographic tools. Preorder searching to avoid duplicates remains a necessity for most libraries although automated on-order files available to selectors negate the need for this searching. Wherever the publishing information is procured, it is important that this information be communicated accurately to the publisher or vendor (bookseller) if accurate ordering is to take place.

Order card preparation involves establishing transaction papers — generally called purchase orders — which allow the library to expend money against library funds. Because this involves creating purchasing agreements as well as making preliminary financial records for payment of the material being ordered, this process often takes place in an acquisitions department. Typically, the acquisitions department transcribes the bibliographic information on one or more internal purchase orders at the same time creating an encumbrance record in preparation for eventual receipt and payment of the material. A more cost-effective approach to creating purchasing papers can be established if the purchase order is filled out at the time of selection. This allows the acquisitions department simply to add vendor and accounting information to the purchasing agreement, but demands more detailed internal recordkeeping of the location of the purchase orders which have not yet been filled out. Once again, automation of the acquisitions process may have some effect on how this process is handled. Some acquisitions departments may use optical scanning equipment to enter purchase records into automated accounting systems. Others may use online ordering systems to transmit orders to vendors, so that no paper orders are sent to the vendor and purchase authorization numbers are assigned internally to purchase requests. Order card preparation is essential for the creation of precise and useful accounting records.

Order placement involves selecting vendors or publishers to fill orders and sending orders out. Two questions are essential to this process: should the order to directly to the publisher or to a vendor? If sent to a vendor, which one should be chosen? Overall policy in these matters optimally lies with the head of the acquisitions department who will base decisions on timeliness of receipt, available discounts, and staff time. Generally, using vendors for acquiring all types of materials is the accepted practice in answering the mainstream needs of a library. Vendor performance evaluation has received a great deal of attention among acquisitions librarians attempting to ensure that ordering is cost-effective.[4] Direct purchase from publishers is done most frequently when special discounts are offered, when timeliness may be a critical factor in satisfying a patron need, or when the library holds a membership in an organization which allows purchase of its publications at special discount prices.

Maintaining files is necessary to any acquisitions program and includes keeping order and receipt files, accounting records, vendor address and terms-of-purchase files, correspondence files, and miscellaneous files such as acquired series. The discussion in Ford's *The Acquisition of Library Materials* of the various files and how they may be organized is a good introduction to the topic.[5] The establishment of files once again depends upon several factors, including the existence of other files within the library and accounting and auditing requirements. The files in acquisitions represent the work of the department and, while they are not necessary patron aids, are fundamental tools for the operation of the library nonetheless.

Claiming, cancellation, and correspondence are necessary adjuncts to the acquisitions process as responses when orders cannot be filled as requested, or cannot be filled at all. An established claiming period for unfilled orders ensures that order fulfillment is actively pursued and provides valuable information about vendor performance. Likewise, cancellation of orders can occur because of duplication, budget problems, or incorrect bibliographic searching. Cancellations account for much of the correspondence kept in an acquisitions department, providing accurate records of requests to vendors or publishers to cancel titles and often providing the basis upon which material can be returned to the vendor or publisher if the cancellation is not honored. Other correspondence generated by an acquisitions department includes letters concerning billing errors, requests for quotations, and agreements concerning terms of purchase.

Receipt of material requires verifying that the material ordered is the material received and establishing that the library is paying a fair price for the material. In most libraries, it also includes updating accounting records so that encumbrances become expenditures and budgets are adjusted accordingly. During the receiving process, materials are identified for return because of damage or because an order has been filled incorrectly. In many respects, this portion of the acquisitions process is the most important for satisfying the collection needs of the library and for correct expenditure of library monies. It is also that portion of the acquisitions process most similar to a for-profit business, because of its work with invoices and statements. The receipt area of acquisitions often deals with many nonbibliographical details such as charges for shipping and handling, adjustments for discounts, and foreign currency conversions.

In some libraries, the receiving process is intimately tied to the billing process although this relationship is dictated in virtually all libraries by the parent organization and by entities such as state, local, or federal governments. Of all the processes for acquiring material for libraries, this is the one least related to the practice of librarianship, dealing as it does with the creation of vouchers, payment checks, and refunds. Whether a librarian is responsible for this aspect of acquisitions depends largely upon the organizational structure. Many of the problems which arise from the receiving and billing process are tied directly to issues of vendor performance and have implications for the maintenance of a strong collection, and, for these reasons, the acquisitions librarian should be involved in the creation and implementation of these procedures. Every library will have its own set of internal procedures for handling billing and invoicing and must be familiar with basic accounting and business practices. From this final process comes the statement of budgets from which collection managers work in selecting new material to acquire, thus beginning the process again.

ORGANIZATION

The procedures described above may be carried out in any number of organizational structures. Some libraries have separate acquisitions departments based on format (such as serial and monograph departments), while others have one unit which handles all types of material requests. Libraries with acquisitions departments based on format argue that because monographs and serials are received in such a different way—monographs require that the order-receipt process happens only once while serials demand a repetition of the receipt cycle—procedures and staffing to answer the needs of the different formats are essential. Libraries with function-based acquisitions departments assert that there is a commonality among all the procedures regardless of the format of the material which precludes the creation of different departments. A series of interesting articles and letters by Potter and Paul in the early 1980s demonstrates how vociferously this organizational question can be argued.[6]

In a typical format-based acquisitions organization, the monographs section may handle monograph and serial orders, monograph claims and receipts, and monograph and serial invoices, while the serials section handles serial receipts and, occasionally, the cataloguing of serials. Many variations of this model exist throughout libraries today. Perhaps the biggest problem in a format-based structure is determining what a serial is. If a selector requests a monograph which is part of a numbered series, the order may be monographic or serial. If the library determines it wants the entire series, the serial department may handle the piece when it arrives; if it decides to treat the title as a monograph, the monograph section will handle the book. The larger the library, the more frequently this will occur; and the relationship between the two different units sometimes will determine how quickly the problem is solved and the user gets the book. Conversely, it has been argued, a function-based acquisitions department may not be prepared to handle the more complex recordkeeping which serial receipts demand. In general, large academic libraries are about equally split on the issue of how to organize acquisitions departments.[7]

Organization should be determined by the size of the library and the materials budget. Small libraries do not require complex staffing and may not need a separate acquisitions unit, while larger libraries will have to establish one or more units to handle their order requests. Whether split by format or function, acquisitions work needs to be organized around the procedures which it embraces, as each procedure is distinctive; and the organization should allow for each procedure to support the next one. Information which is gathered in one area of acquisitions is helpful to another so that sharing problems about claiming, for example, will produce helpful information on vendor selection for the order process.

STAFFING

Occasionally, this question will arise: should the head of an acquisitions operation be a librarian or a business manager? Because of the many business-oriented details of acquisitions work, few of which are taught in library schools, some might argue that an MBA is more suitable than an MLS. In larger libraries, a significant portion of the acquisitions librarian's time is taken up in handling personnel matters, negotiating vendor contracts, and dealing with sales staff from vendors and publishers. Knowledge of these matters can be acquired by a librarian as he or she gains experience in acquisitions work. In addition, there are a number of other tasks which require a sensitivity to the goals of the library and the needs of the library collection which are best addressed by a librarian. Among these are decisions about collection purchases, interaction with selectors and cataloguers, and the creation and maintenance of files which will best support the mission of the library. The acquisitions librarian has to have a foot in the camps of both the for-profit and not-for-profit sectors, and it is this person's job to translate the needs of each sector to the mutual benefit of both.

Many large acquisitions departments have several librarians handling various aspects of acquisitions. Some may have an order librarian, an approval-plans/blanket-orders librarian, a serials librarian, or a receipts librarian. It is important to look closely at the work of librarians engaged in these various procedures, and to determine what, if anything, of a professional nature comprises these jobs. The work of a librarian in acquisitions is almost entirely managerial, and the bulk of the work in acquisitions is almost entirely clerical and paraprofessional. If, as occurs in some libraries, bibliographers are attached to acquisitions, their presence there can be very beneficial to acquisitions, but they should not be engaged in tasks which can satisfactorily be performed by nonprofessional staff. One study determined that for every $1.5 million spent in acquisitions money, two librarians and fifteen nonprofessional staff were needed.[8] Staffing levels need to be determined by work levels, and work levels should be determined by streamlined procedures that have as their sole mission getting material into the collection as quickly as possible.

FUTURE TRENDS

There are several developments in acquisitions which will probably come to fruition in this century. Among these are the increased professionalization of acquisitions work; standardized acquisitions practices among libraries; research with vendors and publishers about the nature of publishing and its effects on libraries; and better training about acquisitions and publishing for the entire profession. Acquisitions will achieve a highly integrated degree of automation as the various routines within acquisitions become computerized and automation standards such as BISAC and SISAC become more prevalent. The natural progression from this will be a high degree of integration with other areas within technical services, such as copy cataloguing. It is not unusual now for some acquisitions systems to provide a more or less fully catalogued record as the order record, a process soon to become a commonplace routine among all types of computer systems and libraries. There is, after all, a commonality of purpose in describing material either for purchasing or for the catalogue.

Many of these changes are occurring because acquisitions has become a more visible part of librarianship. There are now two journals devoted to acquisitions, *Library Acquisitions: Practice and Theory* and *Acquisitions Librarian*, one annual conference in Charleston, South Carolina, an ALA Resources and Technical Services Committee on acquisitions created in 1984, and several subcommittees and task forces appointed to study various issues in acquisitions.[9] In general, the profession is paying more attention to the management of acquisitions issues.

One reason for this upsurge of interest is the increasing price of materials and the shrinking dollars being given to libraries. Successful management of acquisitions can stretch materials money and provide better value from the personnel budget. Acquisitions also shares kinship with collection development activities, themselves garnering more professional attention. Acquisitions and collection development are concerned with money and its successful management and — to varying degrees — with publishing, all of which are important to the health of the library collection.

There is a blossoming interest in the computerization of acquisitions functions, including online ordering capabilities, sophisticated fund management reports, and automated bibliographic files. Publishers and vendors have worked for a number of years to develop MARC-like computer records for monographs and serials, known by the acronyms BISAC (Book Industry Systems Advisory Committee) and SISAC (Serials Industry Systems Advisory Committee).[10] Industry-wide adaptation of BISAC and SISAC will allow all publishers and vendors to transmit publishing information electronically, and eventually permit libraries to transmit orders to vendors and publishers using the same system. Automation of acquisitions has been slow in developing, perhaps because so many widely differing components are needed in a full-fledged acquisitions system. The many system requirements for adequate systems presented by Boss over the past several years have stabilized, and the computer capabilities for responding to these requirements continue to become more sophisticated and to parallel the development of automation in other areas within the library.[11]

The role of the vendor also has had a positive effect on the profession's interest in acquisitions. The vendor of both monographs and serials frequently is trained as a librarian and — even if not a librarian — is able and willing to speak knowledgeably about library concerns. In recent years, vendors have become involved in educating librarians about acquisitions and publishing and are important contributors to conferences and publications. More and more librarians are considering entering the selling and marketing side of publishing and becoming more knowledgeable about bookselling and publishing. This trend will continue to grow with many positive benefits for the library community.

All of these developments indicate the need for better education for acquisitions, both informal and formal. Workshops on acquisitions are enjoying a growing popularity as are conferences on various aspects of the topic.[12] While acquisitions frequently is not taught in library schools as a separate course, it is covered to a certain degree in technical services, automation, and management of library courses, and the growing number of professional education efforts in this area round out the avenues for formal learning about acquisitions.

As the professional roles of librarians develop, so does the role of the acquisitions librarian. Acquisitions is becoming more clearly defined within libraries, and the fundamental processes it handles — ordering, claiming, and receipt — are more streamlined and automated with each year. As acquisitions is better defined, so is its relationship to other processes in the library, including cataloguing, collection development, and binding. After a relatively slow start, this area of librarianship has become an equal and contributing member of the profession.

NOTES

[1]Carter, Mary *et al.* Building library collections. 4th ed. Metuchen, NJ: Scarecrow Press, 1974; Tauber, Maurice. Technical services in libraries: acquisitions, cataloging, classification, binding, photographic reproduction, and circulation operations. New York: Columbia University Press, 1954

[2]Ford, Stephen. The acquisition of library materials. Chicago: American Library Association, 1973; Melcher, Daniel. Melcher on acquisition. Chicago: American Library Association, 1971

[3]Books in print. New York: R. R. Bowker, 1948- . Annual; LIBRIS is an automated acquisitions system available from the vendor Baker & Taylor. Among its services is a bibliographic database.

[4]One of the better-known vendor evaluations is Davis, Mary Byrd. Model for a vendor study in a manual or semi-automated acquisitions system. *Library acquisitions: practice and theory* 3:53-60 (1979)

[5]Ford. *Op. cit.* pp. 169-172

[6]Potter, William Gray. Form or function?: an analysis of the serial department in the modern academic library. *Serials librarian* 6:53-60 (Fall 1981); Paul, Huibert. Automation of serials check-in: like growing bananas in Greenland? *Serials librarian* 6:3-16 (Winter 1981/Spring 1982); 6:39-62 (Summer 1982); Paul, Huibert *et al.* Discussion. *Serials librarian* 7:7-9, 57-60 (Summer 1983)

[7]Schmidt, Karen. The acquisitions process in research libraries: a survey of ARL libraries' acquisitions departments. *Library acquisitions: practice and theory* 11:35-44 (1987)

[8]*Ibid.*

[9]Library acquisitions: practice and theory. New York: Pergamon Press, 1977- ; Acquisitions librarian. New York: Haworth Press, 1979- . Semiannual; The College of Charleston acquisitions meeting is held annually at the college, generally during the early part of November. Synopses of the meetings and papers are available in the book: Library acquisitions: practice and theory.

[10]Book Industry Study Group. BISAC formats. Rev. New York: BISG, 1984; See, for example: Sabosik, P. E. SISAC standardized formats for serials. *Information technology and libraries* 5:149-154 (June 1986)

[11]Boss, Richard W. Automating acquisitions. *Library technology report* 22:479-634 (Sept./Oct. 1986); _____. Developing requirements for automated serials control systems. *Serials librarian* 11:37-70 (Dec. 86/Jan. 87)

[12]As noted earlier, the College of Charleston acquisitions conference reports are available annually in: Library acquisitions: practice and theory. LAPT also covers the reports of acquisitions meetings occurring at the ALA annual and midwinter conferences. The Resources Section of the Resources and Technical Services Division Resources (now ALCTS) of the American Library Association has sponsored traveling workshops entitled "The Business of Acquisitions," beginning in 1987. These workshops focus on building knowledge about publishing, automation, and general acquisitions procedures.

A PERSPECTIVE ON LIBRARY BOOK GATHERING PLANS

EDWARD J. LOCKMAN, with EDNA LAUGHREY and KEVIN COYLE

Libraries purchase books, essentially, in two different ways. They order individual books title by title and they arrange with a bookseller (vendor) to receive certain categories of book *en masse*. The latter method is known as a gathering plan. There are two types of gathering plan. The first, an *approval* plan, is created when a library has a vendor send new publications, usually within specified subject ranges, for the library to accept or reject. For an approval plan to be effective, the rate of rejection ("returns") should be low (5 percent or less). This means that the library has to make its expectations very clear to the vendor. The second type of gathering plan is known as a *blanket order* plan. With this type of plan the library contracts with a vendor to receive all the books denoted by one or more characteristics (e.g., books published in Ecuador, books published by certain university presses, scholarly German publications) without the right of return.

This chapter deals with the advantages and disadvantages of each type of gathering plan and proposes a new approach to this valuable tool in the process of library acquisitions.

The Approval Plan

The approval plan system was created and developed by Richard Abel in the early 1960s in response to a need he recognized in libraries to have books delivered automatically by matching new titles with a predetermined "profile" developed by the book vendor and the library. The growth of this process has been very well documented in library literature. Its success is such that a number of book vendors are offering computer-supported approval plans generating valuable collection development information for the library. The purpose of this chapter is not to explain what an approval plan is, but rather to compare this method of gathering titles with that of the blanket order plan and to propose a new approach to the gathering plan.

Approval plans are found particularly in the academic library world and, more specifically, in research libraries. The approval plan is of great assistance in libraries with policies of comprehensive collection from all countries in broad subject areas. Such a task is, to put it bluntly, impossible without the assistance of a gathering plan. No library has unlimited financial and human resources to accomplish such an undertaking. Approval plans can help a library to develop a comprehensive collection, because they make more manageable the universe of books from many countries covering a dizzying myriad of subjects from which librarians must select. Approval plans offer other benefits as well. For example, using an approval plan a librarian can expect the following.

Quick receipt after publication. Because the book vendor places a standing order for the publisher's new titles, early delivery of new titles which match the approval plan profile can be achieved.

Reduction in required "firm orders." The expense and time involved in processing firm (individual) orders by the library acquisition department is completely avoided as the titles are received automatically in accordance with an agreed-upon profile.

Can be broad or narrow in scope. A library can use the approval plan profile to supplement human resources available to it in the effort to gather new core titles in a selected subject area.

Can be sorted by subject. A librarian can use the approval plan in specific subject areas, allowing for acquisition of titles in other areas through individual orders from book vendors thus avoiding duplication of the approval plan.

Purchase decision is made with book in hand. The greatest benefit of the approval plan is being able to determine the academic value of a new title with the book in hand. This removes most of the guesswork involved in ordering titles from advertisements, blurbs, and so on.

Attractive discounts. Defining the library's expectations through the profile allows the vendor to determine the anticipated profit margin on future deliveries and, thus, to set a firm price on titles delivered within the profile. This allows the vendor the luxury of guaranteed sales at a predetermined level and permits the library to budget a single line for approval plan expenditures.

Helps the library define what it is collecting. Vendors are able to provide development information for the titles they have delivered. This information is often in machine-readable form, therefore the year's acquisitions can be sorted by Library of Congress class numbers, the library's fund codes, and so on.

Electronic invoice loaded into library automation. In some cases, the vendor's invoice is produced in a machine-readable form and can be loaded into the library's automated system on a predetermined schedule. This not only adds the titles to the collection but also updates the expended funds and saves the time and cost of the library staff having to enter the invoices into their system manually.

Although an approval plan offers many benefits, it has some disadvantages which must be considered and addressed by the library staff.

Return of inappropriate titles to vendor. Some books received on the approval plan will be returned. The inconvenience and trouble of returns are intended to be offset by the benefits described above. The costs to the library and the vendor of returns are significant and are often not calculated in determining the true costs of the approval plan.

No reviews available. Titles received on approval must, in general, be accepted on their face value. Although having the book in hand is very helpful, the selector does not have the benefit of supporting his or her initial decision to accept or return a book based on a printed opinion of someone who has reviewed the title and expressed an opinion of its value.

Forms/slips do not give enough information. Often the library will not want to have the actual books delivered to the library. Instead, they request a printed form from which the librarian selects. The form is then returned to the vendor for titles to be purchased. Although this method does eliminate the problems of returns, the form itself does not include as much information as the book in hand or a review in helping the selector make a purchasing decision.

Missed titles not shipped by vendor. The book vendor ships consignments based on the agreed-upon profile which often includes a "do not exceed" dollar amount. Considering all the titles published each year, the vendor must omit some titles which the library will never receive on approval. In addition, some titles will be missed by the vendor, and therefore the library must still review all the new book announcements as if there were no automatic approval delivery service. This is the only way the library can evaluate the success of the approval profile and the vendor and determine which titles should be "firm ordered."

Evaluation and selection of books shipped by the vendor. A well-qualified library staff person has to review each title received. This is a very expensive process considering that such a person would be one of the better-paid workers. In the process of evaluation and selection of a consignment of approval titles, it is sometimes the case that the designated person is unavailable. In that case, the decision to keep or return is made by someone much less qualified.

Not necessarily the "best" books on a subject. Because the vendor makes no attempt to define *best* the fact remains that the vendor's decision on which titles to send on the approval plan includes the terms of sale of each publisher. Some publishers do not allow returns, and therefore the vendor would be foolish to include one of these titles in an approval plan if the library can reject the title and the vendor cannot return it to the publisher. Also, the publisher's discount to the vendor determines if the vendor will deliver the title on approval and at the negotiated discount to the library. As a result, those titles from publishers with restricted return policies and poor discount schedules are not considered for inclusion by the vendor.

All new titles do not fit neatly into profile categories. A lot of gray areas are found in the communication between library and the vendor over which titles are covered by the approval plan profile. This uncertainty confuses the librarian's decision to either place a firm order or hope that a new title will be delivered on approval.

Reliance on one vendor for all new books. One way to prevent firm orders from duplicating approval plan deliveries is to send all orders to the approval vendor. It has been reported that such a consolidation works quite well and, in theory, simplifies book ordering. The assumption is that the approval vendor is proficient in delivering all the library's orders. However, this is not true of *any* vendor. Each vendor has strengths and weaknesses. Therefore, the acquisition librarian will order from multiple vendors to complement strengths and compensate weaknesses. Ordering all titles from the approval plan vendor may eliminate one problem, duplication, but may result in nondelivery of book orders or the loss of higher discounts from other vendors on, for example, trade, scientific/technical, or university press titles.

THE BLANKET ORDER PLAN

There is another approach to gathering books which has met with some success in academic libraries — the blanket order plan. It differs from the approval plan in several ways: it is not subject driven, it excludes or limits book returns, and it does not require a profile. Blanket order plans are becoming quite popular because they are simple to administer and monitor in the library. For example, one can establish a plan for all new titles from a publisher and feel secure that all new titles will be delivered. Approval plans, because they are subject driven, can become very complicated, especially in drawing up the "profile" which matches books to subject categories. This chapter later proposes an alternative approach that could reinvent and revitalize the gathering plan concept.

The rediscovered blanket order (or standing order) plan by publishers has been offered by a few vendors with the intention of providing a library with all the new publications of certain well-known publishers. The library's expectations of the vendor are very well defined, because the scope of the vendor's blanket order plan is limited to only the publishers listed. This sends a clear message to the library as to what to expect or not expect on the plan, and therefore, which titles to firm order from other vendors. Using a blanket order has the following benefits.

Publishers are specified. At the library's request, all new titles from a specific publisher can be delivered. Sometimes, this service can be available to the library directly from the publisher if a vendor's involvement is not desired.

Librarians know what to expect. When a book request is received for one of the publishers covered on the blanket order plan, the librarian knows not to place an individual order, but to anticipate automatic delivery.

Minimal profiling. A blanket order for all new titles from one publisher needs only very limited profiling. Setting a price ceiling or excluding a specific class of book (e.g., textbooks, juvenile literature) would be the extent of profiling required.

No returns to process. Returning books is an expensive process for the library and bookseller. With the blanket order plan, returns should include only volumes received in damaged condition.

No selection forms to process. Since books are delivered automatically, there is neither time nor money spent in reviewing approval selection forms which would need to be returned to the vendor as firm orders.

Attractive discounts. When the vendor knows the type of material to be purchased, a competitive price can be set on all titles received from a preselected list of publishers.

No gray areas of coverage. The understanding between the library and the vendor is very clear. This allows for nearly error-free service from the vendor and the elimination of duplicate orders by the library.

Although the blanket order plan offers valuable benefits, the library must be aware of the difficulties in making this gathering plan work.

Librarian must accept all new titles from the publisher. The library must know that it wants to purchase all the titles from a particular publisher. To ensure that the library would have purchased a very high percentage of a publisher's titles individually, it is necessary to compare the library holdings with the publisher's catalogues for the past few years. Making this comparison is not easy and will require significant time. However, the comparison will confirm that the acquisition department's decision will save time by not having to process firm orders for that publisher's new titles in the coming year.

A NEW GATHERING PLAN PROPOSAL

The primary disadvantage of an approval plan is that the vendor — the bookseller — is the one who determines which books are sent on approval. Basically, the book vendor is in business to make money. He or she buys and selects books most of which are returnable to publishers and will offer a reasonable margin of profit to the vendor. Since these two vendor criteria will influence the titles included in an approval plan, there will inevitably be a number of worthwhile titles that the library will never see on approval. In theory, the library realizes that these particular titles are missing and orders them individually. However, this is not always the case. Perhaps the library selectors will miss advertisements for such nonreturnable, low-margin titles, and by the time the title comes to the library's notice it may be out of funds or the publisher may be out of stock. As a result, many research libraries participating in approval plans have collections reflecting, in large part, a particular book wholesaler's inventory — a situation which clearly does not match the intent of the library.

Libraries using approval plans receive many titles. The idea is that experts in various fields on campus will review these titles, either approve or disapprove them, and keep them or return them to the vendor. In reality, however, three different procedures may occur. First, a knowledgeable person may examine and review each title, approve or disapprove it, keep worthwhile titles and return those which do not fit the library's profile. Second, a librarian can give casual approval without worrying whether his or her choices correspond to the library's collection development policy. Finally, it is possible that no librarian reviews the books at all, or perhaps a staff person without much time does the reviewing. The result of this is, obviously, a hasty and careless approach to both collection development and use of very valuable and limited resources.

The last two situations are all too common. However, because there are supposedly "time-saving" add-ons offered by approval plan vendors, such as taped invoices, approval plans are considered to be easier and simpler than other purchasing methods. Thus, there exists a tremendous amount of "not-by-the-book" purchasing. This naturally raises a major issue concerning the buying and return policies of libraries.

In considering approval and blanket order plans, certain economic conditions exist and must be acknowledged as basic to the acquisitions environment. From the bookseller's point of view, he or she has to make money; has to be able to sell books at a profit; and must be able to limit the returns received because this is the most expensive procedure a bookseller goes through. Further, the vendor's overhead costs incurred by having a professional staff to maintain an approval plan (or, to a certain extent, a blanket order plan) are quite large, a fact that is not appreciated by many libraries. Often libraries dictate the "terms of sale" of an approval plan or a blanket order plan, and for any vendor to remain competitive he or she has to meet those terms. The library expects that a rather handsome discount goes along with any approval or blanket order plan, and the vendor who wants to get into this game has to be willing to offer such a discount. This creates a bidding war between vendors and, more importantly, we lose sight of a more significant feature of this whole business, namely the type of selection or de-selection criteria the vendor is using to determine which books are sent to the library. In essence, the vendor is concerned with sending the most profitable titles, not necessarily the best-quality titles, in order to deliver them at the discounts expected by the library. Put another way, you get what you pay for.

Both approval and blanket order plans are interesting and useful for many libraries, but could be improved. The basic mission of a library remains unchanged: to collect the most pertinent books published each year that complement the existing collection and that conform to the library's collection development policy. As was noted above, no library has unlimited funds to purchase books, therefore each must be very careful in its selection of new titles. These realities signal the need for more of a new qualitative (not quantitative) approach. Is it not time for the library community to finally acknowledge the facts of gathering plans, especially in the light of tremendous cost increases for operations, subscriptions, and monographic purchases?

We offer here a new approach to library selection and buying procedures. First, commercial vendors, particularly booksellers, must be removed from positions in which they control the types of book sent to the library. The vendor has no business in delivering books that do not match the collection development policy of a library or in not delivering books that do. As discussed previously, there is a distinct conflict of interest. The vendor does not pretend to be an authority on the quality of what is published. What is needed is a new environment in which an objective and succinct review of new titles rates them against other titles in the same field. This rating should include the academic level and/or readership level and a comparison of each title with others on the same subject. Is it the best new book written on this subject, or something considerably less? This rating must be communicated to the libraries in a timely manner so they can make intelligent selection decisions.

An independent organization can and should be established to offer this reviewing service. This service will initially focus on a narrow range of subjects, and later expand to comprehensive coverage. Recognized subject experts will be placed under contract to review and rate newly published titles in an agreed-upon and timely manner. The review will then be entered into a database maintained by the core review center (the independent review organization) and stored there. This core review center now has the mission of selling this service to libraries on a subscription basis. The motive for a library to subscribe to such a service is that it will realize that it does not have qualified bibliographers in all subject areas and, therefore, needs some external support. The reviews and ratings would be received on a terminal (and sorted by Library of Congress classes, for example). When bibliographers or subject specialists from the library sit down to review the areas to which they have subscribed, they will have access to the most recent reviews written. The review will report the academic level of the book, rate it, and compare it to others on the same subject. In addition, the author's credentials will be described to enable the library's subject specialists to make an intelligent purchasing decision. The review will be printed on an order slip which is given to the acquisition librarian. The acquisition librarian now can take all of the review slips and buy selected books intelligently from the various vendors. This differs from the approval plans and blanket order plans in which one vendor delivers all kinds of books. Experience shows that no one vendor can give a library the best service on all kinds of books. This is the reason why there are different types of vendors. The art of being an acquisition librarian is to know which type of title should go to which vendor — to be able to say, for example, that the current titles should go to Vendor W, older titles might do better at Vendor X, and popular titles should be sent to Vendor Y. Apart from receiving better discounts from the vendors, this approach allows for better service and a higher fulfillment rate as the librarian is playing to each vendor's strength. The library is no longer held captive by the approval plan or blanket order plan vendor.

We envision this service as being online and on a subscription basis, done commercially by an independent source unaware of what the discount is on each title from the publisher and unaware of which titles are returnable to the publisher. These should not be a concern when assessing the quality of books.

The American Library Association might be exactly the organization to do this. If an ALA division or RLG or OCLC decides that they should be this coordinative reviewing agency, so be it. It could well be based on government funding which will truly leverage the investment that the government is now making via their contributions to libraries of all kinds. The proposed service will provide libraries with the information needed to make more intelligent acquisition and selection decisions and will divorce qualitative assessment from commercial considerations without harm to either.

FURTHER READINGS

Association of Research Libraries. Approval plans: SPEC kit 141. Washington, DC: ARL, OMB, 1988

Association of Research Libraries. Approval plans in ARL libraries: SPEC kit 83. Washington, DC: ARL, OMB, 1982

Cargill, Jennifer S. and Brian Alley. Practical approval plan management. Phoenix, AZ: Oryx Press, 1979

Moline, Gloria. An evaluation of approval plan performance : the acquisition of titles in political science. San Jose, CA: Dept. of Librarianship, San Jose State University, 1975

Rader, Hannelore B. Collection development strategies for academic and research libraries. Lansing, MI: Michigan Library Association, 1981

Schmidt, Karen A. Capturing the mainstream: publisher-based and subject-based approval plans in academic libraries. *College and research libraries* 47, no. 4: 365-369 (July 1986)

Spohrer, James H. *et al.* Guide to collection development and management at the University of California, Berkeley. Berkeley: General Library, U-C, Berkeley, 1986

University of California, Berkeley. Collection development policy statement / prepared by Dorothy Koenig and Sheila Dowd. Berkeley: General Library, U-C, Berkeley, 1980

GIFTS AND EXCHANGES

JOSEPH W. BARKER

Virtually all libraries have programs for gifts, and many operate programs to acquire materials by exchanging publications. The gifts we speak of here are those of books and journals, donated to the library by users of the library and others acquainted with the library's willingness to accept gifts. The exchanges with which we are concerned consist of operations to maintain agreements, called *partnerships*, established for the mutual exchange of publications between the library and various types of institutions. Such exchanges are often called *international exchanges*, although they can also be within a country. Libraries with comprehensive collections find they must maintain at least some international exchanges to obtain certain foreign publications. This chapter will summarize, in general terms, current practices for managing exchange and gift operations in large- and medium-sized academic libraries and then examine emerging trends — the organization, automation, and policy development of these functions — and the impact of the 1986 tax reform and of environmental economic pressures on library budgets. In the future gifts and exchanges will continue to play important roles in technical services and collection development.

EXCHANGES

The core of an exchange partnership is a two-way relationship based on the expectation of sending and receiving future publications. Likely exchange partners include academic libraries and departments, national and provincial libraries, and academies. Some partners may serve as clearinghouses for publications from related or neighboring government agencies. Since international exchange bypasses commerical channels of acquisition, it is a powerful tool for obtaining materials not available for purchase. In fact, exchange may be the best way to collect materials from countries and areas in which commercial trade with the United States is difficult or impossible, the publishing and distribution systems are poorly developed, or print runs are inadequate for external distribution. When political upheaval works against local preservation of printed matter and renders sale of publications impossible, exchanges often continue to function and may save significant research documents for distribution. International exchanges have been known to go on during world wars, political revolutions, and economic depressions, securing materials for libraries that would have been virtually impossible to collect otherwise. Even when purchase is possible, exchanges may be more cost-effective than purchase.

Most exchange agreements are based on the exchange of serials: each partner agreeing to send the other one or more serials as they are published. Current serials are preferred because they involve less recordkeeping and encourage continuity in the exchange partnership. Once receipt and cataloguing records are set up, and once mailing lists to send serials are in place, serials can continue to be exchanged, requiring only the usual claiming, title changes, and adjustments inherent in serials work, and occasional adjustments to the mailing lists. Significant hard-to-acquire monographs and out-of-print items may also be acquired on exchange. However, each monograph received on exchange requires repetition of the entire selection and cataloguing cycle, and supplying monographs involves handling individual requests, orders, and shipments. Records for each title must be created. Furthermore, if a significant number of monographs are exchanged, records must be kept for the value of each piece sent to, and received from, exchange partners. One of the most efficient ways to acquire monographs from partners from whom large quantities of material are sought routinely is to establish blanket exchange agreements based on a subject profile. Although such arrangements still require review and selection of each item upon receipt, checking of exchange lists can be avoided. Out-of-print items and some microfilms are available via exchanges, but arrangements for monographs and noncurrent serials tend to be more costly to operate than serials exchanges.

Balancing exchanges is a necessary part of managing exchange operations adequately. By comparing numbers of items given and received, agreements in need of closer monitoring are revealed. Balancing generally need not be an exact process. The overall program should not show more items received than sent, and individual partnerships should be based on the exchange of roughly equivalent materials. Most institutions determine equivalent value on a title-sent-for-title-received basis. Both sides of the partnership agree that their serials are of more or less equal value, with occasional monographs added as special requests. Dollar-for-dollar balancing is used if the long-range potential cost of an exchange partnership warrants the additional labor required (as in blanket monograph exchange agreements), or if a given partner requires this method. In such balancing the partner and the library both provide lists stating the value of their offerings for a preceding time period. Using equivalent-value or a dollar-for-dollar method, serials exchanges result in fewer items to be reconciled — another reason exchanges based on serials cost less to operate.

To sustain an exchange program, a library must have publications to offer to partners. Ideally, these will be publications of the university press or of other units affiliated with the campus, and made available to the library free or at substantial discounts. These discounts, when available, lessen the cost of acquisition by exchange significantly. The library sometimes earns these discounts if its exchanges distribute publications directly to interested scholars, some of whom are beyond the reach of the publisher's usual marketing and distributing methods. If a library is able to obtain many publications in an assortment of subject areas from its institution and/or its university press, all but the largest exchanges can be sustained with these publications. For many libraries, however, the only way to obtain a guaranteed supply of current publications for exchange is to purchase items at minimal discount or at full cost. There may be no institutional publications available to the library, or, with the increasing commercialization of university presses and other institutional publishers, the library may be ineligible for preferential discounts.

The practice of purchasing commercial publications for exchange partners, called *barter* exchange, increases the cost and complexity of operating an exchange program significantly. Beside the cost of the items themselves, there is the labor of buying them, rehandling them for shipping, and correspondence. Furthermore, exact dollar-for-dollar or title-for-title balancing is almost unavoidable. Bartering of serials, using a serials subscription agent, makes barter exchange less labor-intensive but entails paying vendor service charges. Bartering is, nevertheless, used extensively in some exchange programs, and is used by libraries with extensive university publications to supplement offerings to large and/or important partners. Unselected gifts and withdrawn materials may be offered to partners at less direct cost than purchasing bartered items. However, the savings gained by using this "free" surplus must be weighed against the costs of preparing lists of such materials, of conducting correspondence to determine who wants and is entitled to what, of storing the items, and of packing and shipping them.

Maintaining exchange partnerships is unavoidably labor-intensive. Correspondence with partners about availability of materials, changes in exchange offerings, balancing exchanges, and special requests must often be written in the partner's language if one is to expect a timely and useful reply. Individual (not form) letters are often necessary. Some partners will respond to a letter but not to routine claims. Quite often, partners will supply unsolicited material or new serial titles. A letter must be sent to determine if the material is to be counted as part of the exchange agreement, or if, perhaps, it is part of a new serial or a title change. In order to respond to partners' claims for material not received, records must be kept of all items shipped. A stock of replacement issues/volumes is needed to fill partners' legitimate claims. Once unsolicited material and monographs arrive, they must be reviewed by selectors, and accepted material must be routed for cataloguing and/or preservation as appropriate.

There are two typical ways of fitting exchange operations into the library organization. Frequently they are placed in the acquisitions department as a sub-unit (often grouped with gifts) that works closely with selectors. Alternatively, exchanges may be part of collection development as a unit of the area program or programs most served by exchange. There are five critical elements for which provisions must be made in organizing exchange work:

- expertise in dealing with partners

- specialized knowledge of languages and geographic areas

- adequate handling of correspondence and materials

- routing accepted materials to cataloguing and conservation units

- adhering to and implementing collection development policy

Any form of organization which provides for these elements and is afford-able will be successful. As we will see in discussing present and future trends for exchange operations, a great variety of organizational schemes exist for exchange work, and a number of them appear to be viable.

A fairly high-level (and therefore expensive) staff is needed for exchange work. Knowledge of foreign languages is required, and skills in correspondence are needed. The staff also needs considerable organizational skills, a broad understanding of library procedures, and the ability to use judgment in dealing with partners, collection development staff, and the staff of acquisitions, conser-vation, and cataloguing. If exchanges are located away from collection develop-ment, many libraries believe a librarian or high-level paraprofessional is needed for interpretation of exchange policy and practices and to manage the exchange budget. If exchange is part of collection development, some collection develop-ment time will be devoted to similar exchange management issues.

Many items received on exchange are primary research material and/or writ-ten in languages not widely read. These materials therefore will be less useful overall than many purchased items. For this reason they seem, to some library users and managers, to demand a share of library resources disproportionate to the amount of use. On the other hand, the use exchange materials receive is often for primary research and coincides with an important mission of the research library. As already observed, exchange work is labor-intensive. Some exchange materials require preservation treatment upon receipt, because they are not new, are published on paper of poor quality, or are not bound durably. Furthermore, since these materials are not held by many other libraries, exchanges often need original cataloguing. In libraries in which staffing, space, preservation, and cata-loguing budgets are inadequate for high-use materials, there can be resentment about the resources diverted to handle exchange items. Resolving this controversy requires widespread understanding within the library of collection policies and priorities. Formal policy on the use of exchange and its role in achieving collec-tion development goals will help to clarify the issues.

GIFTS

Gift programs resemble exchange programs insofar as they can be found in different places in the library organization, are labor-intensive, and require a fairly high level of staff. Gifts and exchanges both rely on relationships — not cur-rency — to provide the material they provide, and much of this material cannot be obtained by any other means. Here the resemblance between gift and exchange operations ends. Each obtains a different kind of material. One depends on partners, the other on donors. They generate and use different files and have sep-arate workflows.

Some materials received as gifts are very valuable items virtually unobtain-able in any other way. Gifts are of critical importance in developing special col-lections, can be a significant source of out-of-print materials, and have provided research libraries with many of their unique holdings. Most gifts, however, are not very valuable. Many duplicate existing library holdings. Others are out of the scope of the collections of the library. Because many gifts are not retained by the library, gifts operations often include programs to sell or redirect unwanted gifts and some withdrawn materials. Items not "recycled" are discarded.

The source of gifts is the community of donors and potential donors of materials to the library. The relationship between the donor and the donations is important to the donation process. Some donors value their collections as an investment; some view them as a reflection of their intellectual lives (or of the life of the person who assembled the collection); some hate to throw books and journals away; some believe their collections correspond to the reading interests of library users and will help the library; and many view donations as a welcome tax deduction. When the library is willing to accept the gift, the donation retains much of its value and retains more of its intellectual and/or sentimental meaning than it would if it were sold or, worse, discarded. Even if the library must ultimately discard, give away, or sell much of the donation, the donor is acquitted of responsibility. A responsible and enduring institution has taken charge of the collection's fate, followed policy beyond the donor's control, and issued the necessary acknowledgment to ensure a legitimate tax deduction.

Managing gifts, therefore, involves frequently delicate relationships and understanding of the donor's relationship to the donation, the reason for the donation, the value of the materials, whether they will eventually be added to the collections, and the potential for future donations. Before accepting many gifts, time-consuming interviews and written correspondence are often required. Income tax procedures must often be discussed. Soon after gifts are received, formal acknowledgment is sent to the donor, any required deed of gift is signed, and donor files are updated. Because of the sensitive nature of some donations, the possible tax repercussions, and the question of ownership inherent in any gift, donor files (which identify the donor, describe the gift in general terms, and contain noteworthy correspondence) are usually kept indefinitely.

Since the enactment of the Tax Reform Act of 1984 donor relations and internal recordkeeping have become significantly more complicated and time-consuming. For donors to claim a deduction on their income tax returns, they must complete and submit to the IRS form 8283, and must establish the fair market value of the donations. Appraisals or estimates from the beneficiary of a donation cannot be used to substantiate the value for income-reporting purposes. In addition, if combined donations in one year of any one type (such as books) total $5,000 or more, all the donations must be accompanied by a professionally-written appraisal which identifies the items donated. Copies of the appraisal must be filed with the donee, who must then acknowledge receipt of the gift by signing the form 8283 submitted with the claim for the deduction. Finally, if any part of a gift in the $5,000 category is disposed of within two years after the donation, the donee must file another form (8282) with the IRS, stating the amount for which the materials were sold (zero if discarded). This figure establishes the fair market value of the portion of the gift sold or discarded. Any deduction of income claimed by the donor will be adjusted by the IRS to match it. If the figure reported is substantially lower than the appraisal, it may bring the entire appraisal into question by the IRS. The penalty for reporting items disposed of before the two-year period is $50 (it is not clear whether this penalty applies to the entire gift or to individual items).

The cost implications of these requirements are several. The law has generated more forms to fill out and file, more storage of material not wanted in the collections, and more pitfalls in maintaining donor relations. If a donor is not informed of reporting obligations and of the need for appraisals if annual gifts total $5,000 or more, it is likely that the library will be blamed for this omission. If a library accepts a gift appraised above $5,000 and then decides not to add parts of it, care must be taken that the disposal be deferred for two years, that the appraisal encompass only the portion to be added, or that the donor be prepared to have the deduction adjusted to equal the amount reported on the form 8282. Not only does the gifts unit have to learn and explain the tax requirements, all selectors approached by donors need this information to avoid committing the library to embarrassing, time-consuming, and perhaps costly procedures. Because the law places an increased burden on the donee for keeping track of gifts, most libraries have had to increase their reporting of gifts to the campus development office.

Fairly high-level staff are required to manage a gifts operation successfully. Various management abilities are needed: tact in dealing with donors, a facility for written correspondence, organizational talents to manage donor files and quantities of materials, and thorough knowledge of the policies and regulations of the IRS and the campus development office. In addition, coordinating gifts requires several skills learned best through experience in gift or similar work. A sense for the value of used and rare books and experience with the used book trade are essential, and facility in bargaining is useful when selling surplus items. Gift work requires a broad knowledge of library policies for collection development and of campus policies for gifts-in-kind and disposal of surplus property. Familiarity with several foreign languages at the level to enable bibliographic checking of holdings, and knowledge of foreign publications sufficient to enable recognition of valuable materials are also essential. The degree of expertise needed in the gifts unit varies, of course, depending on the relationship of this position to the collection development experts served by the gifts program, the size and scope of the library, and the nature of its donor population.

As with exchanges, many options exist for organizing gifts operations. Typically, there is a central location at which donors may make inquiries and deposit gifts; permanent donor files are maintained; and such matters as deeds of gift, administering IRS forms, and reporting to the campus development office are controlled. Since these aspects of gifts management must conform to external policies and/or affect future donor relations, they are likely to remain centralized. The sale of unwanted gifts and withdrawn materials may also be subject to campus policies for disposal of surplus property, and may also need to be centralized. The other aspects of gifts work — preliminary screening, checking for duplication, and review by selectors — may be done centrally (as part of the acquisitions or in a separate gifts unit), or may be decentralized to branches and/or area specialists. If gift work is centralized, frequent contact with collection development must be arranged. If gift management is in collection development, provisions must be made for frequent interaction with cataloguing, preservation, and acquisitions. Gifts, like exchanges, require coordination between collection development and technical services.

TRENDS AND LIKELY FUTURES

Many of the changes in gifts and exchanges in the past, and many future trends, arise from attempts by library managers, in both collection development and technical services, to extend their understanding of these problematic and controversial functions and to define the relationship of gifts and exchanges to the rest of the library. What are the possibilities for automation and organizing gifts and exchanges for greater efficiency and fewer staff? As library needs continue to be larger than library budgets, and the purchasing power of the dollar shrinks, how does the cost of these programs compare with the cost of purchase? How does one balance the quantifiable operational costs of staffing gifts and exchanges against their unquantifiable benefits to collections and to future research? How much weight should be put upon area studies collections and the humanities, when scientific and professional disciplines want more support to purchase readily available but expensive new publications? What will be the impact of the 1986 Tax Reform on gift programs? Discussion of issues like these surround the management of gift and exchange programs, and challenge the skills of technical services and collection development managers alike. The diversity of the trends affecting gifts and exchanges reflects the political and technical difficulties of managing these programs. It also reflects the fact that most library managers are gaining understanding and knowledge of gift and exchange programs even as they manage them.

Organizational Trends

Earlier the variety of ways of organizing gift and exchange operations successfully were discussed. In his 1977-1978 survey of ARL libraries' gift and exchange programs, Mark Kovacic noted that approximately 57 percent of ARL libraries had centralized gift and exchange units, 13 percent had two separate units, and 30 percent had integrated gifts and exchange into other units.[1] A 1985 ARL SPEC kit survey reports many organizational changes, all of which seem to have had the effect either of decreasing the size and/or cost of gift and exchange operations or of increasing accountability for these programs. The 1985 survey contains no reports of increased or higher level staff. Of the 63 institutions responding, 17 (27 percent) reported that staffing had been reduced, that gifts or exchanges or both had been merged into other technical service units, and/or that one or both of the functions had been decentralized into collection development.[2]

There is also a trend to individualize organizational approaches to gifts and exchanges. In the 1985 SPEC survey certain themes prevail in the restructuring efforts reported: automation, decentralization, increased use of paraprofessionals in technical functions, and the need to respond to inadequate budgets for the library as a whole. Each reorganization reflects a unique arrangement to accommodate the individual library's way of addressing these themes. As libraries define the level of exchange appropriate to their collections and as they work out their own procedures to provide appropriate levels of collection development and technical expertise in operating gifts and exchanges, more individualized organizational structures are likely to emerge.

Automation Trends

As in almost every other aspect of library work, automation has affected both gifts and exchanges. One trend in automation is to bring gifts and exchanges into larger automated acquisitions/serials control systems. In an equally interesting trend, microcomputers ("PCs") are used to create local automated systems for aspects of gift and exchange work. As experience and technology evolve, the two trends could merge, complement one another, and, thus, automate the whole gift and exchange process.

A number of libraries have found they can exploit the similarities that exist between certain gift/exchange procedures and purchase procedures. By doing this, gift and exchange records can be made to mimic purchase records in most acquisitions systems. "Order" records for gift and exchanges differ from other order records primarily in that no payment is issued. Both purchase and nonpurchase order records can occupy the same files and use many of the same programs as purchased titles. The automated aspects of receiving and routing gift and exchange materials do not need to be different from analogous purchase procedures. The exchange partner or the donor is equivalent to the vendor, an exchange or gift list is handled like a supplier's catalogue or a bibliography, and handling of unsolicited material received through gift exchange parallels the searching and selection review processes for many blanket orders. In most acquisitions/serials control systems, one has a code indicating whether a title is acquired by gift, exchange, or purchase. This code can be used to trigger the necessary adjustments in automated claiming. Some rewording of automatic claims is necessary, price information should be suppressed, and, if initial claims fail, the problem can be referred to appropriate staff for follow-up correspondence.

Certain aspects of gifts and exchanges, however, have no counterpart in the routines of purchase acquisitions. Automating these processes involves creating specialized files and using software not generally used for purchase acquisitions. For example, exchanges must be balanced, publications must be sent regularly and reliably to partners, claims from partners must be answered, and the costs of publications sent must be managed. In exchanges the library buys and reships items almost like a book jobber; this is almost the reverse of the usual purchase acquisitions operation. Gifts also require special files, forms, and procedures — donor files, acknowledgment letters, reports to the development office, lists of gifts received by donor, and reports of revenue from sales or surplus. Both gifts and exchanges require more extensive original correspondence than is normal in acquisition by purchase.

The trend for routines not parallel to purchase acquisitions is toward automating them independently from the main acquisitions system, offline in word processors, in batch printouts, or in linked or stand-alone microcomputer systems.[3] This trend seems to have an active future. The low cost of microcomputers and of software for word processing and file management combined with the difficulty of incorporating much of gift and exchange work into larger automation systems has spawned many imaginative local automation efforts. For the last three years at the meetings of the RTSD RS Gift and Exchange Discussion Group, discussions of local microcomputer developments to automate gifts or exchanges have frequently occupied a prominent spot on the agenda.[4] At the January 1987 meeting of this group at the ALA Midwinter Conference in Chicago, almost all of the forty libraries represented had PCs available for use by gift and/or exchange staff. Many were using them for correspondence, donor files, lists of gifts received, exchange partners, exchange titles received, and materials sent. The 1985 SPEC kit on gifts and exchanges also indicated fairly widespread activity in this area. Ten stand-alone microcomputer systems were reported to be in use or under development among the sixty-three ARL libraries that responded to the questionnaire. Reported applications included partner lists with addresses, publications received and sent, form letters, correspondence, reports, gift acknowledgments, donor files, mailing labels, and lists of exchange requests. Other applications are profiles of libraries to whom unwanted gifts and withdrawn materials can be sent, and fund management for the exchange budget. Stimulated by the creative talents of individual staff members, this trend can be expected to continue because it has the effect of modernizing the approach to the work, enhancing morale, and occasioning review of procedures and files.

Looking further ahead, it seems likely that small databases of gift and exchange data will become automated and linked to files in larger systems. Especially in libraries with relatively large gift or exchange programs, it will make good management sense to take advantage of the existence of machine-readable gift and exchange records in as many applications as possible. Interfaces between microcomputer and larger systems are proliferating. If the data in a stand-alone system are even partly standardized they can be digested by a larger system. Transferring data automatically from acquisitions/serials files and online catalogues to microprocessors is even easier. As capacities for microprocessors grow, enabling them to gain simultaneous access to more than one system, the potential is enormous. One can easily envisage a multiwindowed terminal at a microprocessor workstation online simultaneously to the serials control system, the online catalogue, the correspondence files, a mailing list database, and a word-processing software package. The cost of such linkages may be much lower than the cost of combining the required files in a single, larger system.

Trends in Policy: Costs/Benefits, Assessing and Supporting Real Needs

There are many more written policy statements for gifts than for exchanges. Kovacic noted that half the libraries in his 1977-1978 study had written gift policies while "only a few" had written exchange policies.[5] In 1984 Futas reported ten gift and zero exchange policies among the academic libraries whose policies are represented.[6] In the 1976 SPEC kit, only half of the policy statements represented address exchange policy formally.[7] In the 1985 SPEC kit, a number of gift policies were reported as being revised in the wake of the Tax Reform Act of 1984, but new activity in exchange policy is not mentioned.[8]

GIFT POLICIES

Gift policies have, in the main, been standardized for some time. Such policies state what donors need to know before making a donation (e.g., gifts "with strings attached" cannot be accepted), and that the library reserves the right to make retention decisions, to dispose of unwanted items, and to set processing priorities after receiving the gift. Some gift policies outline the subject and geographical areas in which materials are most welcome (at the risk of offending donors with materials in other fields). Since the Tax Reform Act of 1984, many gift policy statements to donors explain that libraries no longer can provide or pay for appraisals of donations for tax deduction purposes. Some of these policies explain other appraisal possibilities which may be arranged. Some gift policy statements have been revised to inform donors of their reporting obligations and the reporting requirements imposed on libraries under current tax law.

Gift policy statements for internal use may include information not intended to be seen by donors. They may cover the library's policy on soliciting gifts aggressively and they may contain guidelines describing the types of material wanted and/or not wanted as gifts. The policies on bookplating, maintaining donor files, and sharing donor file information with other fund-raising programs may also be spelled out in these internal documents. Written or not, most gift policies are based on a shared body of donor patterns, library procedures, and public relations concerns, and on collection development needs.

A new trend is for gift programs to articulate ways of demonstrating their usefulness to the rest of the library. At recent RTSD RS Gift and Exchange Discussion Group meetings, repeated interest was shown in finding ways to turn more gifts into revenue and to use them to supplement various collection development needs. Sales of gifts and the use of the proceeds to supplement salary, supply, and equipment budgets are topics of recurring interest. Questions about the incorporation of gifts in exchange programs have indicated increased interest in this way of "recycling" gifts. At the Discussion Group's meeting in Chicago, January 1987, it was reported that many libraries had developed procedures to substitute gifts, at least selectively, for worn or stolen copies of the same titles in the collections. In earlier discussions, the shelf checking involved in this substitution was deemed far more costly than the benefits to the collections, but recently increased interest in preservation in many libraries has made this investment of time appear more worthwhile. Similarly, several libraries reported comparing gift receipts systematically with out-of-print desiderata files. One had developed a PC program to do this checking. At least one large library maintains, on a PC, profiles of the needs of smaller institutions to whom unwanted gifts are forwarded. Gift policies governing routine donor and development activity have become stabilized, leaving gift programs freer to explore innovative ways to use microprocessors and to interact with other units of the library.

EXCHANGE POLICIES

The state of exchange policy is much less stable. The purpose of an exchange policy should be to articulate the scope of an institution's need for exchanges and its level of commitment to the program. Before such policy can be constructed, the benefits of exchange for a given library must be determined. To do this, the library must recognize clearly its need for publications obtainable on exchange, and must assess realistically the costs of operating — and of not operating — an adequate exchange program. The process involves undertaking a self-study (formal or informal). These have occurred or are occurring at a number of libraries. To arrive at a formal exchange policy requires yet another process in which collection development and technical services articulate their involvement in, and commitment to, exchanges.

Cost studies published in and before the early 1970s tended to show exchange to be an economical way of acquiring materials.[9] Afterward, a number of converging trends appeared to increase the costs of operating exchanges. With the increased emphasis by library management on automation possibilities, systematic management techniques, systems analysis studies, and operations research, the automation of purchase acquisitions became a priority for many libraries. It was relatively easy to streamline and automate most manual purchase acquisitions functions, and it was not difficult to design a system incorporating those aspects of exchange which are analogous to purchase. However, some of the most costly elements of exchange resisted streamlining and automation: the original correspondence, the exotic language skills, the staff time to provide materials to partners and to balance exchanges, and the frequent consultations with collection development. In the midst of the trend in pursuit of efficiency to automate what could be automated, exchange stood out as an expensive and complex problem for a number of technical services managers. Meanwhile, more of the types of publication acquired through exchanges appeared to be becoming increasingly available by purchase. Commercial trade in Eastern Europe, the Soviet Union, Africa, and Latin America seemed to be opening up, and vendors were promoting their abilities to supply materials from these regions. To make purchase seem even more attractive, the prices of these materials were very low compared to Western publications. Also during this period there was a dramatic increase in the costs to libraries of the publications many of them had been offering on exchange. University presses and other publishing agents within campuses were being called upon to show a profit, were discontinuing low-revenue publications, and would not give the generous discounts previously offered to exchange programs.

Not surprisingly, the cost studies issued during the 1970s reported that exchange had become an expensive way to acquire materials. In the wake of these studies, a number of libraries established policies to obtain a title by exchange only if it could not be purchased, some smaller research libraries simply discontinued acquisition by exchange, and some fostered a policy to use exchange only as a last resort.[10] As a result of these studies, it became fairly well accepted that exchange is, indeed, costly to operate but can be cost-effective — if it avoids acquisition of material easily purchased, if economies of scale can be called upon and procedures streamlined, and if the benefits to research collections are taken into account.

The current trend appears to be toward policies asserting the need for exchange commensurate with collection development policy needs, the cost of materials to offer on exchange, and the commitment from technical services and automation efforts to manage exchange and meet stated collecting needs. Exchange is a necessity if a goal of an institution is to develop research collections containing titles available only by exchange. A few institutions have recently reported increased stability and support for exchanges.[11] Conversely, in light of all that has been learned about exchange costs, those libraries without collection development needs for exchange are unlikely to reopen exchange activity.

Once exchange policy is established, there is a challenge to make exchange efficient, using automation techniques and creative organizational approaches such as those described above. Once policies are established, a comprehensive review of titles received and of overlaps in the array of a library's exchange partnerships can occur.

Other Factors Affecting Trends
in Gifts and Exchanges

Beside the trends originating within libraries that shape gift and exchange programs, certain environmental factors can also have a significant impact on these programs.

THE TAX REFORM ACT OF 1986

It was noted earlier that the 1984 tax reform measure increased library recordkeeping and the complexity of library donor relations significantly. The Tax Reform Act of 1986 did nothing to simplify these requirements. The more recent tax change diminishes donors' ability to claim charitable contributions as income deductions. This may prove to have a negative impact. It may diminish the quantity and quality of gifts, and cause some donors to postpone donations.

Beginning January 1, 1987, only donors who itemize deductions will be able to claim a deduction for charitable contributions. The new law also reduces the number of people who will itemize deductions by greatly increasing the standard deduction available without itemizing. Furthermore, it reduces the attractiveness of claiming a deduction by lowering the tax rates, making the tax savings smaller than under the old law. For those donors with high incomes, the appreciated value of a donation must be declared as income in computing the amount subject to the Alternative Minimum Tax. Most library collections are unlikely to suffer from this ruling, but it will have an impact on beneficiaries of donations of stock or other property which appreciate rapidly. Some special collections and collections gathered in Third World areas, if the donor has a high income, could be affected.

The impact of the 1986 tax reform is difficult to predict. On the one hand, it was not until 1982 that nonitemizers were allowed to claim deductions for charitable contributions, and certainly libraries received many valuable donations before 1982. Donors of small gifts to libraries probably act out of reverence for printed material, and donors of larger gifts will often itemize under the new law. On the other hand, judging from how frequently small gifts are accompanied by requests for a letter of acknowledgment "for tax purposes," there may be a significant number of donations that libraries will cease to see in the future.

EXTERNAL ECONOMIC CONSIDERATIONS

The last few years have seen the gap between library materials budgets and the cost of library materials widen, particularly for serials and particularly for serials from major Western European countries. The purchasing power of the U.S. dollar began to decline relative to the Western European and Japanese currencies in January 1985, and the purchasing power of many Third-World currencies weakened in comparison to the dollar during the same period. Inflation in library materials has been occurring in foreign markets as well as in the United States, adding to the loss of purchasing power in budgets for research collections. For over two years, dramatic increases in the costs of European journals sold in America have been of concern to the American Library Association, and are still being reported. Few research libraries are reporting increases in appropriations for materials commensurate with their losses in purchasing power in these areas. The implications for cost/benefit studies of exchange programs are significant. Policies to use exchange only when purchase of vital research materials is impossible lose some of their strength when purchase budgets are so strained that purchase, too, seems impossible. Increasing use of exchange seems to be a way to spare beleaguered serials budgets. On the other hand, the notion of sheltering titles available on exchange while research libraries do without important titles not available on exchange raises new questions about collection priorities and goals.

GENERAL OBSERVATIONS

Gift and exchange programs did not seem to decline in importance to research libraries in the latter half of the 1980s. On the contrary, some trends pointed to their increased use in some libraries.

Gift operations achieved a small niche in library organizations some time ago as an element of library public relations as well as a method of acquisition. As long as there are donors to libraries, there must be gift operations. Managers of gift programs seem to be trying to raise the profile of their operations by demonstrating their usefulness to the library and by laying claim to their share of automation efforts.

The future trend for exchanges seems to head toward stabilization through policy, but exchange policy has been slower to emerge than gifts policy. Following a trend to reduce costs, examine needs, and narrow programs in the last two decades, managers now seem better able to accept the unique potential of exchange programs in contributing to certain collections in research libraries. Not all libraries need an exchange program. Those that do, however, seem to be inclining toward defining exchange activity at a level proportionate to their collection development requirements and ability to support exchanges.

These trends are not surprising if viewed in a larger context. It may be that a maturation process is being witnessed. As technical services and collection development management come of age, it becomes easier for managers in these fields to recognize and accept their programs' real needs, conflicts, and future options. This understanding makes it easier for gifts and exchanges to function effectively as avenues of acquisition. Along with purchase acquisitions, well-managed and adequately supported gifts and exchanges are becoming accepted as important means of achieving collection development goals.

NOTES

[1]Kovacic, Mark. Gifts and exchanges in U.S. academic libraries. *Library resources and technical services* 24, no. 2: 159 (Spring 1980)

These findings are supported by a SPEC kit: Association of Research Libraries, Office of University Library Management Studies. Gifts and exchange functions in ARL libraries, SPEC Flyer, no. 28. Washington, DC: ARL, 1976. Document 1, Table 1

[2]Association of Research Libraries, Office of University Library Management Studies. Gifts and exchange function in ARL libraries, SPEC Flyer, no. 117. Washington, DC: ARL, 1985. pp. 59-61. Responses to a survey of gift and exchange practices in U.S. research libraries as of 1985.

[3]The automated system at the University of California, Berkeley, is described briefly by: Barker, Joseph W. A case for exchange: the experience of the University of California, Berkeley. *Serials Review* 12, no. 1:69 (1986)

The theory for automating exchange by exploiting its parallels with already automated purchase procedures at the University of California, Los Angeles, and creating stand-alone systems for the rest is set forth by: Jones, Herbert and Margaret McKinley. Automated exchanges control: an interim report. *In* Projects and procedures for serials administration/ ed. by Diane Stine. Ann Arbor, MI: Pierian Press, 1985, pp. 51-60

Surprisingly little has been published on these minor successes in automation.

[4]Libraries whose PC applications have been described in detail are at the University of Utah, the University of California, Berkeley, and Stanford University.

[5]Kovacic. *Op cit*. p. 157

[6]Futas, Elizabeth, *ed.* Library acquisition policies and procedures. Phoenix, AZ: Oryx Press, 1984

[7]Association of Research Libraries. *Op cit*. no. 28 (1976). Document 2

[8]Association of Research Libraries. *Op cit*. no. 117 (1985). p. 2, and SPEC kit pp. 2-41.

[9]Novak, Victor. Let's exchange profitably. *Library resources and technical services* 9:349 (1965) [University of Santa Clara Library]; Galejs, John. Economics of serials exchanges. Library resources and technical services 16:517 (1972) [Iowa State University Library]; Lane, Alfred H. The economics of exchange. *In* Gifts and exchange manual. Westport, CT: Greenwood, 1980, pp. 17-19 [Columbia University Library; adapted from a 1952 paper on exchange costs]

[10]Reports of cost studies which led to policies of retrenchment and use of exchange only as a last resort when purchase cannot be used have been published by: Bluh, Pamela and Virginia C. Haines. The exchange of publications: an alternative to acquisitions. *Serials review* 5:106 (1979) [concerning Johns Hopkins University Library]; Stevens, Jana K. *et al.* Cost-effectiveness of Soviet serial exchanges. *Library resources and technical services* 26:154 (1982) [concerning Duke University Library, and referring to similar policies at the University of Utah and the University of Washington]; Wood, D. N. Current exchange of serials at the British Library Lending Division. *Library acquisitions: practice and theory* 3:108 (1979) [reports a "last resort" policy]

[11]Cautious expansion of exchanges, closely monitored for costs was recommended for the University of Illinois at Urbana-Champaign Library by: Yu, Priscilla. Cost analysis: domestic serials exchanges. *Serials review* 8:80, 82 (1982)

The University of California, Berkeley, has approved a formal exchange policy, described by: Barker. *Op. cit.* p. 68; McKinley, Margaret. The exchange program at UCLA: 1932 through 1986. *Serials review* 12:78-80 (1986) [reports that the University of California, Los Angeles, having recognized its need for a sizable exchange program, is proceeding to provide additional automated support to make the program more efficient).

At least one of the libraries that adopted a "last resort" policy in the wake of an earlier cost study reported at the 1987 ALA Midwinter Conference that it had identified the need to enlarge its exchange program under recent pressure from collection development officers for materials available only on exchange.

FURTHER READINGS

Bandara, S. B. Dormant exchanges: a suggestion for less wasteful exchanges. *Libri* 28:313-322 (1978)
Suggests agreements to exchange only when publications are urgently needed, in order to avoid sending partners publications that will get little use.

Kovacic, Mark. Acquisition by gift and exchange. *In* Acquisition of foreign materials for U.S. libraries. Metuchen, NJ: Scarecrow Press, 1982. pp. 34-41
Provides general guidelines for use of exchanges and gifts.

Payne, John R. A closer eye on appraisals. *College and research libraries news* 46:52-56 (1985)
Discussion of the implications of the Tax Reform Act of 1984 on appraisals for gifts in kind to libraries. See also his:
A closer eye on appraisals: a clarification. *College and research libraries news* 46:174-175 (1985)

Reid, Marion. Technical services management: the gifts and exchange operations: considerations for review. *RTSD Newsletter* 10:21-24 (1985)
Outlines general options for organizing and managing gift and exchange operations.

Schenck, William Z. Evaluating and valuing gift materials. *Library acquisitions: practice and theory* 6:33-40 (1982)
Although pre-1984 tax reform, contains useful advice on appraising and acknowledging gifts.

Volkersz, E. Gift development realities in academic libraries. *In* Academic libraries: myths and realities, proceedings of the Third National Conference of the Association of College and Research Libraries. Chicago: ACRL, 1984. pp. 290-292.
Discusses important truisms about cultivating and maintaining productive donor relationships, with emphasis on special collections and relevance to other gifts operations.

SERIAL ACQUISITIONS:
Trends and Prospects

Many of the social, economic, and technological developments that have influenced the direction of libraries over the past twenty-five years are illustrated vividly in the area of the acquisitions of serial publications. Ordering, claiming, and inventory control are the processes involved. However, the forces that influence the acquisition and control of serials include the nature of intellectual inquiry and knowledge dissemination; the vagaries of inflation, currency valuation, marketplace competition, and library budgets; and a host of technological factors facing all parties to the chain of knowledge/information dissemination. Serials are published by commercial and university presses, learned societies, academic departments, small presses, commercial firms, and government agencies in response to motives that range from the urge to share knowledge to "publish or perish" pressures to a greed for profit. Decisions to purchase serials lock libraries into large annual commitments of funds. Thus, materials that are, often, little used are now gobbling up huge chunks of our budgets owing to steep price increases and a weakening dollar. As this happens, serial expenditures squeeze out discretionary funds for monographic purchases, a phenomenon that may alter the nature of library collections significantly. At the same time, automation is having a radical effect on the way in which serials are published, marketed, and managed.

In the late 1980s, these factors have brought us to a pivotol position. Libraries can no longer carry the enormous financial burden imposed upon them by skyrocketing subscription costs and the proliferation of new serial titles. The current literature is increasingly peppered with cries for librarians to become critical consumers. Rather than behaving passively and paying stiff renewal invoices year after year, librarians must become partners of publishers and serial vendors not only to manage the economic burden better, but also to explore new ways of disseminating and preserving the knowledge and information traditionally gathered in the printed serial. Automation has finally made significant strides into serials acquisitions and control. After more than a decade of huge monetary investments

38

in research and development, large serial vendors are now highly automated and libraries are reaping the benefits of that automation. Automated serial control systems have now proliferated and are found in a variety of micro-, mini-, and mainframe computer manifestations. *Interface* is the contemporary buzzword. We have developed and adopted a variety of standards for serials, and vocal serials interest groups are flourishing. In the coming years, librarians and serial publishers and vendors will have the challenge of forging new relationships out of their natural interdependence.

TRENDS IN JOURNAL PUBLISHING AND PRICING

Since the mid-1970s, serial publishing and pricing have kept librarians climbing higher and higher up a veritable Jacob's ladder (one, alas, that has not taken them to heaven). The Faxon company reported that between 1975 and 1985 the journals recorded in its bibliographic database increased in price by 174.1 percent.[1] In 1987, college and university libraries paid an average subscription price of $104.69 compared to $45.16 in 1977.[2] In 1987, these libraries had to deal with an overall increase in average subscription cost of 13.4 percent, nearly double the previous year's increase of 7.2 percent.[3] Not everything in the world of serials is going up, but those indicators that are falling—the rate of real dollar increase in library budgets and the value of the U.S. dollar against foreign currencies—only serve to push us further up our Jacob's ladder.

How did we get to where we are? In his 1977 article "Escalating journal prices: time to fight back," De Gennaro describes the relationship between libraries and serial publishers prior to the affluent 1960s as a genteel scholarly partnership.[4] Libraries had little money and publishers neither glutted the market nor priced serials beyond the reach of library budgets. During the 1960s, higher education received enormous increases in funding. Library budgets grew and scholarly publishing became a big business. The complicated factors that culminated in our present state of affairs were set in motion in the 1970s. In his excellent study, Taylor describes the social and economic factors that led to a dramatic proliferation of scholarly journals and a concomitant escalation in their prices to libraries.[5] Instructional staff in colleges and universities increased steadily. As academic research flourished, so did the need to communicate research findings. Ever more specialized fields of enquiry branched off from main disciplines. This resulted in the growth in the number of specialized and (because the audiences were small) very expensive journals to communicate research findings. Commercial publishers entered the scholarly market in increasing numbers because they could more easily afford to take the financial risks involved and because they discovered, to quote De Gennaro, that "librarians have a weakness for journals and numbered series of all kinds. Once they get volume 1, number 1 of a series, they are hooked until the end."[6]

As journal publication increased, the economic climate of the 1970s was also causing subscription prices to increase dramatically.[7] Publishers' costs rose because of declines in revenue from advertising and page charges. During the 1960s, page charges were a major source of publisher revenue and were generally covered by research grants. In the mid-1970s, the amount of federal support for academic research declined precipitously and, thus, publishers lost this valuable source of income. The costs of paper and printing were also rising. As publishers' costs increased and revenue from other sources declined, the institutional sub-scription rate that is such a burden today became an increasingly important source of income for the publishers. Publishers justified this higher rate by assert-ing that library subscriptions were used by many more than one person. In the early 1960s, publishers' commissions to subscription agencies were sufficient for the latter to make a profit. By the late 1960s, publishers began to withhold these commissions because of rising costs. Therefore, between 1965 and 1973 serial vendors began to apply service charges to library subscriptions in order to reach sufficient operating margins.[8] Although library budgets increased during the 1970s, the purchasing power of the library dollar declined. This phenomenon continued into the 1980s and now has been exacerbated further by discriminatory pricing by foreign publishers and the decline of the U.S. dollar against other currencies.

Some foreign publishers have had, since the mid-1970s, two different prices for their domestic and foreign subscribers. Some moved, in the 1980s, to a three-tiered structure—different prices for domestic, North American, and all other foreign subscribers. Such market-based pricing aims to price goods at the level the seller believes the buyer will bear. Between 1982 and 1984, the U.S. dollar was strong against many foreign currencies, particularly the British pound sterling, a situation that should have favored American libraries. However, as the 1984 study by Hamaker and Astle revealed, North American libraries paid an average of 66.7 percent more for the titles surveyed than U.K. libraries and 34 percent more than other overseas libraries.[9] This overcharging resulted directly from pub-lishers establishing a fixed dollar rate for North American libraries rather than allowing them to pay a convertible pound sterling rate. As a result, as Hamaker and Astle point out, "through setting an unrealistically high valuation of the pound against the dollar, many British publishers had found a way to increase their sales without a corresponding increase in market penetration."[10]

The dawning awareness of such discriminatory pricing galvanized the Ameri-can library community which was already staggering under the burden of stiff yearly price increases. Hamaker and Astle's study, public discussion of the problem at ALA meetings beginning in 1984, and other pressures brought to bear on British publishers by librarians met with success. Two years after their original survey, Astle and Hamaker did a follow-up study. They reported that, in 1986, the price differential between North American and domestic British libraries had dropped 45.3 percent as compared to 1984 and the differential between North American and other overseas libraries by 49.2 percent.[11] Unfortunately, this was not due to a drop in North American prices or publishers' profits, but to increases of 21 percent and 17.3 percent respectively for British and other overseas sub-scribers.[12] The problem of discriminatory pricing has not gone away, but over the past few years North American subscribers have shouldered a lower percentage of the overall publication costs of foreign (especially British) journals than they did in previous years.

In the fall of 1985, the U.S. dollar began to weaken against other currencies as the result of the Reagan administration's effort to stimulate the U.S. economy. This process has continued and, despite some ups as well as downs, the dollar is significantly weaker now (1989) against many major currencies. This fact, com-bined with small or no increases in library budgets, has had a devastating finan-cial impact on U.S. libraries.

Actual price increases in 1988 for journals from the Netherlands, Swit-zerland, and West Germany averaged about 5 percent. However, when the rate of currency exchange is figured in, total 1988 price increases for these countries were, respectively, 29, 25, and 27 percent.[13] Since 1980, price increases for U.S. journals have steadily outdistanced general inflation rates as measured by the U.S. Consumer Price Index.

Can these trends be slowed or reversed or will they be continued until every penny of the library's materials budget is being spent on serials? That day cannot be too far away for large academic libraries which have been increasing their serial expenditures by several hundred thousand dollars a year, largely at the expense of their monograph budgets. Some libraries have undertaken massive serial cancellation projects and are still coming up short. Reports of the cancelled titles are indicative of the double bind in which libraries find themselves. Faxon reported that the 1988 cancellation rate for domestic titles was somewhat lower than that for foreign titles and that new orders to major European publishers far exceeded cancellations of titles put out by those publishers.[14] This would appear to indicate that the increasingly expensive titles from big European publishers are the ones that libraries can least afford (from a patron service viewpoint) to cancel. Publishers know this too.

One of the most impassioned arguments on the "something *can* be done" side is by Houbeck, a serials librarian at the University of Michigan.[15] He feels little sympathy for commercial publishers whose price increases far outstrip inflation and, in his view, their own cost increases. He believes that big commercial and society presses are lax in controlling their internal costs and casually pass these costs on to libraries. Foreign publishers, he notes, "appear to be using increasing portions of their revenues to finance corporate growth [by purchasing U.S. companies]" and he is angry that "the escalating prices that we are paying are being used ... to help big boys get bigger." Houbeck urges librarians to be less naive and suggests that our naivete has been "one of the key variables driving this market." He suggests that libraries could foster competitive pricing by using some serial monies to invest in small entrepreneurial publishers who have the incentive to produce similar journals at lower costs. He further urges library buyers to confront foreign publishers on the question of exchange rates.

Houbeck's suggestions are sound and should be heeded. However, we should be wary lest we degenerate into counterproductive publisher-bashing. The crisis will be solved only if we engage and persist in informed dialogue with journal publishers and with the vendors who can be strong allies. As with all wise consumerism, we must use our most powerful tool — our checkbook — to drive the point home. Libraries should undertake serious use studies to identify costly and little-used titles in their collections and explore other ways of gaining access to those materials — such as cooperative collection development programs supported by online databases and the now ubiquitous "fax" machine. Better managerial tools that enable us to project and track expenditures and use patterns will be ever more important.

SERIAL VENDOR SELECTION, SERVICES, AND EVALUATION

Few libraries have the financial or human resources necessary to perform the paper- and labor-intensive activities associated with ordering serials directly from their publishers. In any event, the rationale for direct ordering has been weakened by staff reductions, the increase in the sheer bulk of serial publishing and purchasing, and the professional service orientation of the large serial vendors. Many publishers of popular periodicals will not deal directly with subscribers but contract those services to highly automated "fulfillment centers," which are good at fulfilling individual orders and abysmally bad at providing library service. When a major publisher adopts a direct order policy (as R. R. Bowker did in 1986) thus bypassing the serial vendors, the library community protests and predicts massive customer service problems.

In the past twenty years, two domestic subscription agencies—EBSCO and Faxon—have emerged as industry leaders. Thyden and Lenzini have described the factors leading to the evolution of subscription agencies from mere clearinghouses to the highly automated and service-oriented companies we know today.[16] Libraries, faced with all the problems detailed above, began to make greater demands for services on the serial vendors. Successful agencies survived and thrived by charging service fees and reinvesting profits in the automation that became the basis of the broad range of services they now offer. These services, performed with economies of scale by subscription agents, have lifted the burden of many paper- and labor-intensive activities from the backs of libraries.

The basic advantages of using subscription agents—consolidation of ordering, payment, renewal, payment, and claiming activities—are well known and little disputed. However, what we see today are increasing incentives and increased pressure to use fewer and fewer agents. Though our foreign vendors are not yet trying to sell us domestic serials, our domestic vendors are trying for a bigger chunk of our foreign business. Some of the domestic vendors are able to compete with foreign vendors by obtaining and locking in a favorable exchange rate with publishers shortly after they set their prices. Periodical vendors are starting to compete aggressively for standing order business, long the purview of book vendors.

Legal requirements force some libraries into annual bids for their business, thus removing most of their discretionary judgment. For those who can make independent judgments, there are many pressures to consolidate with one or two vendors, despite the fact that many librarians have a gut instinct against putting all their eggs into one basket. As staff losses continue, the prospect of fewer invoices to approve, fewer checks to cut, and fewer sources from which to claim is quite attractive. As we rely increasingly on vendors for management information (e.g., price comparison studies), it would seem preferable to obtain such information from one source rather than compiling it from several sources. Another perceived advantage of consolidation has to do with serials automation. Bibliographic data can be transferred from the agent's database into the library's database without rekeying. Claims and invoicing information can also be transmitted from computer to computer, all at great savings of time and money.

Despite the pressures to consolidate, vendor selection has to remain a careful process that is evaluated regularly in the light of the library's objectives and priorities. The library has to decide the priority it places on the following factors—cost (discounts and service costs), fulfillment percentage, claiming effectiveness, and managerial information. The scope, size, and complexity of the serials collection have also to be considered.

Vendor selection based primarily on type of material or publisher is not necessarily wise. A good mix of orders usually results in a lower service charge overall. In *A Librarian's Guide to Serials*, Faxon lists publishers whose journals can lower Faxon's service charge significantly. There is, as yet, no serious study comparing fulfillment and costs of domestic and foreign vendors for foreign serials. Domestic vendors have the jump on foreign vendors when it comes to automation and its byproducts, but the foreign vendors are picking up speed and will need to do so if they are to compete successfully with U.S. agents. Two excellent articles deal with serial vendor selection and performance evaluation. Derthick and Moran discuss the results of a 1985 Association of Research Libraries study of its members use of subscription agents. Bonk's paper is a valuable effort to outline a methodology for a systematic evaluation of vendor performance.[17]

Cargill offers a good (though somewhat outdated) survey of vendor services.[18] Though this paper cannot attempt an exhaustive examination of vendor services, a few services that pertain to trends noted elsewhere in this chapter are worthy of mention.

Increased electronic transmission of data between library/vendor and vendor/publisher is a trend that will have major implications for speeding up processing time and increasing accuracy. Transmitted data includes orders, publication and pricing information, claims, and general queries. Data can be transmitted via magnetic tape, online access, and electronic mail. Lennie describes the most effective types of application for each: "The timing of exchanges depends on how much data must be transferred and how fast. Sending orders from agents to suppliers is an infrequent but high volume exchange, suitable for magnetic tapes. Online access to a remote system is needed for interactive communication, such as searching through a file. Electronic mail is suitable for short, but frequent, communication and is a very economic service."[19] Many agents now routinely transmit orders to publishers via magnetic tape. Faxon reports that it processed 60 percent of its 1988 orders in this manner.[20] Currently, forty publishers can accept magnetic tape orders. This number is unlikely to increase without an industry standard for ordering and claiming, such as the one the Serial Industry Systems Advisory Committee (SISAC) is now working on. Some domestic and foreign agents also offer libraries the option of receiving their annual renewal invoice on magnetic tape which can then be run into a library's own accounting system. Both EBSCO and Faxon, through their electronic databases, EBSCONET and LINX, offer online transmission of orders and claims between library and vendor. Faxon also has online communications with many publishers through PUBLINX. Pergamon reports similar online connections with agents in Japan, Europe, the United Kingdom, and the Americas.[21] One area in which such online connections are having significant impact is in serial claims processing, long a bugaboo for libraries, vendors, and publishers. Local check-in systems can generate a file of claims which can then be transferred electronically to the vendor's mainframe and, thence, transmitted electronically to publishers.

One of the most important byproducts of automation has been the wide variety of managerial reports vendors can supply. EBSCO's Historical Price Analysis Report and Faxon's SCOPE Report (three years of comparative pricing information) are both excellent tools for analyzing and projecting serial expenditures. Faxon can also provide their report arranged by country of publication to enable libraries to track expenditures against foreign currencies.

Two agents, Faxon and Nijhoff, offer interest programs for early prepayment of renewal invoices. The vendor pays interest on the principal between the date payment is received and the date it is due. These programs offer libraries a valuable opportunity for recouping a percentage of their serial expenditures.

Future vendor services will probably include more sophisticated interfaces and electronic connections with both libraries and publishers. Faxon is already branching out into the document delivery business in conjunction with Information on Demand, Inc. Users of Faxon's automated system (LINX) can order laser-printed copies of articles from more than 200 biomedical journals maintained on the ADONIS CD-ROM database.

Serial vendors have always served as mediators between libraries and publishers, and it will be interesting to see how this relationship evolves. Publishers accept business from vendors for the same basic reason that libraries give business to vendors — a transfer of the costly labor-intensive activities associated with order fulfillment from their shoulders to the vendors'. In this time of skyrocketing journal prices, libraries are increasingly asking vendors to run interference for them with publishers. In many instances vendors have gone to bat for libraries by conveying the concerns of libraries, asking publishers to keep price increases within reason, and providing publisher-specific pricing information to libraries. Some vendors have even participated in "buying around" activities in order to provide U.K. publications to U.S. customers at U.K. rates. Can vendors remain neutral observers in the price wars? What is the role of vendors as more publishers move into electronic publishing? Will they become retail agents for publishers of electronic information? Much, of course, depends on technology and economics. As long as agent services are economically beneficial for publishers and libraries they will continue to be used. However, if technology makes it easier and more cost-effective for producers of information to deal directly with end users, the vendor's role may be limited.

Libraries, vendors, and publishers are still very interdependent. Librarians should not simply wait for vendors to come to them with new services; they should become actively involved by suggesting new services and improvements to existing services.

SERIALS AUTOMATION

In the early 1980s, the automation of serial processing was likened by some librarians to "growing bananas in Greenland" or "nailing jello" — a task both fruitless and unwise. Although the automation of serials control came later than other library automation, by 1984 twenty of forty-seven bibliographic networks, subscription agents, automated systems vendors, and software developers surveyed by Information Systems Consultants, Inc., had operational automated serials control systems. Twelve hoped to offer this service by the end of 1985, and ten others reported future development plans.[22] The question for most libraries now is not *whether* they should automate but *which* of the plethora of main-frame, mini-, or micro-based systems they should choose. Serials control has always been a problem for libraries, largely because of the erratic nature of serials themselves. Automated serials control systems have provided a viable alternative to chaos at the Kardex, liberated many libraries from cumbersome and specialized manual files, and redefined the nature of professional duties associated with serials acquisition and control.

Several factors had to converge before serials automation was feasible. Cataloguing, circulation, and public access catalogues had all been successfully and extensively automated by the early 1980s and the expertise gained in these areas could then be focused on one of librarianship's major problems. The quantity and expense of serial publications had increased dramatically. As library expenditures for serials increased, so did the need for better managerial information about those expenditures. The demand for journal literature was growing. Automation had in many areas blurred the distinction between technical and public services. Expectations of computer-literate patrons were rising. In an automated environment, emphasis had begun to shift from librarian-oriented bibliographic control to patron-oriented bibliographic access. More sophisticated computing capabilities were becoming available to support the complex data manipulation and computer-to-computer communication necessary for automated serials control.

Most libraries that automate serials control wish to gain the ability to maintain large quantities of information more effectively, to improve staff and patron access to serials records, to obtain faster and more efficient check-in and claiming, and to have better managerial information about serial expenditures. Although reorganization of serial processing within the library is not always a goal of automating serials control, it is an inevitable result of doing so. Many of the activities formerly associated with professional serial specialists become routine computer processes. As a result of serials automation, Gorman foresaw the replacement of professional serials librarians by an emerging semiprofessional and clerical class — "technicians dealing with the ordering, claiming, receipt, copy cataloguing of, and payment for library materials of all kinds" working "within frameworks devised by librarians and, in many cases, under the direction of librarians."[23]

TRENDS IN SERIALS AUTOMATION

A survey of available automated serial control systems is not within the scope of this chapter. Descriptions of systems and their implementation in various libraries abound in the literature. However, several evident trends in this area are appropriate for discussion.

Early visions of those involved in the design of bibliographic networks pictured totally integrated library systems. In 1968, Kilgour envisaged the future of OCLC: "The entire system, including shared cataloging, bibliographic information retrieval, circulation control, serials control, and technical processing, will be based on one file, thereby achieving a truly comprehensive system."[24] In fact, OCLC's mainframe-based Serials Control System (SCS) was long awaited, largely unsuccessful, and short-lived. In 1985, OCLC announced that it would no longer support SCS after the summer of 1987. Instead it offered SC350, a micro-based serial control system to which its customers could migrate. By that time, SCS users could also choose one of several other micro-based systems newly on the market.

What happened with OCLC illustrates an important technological trend in serials control — a trend away from serials control as part of a totally integrated system toward a modular design of serial control systems that interface with online catalogues, circulation systems, and vendors' mainframes. The enormous advances in microcomputing capabilities and telecommunications protocols that make possible sophisticated computer-to-computer communications have been central to this trend. It is now completely possible for serial check-in to be performed locally on a microcomputer and, through an interface, to transfer current issue information into an online catalogue. Access to that catalogue could in turn be gained by other libraries in a state or regional consortium. The data-intensive work is done in the least expensive computing environment, thus realizing large savings in telecommunications charges. Faxon's and EBSCO's mainframe-based serial check-in systems were among the first commercially available systems. Now both companies have introduced micro-based systems. Faxon's Microlinx is an excellent example of efficient use of computing services.

Interface has become the buzzword among today's serial and serials systems vendors. This is an intriguing twist in a competitive and profit-making environment. Faxon, both a materials and a systems vendor, has been most active in this area and has created an entire division devoted to library/vendor interfaces. A GEAC interface allows users to alternate between Faxon's Microlinx check-in and the GEAC online catalogue. Another interface allows Faxon invoice renewals to be automatically transferred into the NOTIS system. Faxon and Innovative Interfaces are working on an interface between their two systems.

Another important trend affecting serials automation is the development and use of standards. Standards have been a driving force in automation efforts and will certainly shape future developments in automated serials management. Standards play an important role in bibliographic description of serials and in their processing. Their purpose is to assist in the identification and exchange of information between computers and in the uniform interpretation of that information by users of more than one system. They are essential to all automation, resource sharing, and data conversion activities. The two most important efforts made in the area of serial standards in recent years have been those of SISAC and the US MARC Format for Holdings and Location.

SISAC is a forum for serial publishers, vendors, retailers, librarians, and database producers to develop industry-wide standardized formats. SISAC had three objectives when it was formed in 1982: standardized formats for computer-to-computer ordering of serials, standardized coding for serial issues to promote automated check-in and circulation, and standardized coding of serial articles to aid in the payment of royalties through the Copyright Clearance Center and the identification and retrieval of articles in full text and bibliographic databases.[25] The SISAC machine-scannable bar-code format was slow to catch on at first, but the number of publishers who print the bar code on their journals is increasing. Initially, the SISAC code will probably be most used for issue identification, and bar-code scanning capabilities have been built into most automated serials control systems. The SISAC Test Report, issued in early 1987, reported that libraries, publishers, and system vendors who participated in a test of the bar code found it readable, functional, and flexible. For libraries in the test, the bar code significantly reduced the time and increased the accuracy of check-in by eliminating keying errors.[26]

The US MARC Format for Holdings and Location, development of which began in 1982, is a communications format for carrying holdings and location data from computer to computer. To date, the emphasis in developing the format has been in relation to serials holdings information.

> The most crucial need is for the ability to communicate and exchange
> holdings and location data in a standard manner. Such information is
> a necessary component of online catalogs and is an essential ingredient

in such applications as cooperative acquisitions, collection development, preservation programs, national union catalogs, and union list activities, and is a link in fully automated interlibrary loan/document delivery systems.[27]

Several automated serials control systems have already implemented the MARC holdings format in their systems.

Contemporary automated serial control systems are designed for management of serials in print format. The future of automated serials control is inextricably tied to the technological, economic, and social factors that may converge to alter the nature and distribution of serial literature as we now know it. Libraries can no longer afford to shoulder the financial burden of growing numbers of serial publications at higher and higher prices. The low use of this costly and cumbersome material only serves to heighten the need to re-evaluate the traditional journal as an effective vehicle for communicating research findings. As full-text databases and electronic document delivery systems develop further — a direction which libraries should encourage, in part to avert the journal crisis we face — we may find our financial resources directed away from the bottomless pit of serial expenditures and automated systems to control print serials. In their place may come more office equipment — microcomputers and printers — to give access to full-text computer databases and to order or print out copies in response to actual user demand. Libraries have an important role to play in this development. Electronically produced and maintained information carries the risk of restricting access by requiring computing equipment and fees. Libraries can reallocate traditional serial expenditures and intervene to ensure access to new information sources for all interested users. This is an exciting time to work in serials acquisitions. Librarians, publishers, and vendors all have important roles in influencing future directions in the publication, distribution, and collection of serial literature.

NOTES

[1]Lenzini, Rebecca T. and Judith Horn. 1975-1985: formulative years for the subscription agency. *Serials librarian* 10:225 (Fall 1985/Winter 1985-86

[2]Lenzini, Rebecca T. Periodical prices 1885-1987 update. *Serials librarian* 13:53 (Sept. 1987)

[3]*Ibid*. p. 50

[4]De Gennaro, Richard. Escalating journal prices: time to fight back. *American libraries* 8:70 (Feb. 1977)

[5]Taylor, David C. Managing the serials explosion: the issues for publishers and libraries. White Plains, NY: Knowledge Industry, 1982. pp. 26-36

[6]De Gennaro. *Op cit*. p. 69

[7]Taylor. *Op cit.* pp. 20-25

[8]Thyden, Wayne. Subscription agency size: threat or benefit? *Serials librarian* 7:30 (Spring 1983)

[9]Hamaker, Charles and Deana Astle. Recent pricing patterns in British journal publishing. *Library acquisitions: practice and theory* 8:229 (1984)

[10]*Ibid.* p. 226

[11]Astle, Deana and Charles Hamaker. Pricing by geography: British journal pricing 1986, including developments in other countries. *Library acquisitions: practice and theory* 10:170 (1986)

[12]*Ibid.* p. 173

[13]Faxon Company. Budget planning for Faxon clients. Westwood, MA: 1988

[14]Rowe, Richard. Remarks at LINX Users Meeting Breakfast, San Antonio, Jan. 11, 1988

[15]Houbeck, Robert L. If present trends continue: responding to journal price increases. *Journal of academic librarianship* 13:214-220 (Sept. 1987)

[16]Thyden. *Op cit.* pp. 29-34; Lenzini and Horn. *Op. cit.* pp. 225-238

[17]Derthick, Jan and Barbara B. Moran. Serials agent selection in ARL libraries. *In* Advances in serials management. Greenwich, CT: JAI Press, 1986. pp. 1-42; Bonk, Sharon C. Toward a methodology of evaluating serials vendors. *Library acquisitions: theory and practice* 9:51-60 (1985)

[18]Cargill, Jennifer. The vendor services supermarket: the new consumerism. *In* Serials and microforms: patron oriented management. Westport, CT: Meckler Publishing, 1983. pp. 97-109

[19]Lennie, Michael. The emerging publisher network (cont'd). *In* Proceedings of the Sixth Annual LINX Users Meeting. Westwood, MA: Faxon Company, 1987. p. 51

[20]Appleton, Diane. The emerging publisher network. *In* Proceedings of the Sixth Annual LINX Users Meeting. Westwood, MA: Faxon Company, 1987. p. 48

[21]Lennie, *Op cit.* p. 53

[22]Boss, Richard W. Developing requirements for automated serials control systems. *Serials librarian* 11:37 (Dec. 1986/Jan. 1987)

[23]Gorman, Michael. Dealing with serials: a sketch of contextual/organizational response. *Serials librarian* 10:17 (Fall 1985/Winter 1985-86)

[24]Kilgour, Fred. Initial systems design for the Ohio College Library Center: a case history. *In* Proceedings of the Clinic on Data Processing. Urbana: University of Illinois Graduate School of Library Science, 1969. pp. 86-87

[25]Serials Industry Systems Advisory Committee. Report. *SISAC News* 1:3-4 (Oct. 1985)

[26]Serials Industry Systems Advisory Committee. SISAC Test Report released at ALA Midwinter (press release), January 1987

[27]US MARC Format for Holdings and Location. Washington, DC: Library of Congress, Network Development and MARC Standards Office (Final Draft 1984). pp. 1-2

MONITORING THE INFORMATION RESOURCES BUDGET:
Acquisitions Accounting

JENNIFER CARGILL

A library exists to provide information services for an identifiable client group. It is a nonprofit entity that generally receives its funding from a parent organization such as a government agency or municipality, or a private educational institution. That portion of the budget which is devoted to the acquisition of materials (in traditional and new forms) is commonly called the materials budget. For reasons explained below, it is referred to in this chapter as the *information resources budget*.

The library will receive its funding via one of the following different budgeting methods.

Line-item budget. In a line-item budget the anticipated expenditures are grouped by categories.

Lump-sum budget. The total budget for the library is identified. The library can then determine what will be spent in different expense categories: operating, personnel, and materials acquisitions.

Program budgets. Allocations are identified for specific programs or activities such as database searching, rather than by accounting categories. Thus emphasis is on what is accomplished with money requested.

Program Planning Budget Systems (PPBS). A refinement of program budgeting. The budget is allocated into all expenditure categories or programs. Each program's existence and implementation is justified with continual evaluation.

Zero-based Budgeting (ZBB). Each budget category is started with zero, with justification required for all allocations.

Libraries commonly use the previous year's budget as a starting point for budget justification for the upcoming year. It is usually realistic to plan budgets in this manner since a library will have certain continuing commitments. This is certainly true of the information resources budget.

IMPORTANCE OF MONITORING

Libraries have a continuing responsibility to ensure that information resources monies are dispersed to the appropriate individuals, monies are encumbered and expended properly, and institutional financial policies and procedures are followed both to the letter of the law and in the spirit intended. The responsibility for many of the financial procedures and the information resources funds usually resides, completely or in part, in the acquisitions department.

To discuss and explain acquisitions accounting adequately is a lengthy process. Sources of detailed policies and procedures with practical examples are listed in Further Readings at the end of this chapter. The books by Alley, Smith, and Ramsey provide relevant advice and examples as well as cover the topic in greater depth. The books by Auld and Swersey are examples of the recent books available on the use of spreadsheets on microcomputers.

Considerations in establishing and maintaining an acquisitions accounting system and the future of such systems will be discussed in this chapter. It will deal primarily with the fundamentals of acquisitions accounting, concerns and guidelines within the process, and developing trends.

FROM THE MATERIALS BUDGET TO THE INFORMATION RESOURCES BUDGET

When libraries and librarians have thought of the materials budget—the funds set aside for acquisitions—the focus has traditionally been on the purchase of books, serials, microforms, and on expenditures for binding. In the late 1980s, information is increasingly available in a variety of types of recently developed technological media. Emerging technologies promise to provide even more methods of distributing information. Access to information is no longer totally dependent on print in its various forms. Databases available online electronically are accessible within the library setting as well as from the microcomputer or terminal housed in the user's office. Indexes traditionally available in paper or hardback, housed on rows of index tables, are now available online or on CD-ROM, accessed through use of a microcomputer. Some libraries can now consider cancelling subscriptions to indexing and abstracting services in favor of the availability of online or CD-ROM access.

We can now also order materials through electronic mechanisms as a matter of routine whether these are materials for permanent retention in the collection or are items acquired via interlibrary loan for patron use. Thus, through an increasingly varied mélange of information transmission media available to us, library funds are being used for the acquisition and dissemination of information rather than solely for the addition of materials to the collection.

The portion of the library budget that is spent on library materials will change as libraries move away from being warehouses for quantities of materials.

Instead libraries increasingly will be providing access to online databases or acquiring databases that can be accessed in-house rather than relying upon hard copy or information being available in hard copy. Quantity will cease to be a measurement; quality and effective access to and dissemination of information will become the focus.

While it is unlikely that we will become a paperless society, we will become more reliant upon electronic means to acquire and retain information. As libraries move to the primary emphasis on dissemination of information through different modes, including remote access, we must begin thinking of the acquisitions funds as the information resources budget, not the materials (acquisitions) budget.

ACCOUNTING WITHIN THE LIBRARY

The library will receive its information resources funding through one of the budgeting mechanisms listed above. The library must then decide to what extent it will perform accounting activities within the library. If the library elects not to monitor its own funds but rather to rely on the reports of the parent institution, the library should recognize that there will be lag time that may lead the library to overextend itself financially.

Usually the parent organization is only concerned with the overall library accounts; as long as the library adheres to established institutional guidelines, there is little concern for how much is expended within specific disciplines or acquisitions categories. The library, however, may want to have a more detailed allocation system, especially for acquisition of materials or information. This will not only assist in collection development and management but will provide data that is needed by the accrediting groups to which colleges and universities are subject. Knowledge of spending patterns will be useful in designing programs to meet the needs of specific patron categories. For our purposes, monitoring of acquisition allocations is referred to as acquisitions accounting.

Acquisitions Accounting

What is acquisitions accounting? Basically, it is the tracking of encumbrances (orders and other obligations) and expenditures against information resources allocations. This may be done by the acquisitions department itself or through the acquisitions process within a library or a library system. How this is handled will vary depending on the category of library, the governing agency, and the type of financial support. Different methodologies may be used within the acquisitions accounting process but the basic concept—effective monitoring of the encumbrances and expenditures while adhering to the institutional financial guidelines—remains the same.

Libraries have a specific amount of money that they or their parent institution designate for acquiring information resources for the library. Up to now, these resources have primarily been in the form of books, periodicals, and microforms. This is now being broadened to include information in different formats. The expenditure of acquisitions funds to gain access to, or to acquire, educational and research information from databases will become increasingly important.

Who determines the portion of the total budget used for the acquisition of materials and information? Libraries have to meet personnel and operational commitments. The remainder of the budget can be designated for the acquisition of information resources. The amount spent on acquisitions is based on continuing commitments, such as those for serials or binding, as well as on collection needs.

Once the total budget for acquisitions is designated, who determines how the acquisitions budget is divided? If there is a collection development officer, that individual may be responsible for the allocations within the acquisitions budget. In some libraries this person will also be the acquisitions librarian. In other libraries the head of the library retains complete authority to allocate the acquisitions budget.

No matter who allocates the acquisitions budget, certain factors enter into the decision-making process. Specifically, the person dividing the budget must first know exactly what the continuing commitments will be:

- How much is needed for renewal of periodical subscriptions?

- What must be expended on the binding of periodical volumes, other preservation programs, and the acquisition of journals in microform?

- Is there an approval plan? If so, how much does it cost?

- What is the amount needed for standing orders (continuations)?

Once these continuing commitments have been met, the remainder can now be allocated for information resources.

How these remaining funds are allocated depends upon the type of library and the spending philosophy. A public library, for example, may divide funds between fiction and nonfiction or among adult, adolescent, children's literature, and reference materials. In a college or university library the emphasis will usually be on purchasing by discipline or academic program. There is a determination of how much will be spent for each subject area as designated by academic program structure or by broad grouping such as sciences, social sciences, and humanities.

Location

Does the accounting process have to be in the acquisitions department? This will be dependent on the type of library, the legal requirements within the institution, and the competence and understanding of the acquisitions staff. Even if the bookkeeping activities are not the official responsibility of acquisitions, the status of individual funds must be readily available to the staff responsible for processing requests, placing orders, receiving items, and authorizing payment.

Although the information resources budget is a large portion of the total library budget, it is typically encumbered and expended in relatively small amounts. The library must have an accurate and current accounting of how much is being spent on the acquisition of new materials and services for the library.

The encumbering process is important to acquisition accounting. Encumbering, usually an internal library process, identifies costs that are anticipated and for which purchase orders have been initiated. This money is reserved for the anticipated expenditure and the allocation is reduced by the encumbrance total. When payment is made, if the actual cost differs from the encumbrance, an adjustment is made. Expenditures, not encumbrances, are usually the figures of primary concern to the parent organization.

Accountability

Who is responsible for accounting for expenditures against the information resources budget? Is it centralized within a library accounting office? Are all institutional funds controlled and monitored in a central accounting office? Does the acquisitions department have the responsibility for the funds? Is a collection development office responsible for overseeing acquisitions accounting activities? No matter where the monitoring function is located, the acquisitions staff itself is responsible for the accurate and careful ordering of materials and the approval of invoices for payment for materials that have been received.

The acquisitions accounting process begins with the placement of an order with a publisher or vendor. It is followed by receipt of the ordered items and the recording of that receipt in the order records. That is followed by the approval of the invoice for payment. While this is taking place, the individual orders must be tracked within the total library accounting picture so that outstanding commitments and the amount of funds actually expended are known.

Access to Accounting Information

Who should have access to the acquisitions accounting records? The acquisitions staff itself must have access to this information since it is the responsibility of that staff to not overextend commitments for funds. Orders should not be placed when funds are no longer available, funds have been blocked, or monies committed or expended have reached an agreed-upon level. In addition, the administrators of the library must have access to the fund commitment totals so that they can track the growth of the collection, be assured that the funds are being spent appropriately, and restructure the budget as changes occur. Collection development staff must have access to information for the fund for which they are responsible.

What to Monitor?

Which accounts should be monitored? If the acquisitions budget is divided into separate serial and monograph acquisitions funds, obviously those budget totals must be monitored. In addition these funds may be broken into allocations for specific subject areas or types of materials.

Every time an item is ordered, the funds should be encumbered against the appropriate account. The full price should be encumbered. Similarly, when materials are received, the expenditure must be levied against the correct account.

If a discount is received for an expenditure, the discount should be credited to the encumbered fund. Additional charges, such as increased prices, should be expended against the encumbered fund. Refunds for materials returned to vendors should be credited to the encumbered account. Shipping may be charged against the fund or to a specific shipping account.

Payment documents must be generated and payment records must be monitored to ensure that vouchers are recorded against the total budgeted fund.

If an institution codes payments by type of purchase, this may be done by the central purchasing office or by the library. If the library does not have an automated fund accounting system that generates payment requests, an alternative is an electronic (memory) typewriter or a microcomputer program in which constant data can be entered and the operator need enter only variables (e.g., vendor, invoice number and amount).

Usually the total library materials budget will be all that concerns the parent institution. It will be against that fund that the payment records and payment vouchers are recorded. The library itself will be concerned about the individual accounts; a well-rounded collection must be acquired and monies designated for specific areas must be committed to those areas.

If stringent state regulations, especially contracts, apply to materials purchasing, the person doing the accounting must monitor for the contract vendor being used, contract discount and other conditions being observed, and contract renegotiation when expiration date is reached.

Work Flow

In order to have an effective acquisitions accounting system, work flow must be analyzed and carefully planned. Work flow considerations include:

- designation of price on order

- encumbrance of order price before order is placed with vendor

- follow-up on delayed orders (claiming)

- expenditure for received items

- generation of payment

- follow-up on statements

- credits for returned items

Institutional procedures and policies may add other steps to the work flow.

Staffing

When planning for an acquisitions accounting system, the personnel involved and the amount of money involved are major considerations.

Selecting and hiring personnel to perform accounting tasks should be approached seriously and carefully. The individual hired to do accounting for the information resources budget may also be the person who does the accounting for the total library budget. A great deal of responsibility for details will rest with him or her. The person should know basic accounting concepts. Today, he or she should also be familiar with the use of computers for accounting purposes. Candidates for such a position should have the ability to handle detailed work that is usually routine, often tedious, and always repetitive.

The actual level of staffing may be determined by the amount of money and number of accounts to be handled by the staff. In most libraries, using off-the-shelf accounting software programs or an online accounting system, one individual can usually handle the accounting functions for all the funds. If the process is well organized and adequate hardware and software support is available, he or she can also perform other secretarial or clerical duties.

There should be a current position description detailing the purpose and scope of the position, required and desirable qualifications, supervision given and received, and the accountability mechanism. Some of the tasks the person may be expected to perform include:

- posting journals, ledgers, or other records from supporting data

- classifying expenditures by accounts

- preparing routine reports pertaining to the information resources budget

- making deposits

- setting up account records at the beginning of each fiscal year

- closing records at the end of the fiscal year

Qualifications, minimum training, and experience should include:

- knowledge of the application of bookkeeping principles to accounting transactions

- knowledge of modern office methods and procedures

- ability to make and verify numerical computations accurately and rapidly

- skill in the operation of calculators and related office equipment

- proficiency in written and mathematical skills

- experience in bookkeeping and related office activities

The administrator or account manager must know or learn the financial layers within the entire organization, must know what the library is responsible for, and must be aware of the procedures to be followed.

The accounting staff should report directly to the administrator who is ultimately responsible for the funds, that is, the account manager. If different persons monitor the acquisitions budget and the total library budget, the individual who is responsible for the total library budget must also have some supervisory or liaison responsibility for the account clerk handling the information resources budget.

The administrator or account manager — to whom the person responsible for accounting reports — should take the time to explain the institution's financial structure and the monetary responsibility that rests with the library. The administrator or account manager should be sure that the account clerk understands how the library budget fits into the institutional picture.

System Planning

After staff and funding, the next major consideration is planning how technology can be incorporated into the monitoring of the information resources monies. The system is the basis for determining whether the acquisitions accounting process is effective.

If the library has an online acquisitions system it may have an accounting module available which will track funds as orders are placed and received. If the acquisitions system itself has a module that will monitor funds, capitalize on this and use the software to your advantage rather than creating and maintaining a parallel automated or manual system.

Such an online system will probably be based on a minicomputer or a mainframe which may or may not be housed within the library. Such a module should include the printing of payment documents. Access to the accounting module should be controlled, for only authorized and trained personnel should manipulate records and input data.

If, however, the online acquisitions system lacks an accounting module, and a separate program for monitoring the funds is necessary, use of an off-the-shelf software package such as Lotus 1-2-3 or VisiCalc will provide a means of performing effective monitoring with minimal effort. Only authorized individuals should have access to the data disks and permission to manipulate records.

The library may be part of a local network within the institution; the accounting function may simply be a node on that library or institutional network. Increasingly, libraries have access through an electronic mail system or other online access to the institution's central accounting system. While the library may not be given the authority to input or correct data within the central accounting system, the library can at least check the status of accounts and initiate corrective action when errors are discovered. Since, in many institutions, the central accounting system for the institution often lags far behind the reporting of the expenditure of funds within the individual departments, it is important to have this online access to central accounting while maintaining internal records of account status.

Whichever accounting system is used, only trained, authorized individuals should have access to the actual records.

Which is more effective: an automated accounting system or a manual system? Generally, a well-designed and carefully planned and implemented automated system can track the expenditure of funds effectively in a fraction of the time that a manual system will take. A very poorly designed automated acquisitions system will, however, create many built-in problems and errors, in which case a manual system may be a more effective use of resources. Do not, however, maintain a manual system that parallels an operating automated system. Such parallel systems are never cost-effective.

Statistics and Reports

A desirable byproduct of any acquisitions system is the provision, in appropriate formats, of reports and statistics required by state, local, or national agencies. The recipient of these reports will be determined by authorization levels. The distribution of the reports and the information contained within the reports may be regarded as a source of power for the person who makes the distribution decision and the people receiving the reports. This can become an undesirable political ploy.

Those responsible for monitoring the funds on a daily basis will need to see reports as frequently as possible. Other people may be able to work effectively with only monthly reports. External agencies may only need annual reports, if any at all. When determining the type of acquisitions accounting system for a library, first decide which statistics will need to be gathered for reports and then create the capability for gathering those statistics.

Other Issues of Concern

CHECKS AND BALANCES

There should be adequate checks and balances to ensure that the funds are encumbered and expended accurately and speedily and to detect errors. If one person posts data, and another checks the data, errors are easily identified and corrected. If only one person does both, the need for care should be stressed.

AUTHORIZATIONS

There must be clear-cut guidelines designating who can authorize expenditures. Within the acquisitions budget there should be assignments determining who is responsible for each subject area or allocation. For other accounts, the account manager authorized to approve the purchase orders and vouchers should be designated. The parent organization will probably require filing of signature authorization for each account manager.

CARRY-OVER OF FUNDS

Some institutions will allow a library to carry over unexpended funds to the next year while other institutions will allow the library to carry over only those funds that have been encumbered. Still other organizations will insist that every cent allocated to the library must be totally expended by the end of the fiscal year, a particularly difficult situation for library acquisitions. The person responsible for the acquisitions account should be familiar with the regulations of the institution, and plan the process accordingly. When preparing for a new fiscal year, determine how funds left over from the previous year will be monitored and expended before setting up accounts for the new fiscal year.

STATEMENTS

Following up with vendors is part of the accounting function. When statements arrive, they are often checked to see if the vendor has indeed submitted an invoice, whether it and the materials ordered have been received, and if payment has been initiated. Statements are generated quickly by vendors; every statement need not be followed up. In general, statements should be checked only if urgency is noted. The person responsible for this follow-up should also know approximately how long it takes for payment to be made. In some organizations payment may be made within two or three weeks of receiving the invoice. In others, particularly those with cumbersome state regulations, payment may not be made for weeks or even months. The number of statements received will be drastically reduced if the library and the institution process payments quickly.

AUDITS

Audits are a fact of life. They may be library initiated, that is, the library does its own audit periodically to ensure that the accounting is being done properly, following institutional guidelines and standard accounting practices. They may be institutional; the parent institution sending an internal auditor into individual departments, including the library, to determine that appropriate accounting guidelines are being followed. In addition, there may be auditors from the state government to determine that state financial regulations are being followed.

An audit can be viewed as a negative experience and be a source of great anxiety. However, if the audit is approached as a constructive exercise in which the auditor will be able to offer advice on how to perform the accounting task better, the library will benefit from the audit. It is a good idea before an audit takes place, or before you even know that an audit is expected, to meet the internal auditor for the parent institution and determine exactly which guidelines he or she expects to be followed. A friendly audit can be requested in which the auditor will apprise the library of potential problems. The library would then have the opportunity to correct problems before an official audit takes place.

INTERACTION WITH CENTRAL BUSINESS OFFICES

There are various interactions with the purchasing and central accounting offices of the parent institution. A library will usually do its own purchasing since most central purchasing offices do not want to be bothered with the numerous individual orders that a library generates. However, the library will be expected to follow common purchasing practices and stay within the institutional purchasing guidelines.

Libraries usually do not issue checks against invoices themselves. The central accounting office for the parent organization will have this responsibility. While the library will place orders and authorize the payment of invoices, the central accounting offices will actually be sure that the checks are issued and mailed. These checks will usually be printed in batches. In some organizations this may be done once or twice a week. Since this may affect the time it takes for payment to reach the vendor, the library should be aware of the check printing schedule.

MAINTENANCE

No matter which kind of accounting system the library uses, procedures should be examined periodically to be sure that the system is functioning as intended. Are encumbrances and expenditures being input regularly? Are invoices being processed for payment quickly so that statements are not received as a result of slow payment? Is the system accurate? The system should be audited periodically for accuracy—a good preparation for an official audit.

SUMMARY AND PROSPECTS

In general, libraries rely more and more on automation to monitor the expenditures of all types of funds, including those that are used for information resources. They also acquire information in different formats (e.g., CD-ROM software or access to databases). These are all ways of acquiring additional information for the patrons; though, philosophically, librarians have often been opposed to paying for database access on the acquisitions budget. Increasingly, there will be different formats requiring expenditures from the information resources budget. Librarians responsible for monitoring the information resources budget should remain alert to technological trends and be willing to change their own internal practices in order to use library funds more effectively.

In the future, an important part of the acquisitions accounting process will be billing for access to databases. Acquiring updates of databases or upgrades of software may also become a part of the information resources budget.

As use of funds for information resources evolves, the necessity for careful monitoring of those funds will become more critical because the funds must be spread over several information access and distribution media.

FURTHER READINGS

Alley, Brian and Jennifer Cargill. Keeping track of what you spend: the librarians' guide to simple bookkeeping. Phoenix, AZ: Oryx Press, 1982

Auld, Lawrence W. S. Electronic spreadsheets for libraries. Phoenix, AZ: Oryx Press, 1986

Bens, C. Library budgets: hard sell for a soft service. *Ontario library review* 65:88-100 (June 1981)

Bloomberg, M. and G. E. Evans. Accounting and bookkeeping. *In* Introducduction to technical services for library technicians. 4th ed. Littleton, CO: Libraries Unlimited, 1981, pp. 120-130

Chandler, J. S. and T. N. Trone. Bottom-up budgeting and control. *Management accounting* 63:37-41 (Feb. 1982)

Chen, Ching-chih. Zero-based budgeting in library management: a manual for librarians. Phoenix, AZ: Oryx Press, 1980

Collins, F. Do managers play games with their budgets? *Managerial planning* 32:28-34 (July-Aug. 1983)

De Gennaro, Richard. Marketing commitments to needs and resources. *Journal of academic librarianship* 7:9-13 (Mar. 1981)

Echt, S. *et al.* Save time, simplify procedures, get better statistics. *Online* 5:21-35 (Apr. 1981)

Gambino, Anthony J. and Thomas J. Reardon. Financial planning and evaluation for the nonprofit organization. New York: American Association of Accountants, 1981

Guess, G. M. Budget preparation and academic literature. *Bureaucrat* 12:61-64 (Summer 1983)

Hayes, Robert M. Managerial accounting in library and information science education. *Library quarterly* 53:340-58 (July 1983)

Hoffman, Herbert F. Simple library bookkeeping. Newport Beach, CA: Headway Publications, 1977

Koenig, Michael. Budgeting techniques for libraries and information. New York: Special Libraries Association, 1980

Lee, Sul H., *ed.* Library budgeting: critical challenges for the future. Ann Arbor, MI: Pierian Press, 1977

Lyndon, Frederick. Library materials budgeting in the private university library: austerity and action. *In* Advances in librarianship, vol. 10. New York: Academic Press, 1980, pp. 89-154

Pakmour, Vernon E. *et al.* A planning process for public libraries. Chicago: American Library Association, 1980

Poole, Jay Martin and Gloriana St. Clair. Funding online services from the materials budget. *College and research libraries* 47:225-237 (May 1986)

Prentice, Ann E., *ed.* Budgeting and accounting. Special issue of *Drexel library quarterly* 21 (Summer 1985)

Ramsey, Inez L. and Jackson E. Ramsey. Library planning and budgeting. New York: Franklin Watts, 1986

Ramsey, Jackson E. and Inez L. Ramsey. Budgeting basics. New York: Franklin Watts, 1985

Sanders, N. P. Review of selected sources in budgeting for collection managers. *Collection management* 5:151-59 (Fall/Winter 1983)

Schauer, Bruce P. The economics of managing library service. Chicago: American Library Association, 1986

Shields, Gerald R. and J. Gordon Burke. Budgeting for accountability in libraries: a selection of readings. Metuchen, NJ: Scarecrow Press, 1974

Smith, G. Stevenson. Accounting for librarians and other not-for-profit managers. Chicago: American Library Association, 1983

Stueart, Robert P. and J. T. Eastlick. Budget and justification forms. *In* Library management. 2nd ed. Littleton, CO: Libraries Unlimited, 1981. pp. 265-85

Sweetman, Peter and Paul Wiedemann. Developing a library book-fund allocation formula. *Journal of academic librarianship* 6:268-76 (Nov. 1980)

Swersey, Patricia. Spreadsheets for the IBM: librarian's guide. Westport, CT: Meckler Publishing, 1986

Trumpeter, Margo C. and Richard S. Rounds. Basic budgeting practices for librarians. Chicago: American Library Association, 1985

Bibliographic Control

DESCRIPTIVE CATALOGUING:
Its Past, Present, and Future

MICHAEL GORMAN

The term *descriptive cataloguing* is somewhat ambiguous. It is often confused with *bibliographic description*, which is a significant part of descriptive cataloguing but not the whole. In this chapter *descriptive cataloguing* signifies the activities connected with the bibliographic description of library materials, the assigning of access points (previously called *headings*) to those descriptions, the construction of authority records containing access points and references to those access points, and the MARC tagging and coding of bibliographic descriptive data and authority records. This definition goes beyond the traditional because it deliberately embraces the effects of computer technology on descriptive cataloguing rather than, as is mostly the practice, assuming that cataloguing is essentially unaffected by, and separate from, the major change in the medium through which cataloguing data is transmitted and stored. The truth of the matter is that one cannot think about any aspect of cataloguing, except at the most rarified and abstract level, without taking the effects of the MARC record into account.

A catalogue entry, irrespective of the form of the catalogue, comprises three parts:

- the name and/or title *access point* (heading) which allows the catalogue user to find the entry

- the *bibliographic description* which describes a piece of library material (book, serial, map, etc.)

- the *location* which enables the catalogue user to move from the catalogue to the desired object

The first element (the access point) relates to the work of which the book (etc.), is a manifestation. The second element (the bibliographic description) relates to the physical object (book, etc.) itself. The third element (the location) can be be any code that signifies the physical placement of the book (etc.), and is often based on the classification number. The first two elements of the catalogue entry (the access point and the description) have been the subject of cataloguing codes from at least the 18th century until today. A cataloguing code (or, more formally, set of "rules for descriptive cataloguing") is a national or international set of rules for describing library materials and for assigning access points (headings) to those descriptions. For the purposes of this chapter, the British and/or American codes from Panizzi (1841) onward constitute what Dr. Leavis, in another and utterly different context, called the Great Tradition.[1]

This chapter will deal with four areas (description, access points, authority files, MARC format) in turn. In each case, I will outline the past and present and, in a concluding section, give my views on the future. The chapter "Authority Work, Authority Records, and Authority Files" by Arnold Wajenberg (p. 86) details the concept and application of such records. Later in this chapter I shall, without repeating his analysis, fit those concepts and practices into the wider picture of descriptive cataloguing.

Although this book is aimed primarily at a North American audience, it is vital, especially in the context of descriptive cataloguing, that we understand the international dimensions of our topic. Descriptive cataloguing in the English-speaking world today is dominated by three bibliographic standards—the *International Standard Bibliographic Description (ISBD)*; the *Anglo-American Cataloguing Rules, Second Edition (AACR2)*; and the family of MARC formats.[2] The *ISBDs* constitute the true worldwide standards in that they are available in the same form (though in translation) throughout the world. *AACR2* is used throughout the English-speaking world and, in English or in translation, in many non-English-speaking countries. In yet other countries, however, completely different cataloguing codes are used. The MARC family consists of numerous variations on the theme of the original MARC format developed at the Library of Congress in the late 1960s. Though the various national MARC formats share a common structure in that they are all based on an International Standards Organisation standard (ISO 2709), the differences between them are significant. In addition MARC is not used as a standard format in some non-Western countries.

BIBLIOGRAPHIC DESCRIPTION

Bibliographic description is the core of the catalogue entry. It consists of the recording of data about physical objects (books, maps, sound recordings, graphic materials, computer files, etc.) collected by libraries. The information given in the descriptive part of the catalogue entry is, in great part, derived from the object itself.

Bibliographic description was, for a very long time, the poor relation of cataloguing. In the 19th century, when the codes of Panizzi (1841), Jewett (1852), and Cutter (1876)[3] appeared, controversies and speculations were almost all about the nature and form of the headings. The description of books and other materials was almost an afterthought. The rules for description that were given represented a watered-down version of analytical and historical bibliographic practice. The resulting descriptions, as can be seen readily in catalogues and bibliographies of the period, confused the average catalogue user and often lacked detail. Furthermore, the rules for description were based on the physical characteristics of books. When applied to even the "traditional" kinds of "nonbook" materials (manuscripts, maps, music scores, etc.), the old rules for description resulted in some rather peculiar catalogue entries. In the first of the Anglo-American cataloguing codes (1908), the rules for description occupied fewer than fourteen pages (out of seventy-five).[4] They were entirely book based and divided the description into the following: Titles, Imprint, Collation, Series note, Contents, Notes. Such familiar and important elements of modern descriptions as statements of responsibility and editions were subsumed under "Titles," and areas that are the subject of a series of rules today were dismissed briefly or even dealt with only by inference. The 1908 rules for description had the merit of brevity—a brevity that was possible when standardization between libraries was felt to be of little or no importance.

The question of standardization is central to the understanding of cataloguing rules and the necessity for those rules. The time is long past when a library could busy itself about its own concerns without reference to any other library. Standardized cataloguing was born in the United States when the Library of Congress began to distribute its catalogue cards at the turn of the century. Libraries in droves wished to take advantage of the economies offered by purchasing cataloguing rather than creating cataloguing. The one drawback to this arrangement was that the Library of Congress did not, and could not, catalogue everything. If any coherence were to be possible in the local catalogue, items that were catalogued locally had to conform to the standards set by the Library of Congress. It was centrally provided cataloguing that gave the first impetus to cataloguing standardization. There is another reason, less obvious though no less compelling, for standardization. It lies in the use by individuals of more than one library. A catalogue entry is a complicated thing. It uses conventions (layout, punctuation, abbreviations, etc.) that are far from natural language. Though they are well known to those of us who work in libraries, those conventions are something that the average catalogue user has to learn. That learning task is rendered very difficult, if not impossible, if the conventions vary from library to library or even within one catalogue. Standardization in cataloguing, then, is demanded when libraries share cataloguing and to enable the library user to comprehend the catalogue entry.

In the years between the 1908 rules and the publication of the Library of Congress *Rules for Descriptive Cataloguing (RDC)* (1949), the whole process of cataloguing was dominated by the practices of the Library of Congress.[5] Their 1949 rules for description (note that they are using *descriptive cataloguing*, in the title of their rules, to mean *bibliographic description*) represented the summit of that process. The rules covered every tiny detail of description in catalogue entries to the point at which the 1949 rules were a manual on the production of LC catalogue cards. In turn, the 1949 rules of LC practice were the basis for the rules on description in the *Anglo-American Cataloging Rules (AACR)* (1967).[6] For nearly seventy years the in-house practice of the Library of Congress had defined description in cataloguing without ever resolving the tension between classic description of books based on traditional bibliographic practice, on the one hand, and the need for medium-neutral standardized descriptions, on the other hand. To take just one example, classic bibliographic description called for the descriptive data to be given in the order in which they appeared in the book and standardized description calls for the data to be given in an invariable standard order. LC practice represented an uneasy compromise between the two, one that never came to grips with the problem of describing *nonbook material*. They operated on the "deformed book" theory of description which treated all nonbooks as if they ought to be books. All of this was to change very rapidly with the advent of the *International Standard Bibliographic Description (ISBD)*.

In 1969, IFLA convened the International Meeting of Cataloguing Experts (IMCE) in Kobenhavn, Denmark. The IMCE had two purposes — to consider the *Paris Principles* (a broad set of agreements on access points intended to induce international agreement and, hence, harmony between the cataloguing codes of different countries)[7] and to consider an analysis of bibliographic descriptive data produced by national bibliographic agencies worldwide prepared by Michael Gorman. The result of the latter discussion was the establishing of an international committee charged with preparing a draft international standard for descriptive data in catalogue entries. In 1974, the first definitive *ISBD* was published.[8] It dealt with printed monographs only but embodied the two characteristics of the *ISBD* program. The first important characteristic is a set and invariable order of elements in the description (those elements are grouped into eight "areas"). The second is the use of unique and invariable punctuation to introduce (or, in some cases, enclose) each element. The *ISBD* resolves the tension between classic bibliography and standardized description by coming down firmly in favor of complete standardization in both the order and the presentation of bibliographic data.

Here are two bibliographic descriptions demonstrating the order of data in, and punctuation of, the *ISBD*.

> The elements of mechanical engineering / Herman B. Strong ; illustrated by Philomena and Phoebe Barrett. — 3rd rev. ed. / edited by Norbert Chalmers. — London : Parrott and Hawkes ; New York : Mangrove Press, 1989. — xvii, 397 p. : ill. (some col.) ; 29 cm. — (Engineering for today ; v. 17). — Previous ed. 1981. — ISBN 0-123-34125-1 : $85.00

> Time and the tailor [sound recording] / Sid Uranium and the Elements. — [New York] : Rave-Up Records, p1989. — 1 sound disc (49 min.) : digital, stereo. ; 4¾ in. — Reissue of: Sunspot SM 195 (1980). — Compact disc. — Issued also as analog disc and casssette

The *ISBD(M)* formed the basis for a published revision of the chapter (chapter 6) on the description of books of the 1967 *AACR*. There then followed *ISBD*s for serials, nonbook materials, maps, and so on, and, in a remarkable example of the horse coming after the cart, the *General ISBD* which represented a distillation of the elements and their punctuation for all library materials, regardless of their physical form.[9]

Despite an initial flurry of opposition (most of it on grounds too ludicrous to record for posterity), the *ISBD*s were adopted by cataloguing agencies throughout the world. Part 1 ("Description") of the 1978 *Anglo-American Cataloguing Rules, Second Edition* is based squarely on the *ISBD* program.[10] It opens with a general chapter based on the *ISBD(G)*. That chapter is followed by ten chapters dealing with elaborations of the basic rules for different physical kinds of library material (books, maps, manuscripts, music, sound recordings, films and video recordings, graphic materials, computer files, three-dimensional objects, microforms) and two chapters dealing with pervasive descriptive problems (serials, analytical entries). What has happened in this transformation is that the descriptive rules are now neutral, that is, they apply equally to all kinds of library material, and that the descriptive part of the catalogue entry follows exactly the same pattern of presentation, irrespective of the country in which the item is being catalogued and irrespective of the physical form of the item being catalogued. This has aided in the comprehensibility of catalogue records (even across national and language boundaries) and has facilitated cooperative cataloguing within countries and between countries.

There is an ideal set out in a plan called Universal Bibliographic Control (UBC) that has as one of its components the idea that each item should be catalogued only once and that cataloguing should occur in its country of origin.[11] The standardization wrought by the *ISBD* program has been a giant step in the direction of that ideal.

ACCESS POINTS

From Panizzi's ninety-one rules for the British Museum (1841) to the latest (1988) revision of the Anglo-American cataloguing rules, cataloguing codes have been preoccupied with questions revolving around the name and/or title access points (headings) by which descriptions are filed and by means of which descriptions may be retrieved. In the case of description, the data given in the catalogue entry are derived from the physical item being described. In assigning name/title access points, one is not generally considering the physical object but the work of which that object is a manifestation. To give a simple example, there is a work called *Hamlet* that is known to be by William Shakespeare. A cataloguer may, in the course of time, have to catalogue an English text of the play called *The Tragedy of Hamlet, Prince of Denmark, by Shakespeare*; an Italian translation of the play called *Amleto di Shakespeare*; a videotape of the Laurence Olivier film of the play; and a sound recording of the Royal Shakespeare production of Hamlet. What these objects (each of which is *described* in its own terms) have in common is that they are all derived from the work that we identify with the person William Shakespeare and to which we have assigned the standard title *Hamlet*. In other words, irrespective of the form of Shakespeare's name on the individual items and irrespective of the title that appears on those items, we will always use the same name/title access point—that is, "Shakespeare, William. Hamlet."

The four kinds of access points that result from descriptive cataloguing are listed below, with examples of each.

- personal name access points

    Wodehouse, P. G.

    Joan, of Arc, Saint

- corporate name access points—including those based on the names of conferences and of governments, many of which are geographic names

    British Museum

    Conference on Nematodes (5th : 1988 : Chicago, Ill.)

    Fresno, Calif. City Council

- uniform titles

    Bible. New Testament

    Song of Roland

- name and title access points

    Shakespeare, William. Hamlet

    Caesar, Julius. De bello Gallico

Historically, the choice of access points to be applied to a particular description has been based on the idea of *authorship*. In the latest cataloguing rules (*AACR2*), an author is defined as the person who is chiefly responsible for the intellectual or artistic content of a work. Note that one has to consider the *work* in deciding on authorship and not just the item that one has in hand. Note also that, according to modern thought, only a *person* can be an author. This has not always been the case. From Cutter's rules (1876) to the first *AACR* (1967), the Anglo-American tradition treated corporate bodies as authors in the same way as persons.[12] This was an absurdity on the face of it and one that led to many elaborate and, often, self-contradictory rules. It is easy to ask why the concept of authorship has any importance at all, but it is difficult to come up with a comprehensive and coherent answer. Established doctrine has it that the way to assign access points is to find the "author" and to make that person's name the basis of the main entry heading. Other persons, bodies, and titles connected with the work can then be considered as the possible bases for added entry headings. If there is no author (as in the case of anonymous works, works that are compilations of one kind or another, and works in which the authorship is diffuse—e.g., movies), the title is preferred as the main entry heading, and added entry headings are assigned as in the case of works with "authors."

It is my firm belief that this notion of *main entries* (though enshrined both in cataloguing codes and in the MARC formats) is, essentially, outdated flummery that has no relevance to the realities of modern catalogues. If one is going to allow access to a particular description by two or more access points and if each of those access points allows the system user to get to the description with equal dispatch, what is the point in pretending that one access point has more importance than any other? The main entry idea arose in a time of book catalogues in which time, space, and expense militated against having more than one full entry for each book (the other "entries" were little more than references). That rationale was weakened considerably in the era of the multiple card set for each item and has been destroyed entirely by the advent of the online computer catalogue. However, since our cataloguing codes and the MARC formats insist on cataloguers making that distinction, the weary farce of the main entry will continue indefinitely.

Having, by whatever means, chosen *which* access points are going to be used for an item, the cataloguer has next to decide on the *form* of each of those access points. Below are some of the problems with which cataloguers are faced.

People and corporate bodies change their names. The man once known as "Angelo Giuseppe Roncalli" became more widely known as "Pope John XXIII"; the body once known as the "Information Science and Automation Division of ALA" is known now as the "Library and Information Technology Association."

People and corporate bodies are known by different names in different countries. Our "Saint Joan of Arc" is known in her native country as "Sainte Jeanne d'Arc"; our "Red Cross" is known in France as "Croix Rouge."

People and corporate bodies are known by shorter and fuller forms of their names. Is it "W. H. Auden" or "Wystan Hugh Auden"; "NATO" or "North Atlantic Treaty Organization"?

For modern persons living in a Western culture, the first word of the access point is generally easy to discover. We have little trouble in deciding on "Shakespeare, William" and "Christie, Agatha" as access points. Even for that group, though, the entry word is not always easy to discern. Is it "Joyner, Florence Griffith" or "Griffith Joyner, Florence"; "De Gaulle, Charles" or "Gaulle, Charles de"? For persons from other times and other cultures, such problems are multiplied. How does one enter "Leonardo da Vinci" or "Mao Tse-tung" or the Roman poet "Quintus Horatius Flaccus" (better known to English speakers as "Horace")?

These and numerous other problems concerning access points are all addressed at length in Part 2 of *AACR2*, as are other matters such as the use of uniform titles (a standard title — e.g., "Hamlet" — chosen as the filing and retrieval title for all manifestations of a particular work). It should be noted that uniform titles are sometimes used alone (as in the case of ancient anonymous works — e.g., "Beowulf" — and sacred scriptures — e.g., "Book of Mormon") and are sometimes added to a name access point (in which case, the convention is to enclose them in brackets — e.g., "Dickens, Charles [Pickwick Papers]"; "Church of England [Book of common prayer]").

AUTHORITY FILES

The last chapter of *AACR2* addresses the question of name and title references. These references, as is familiar to all who have used card catalogues, are of two types. The first type of reference is a simple direction from one form of a name or title (not used as a heading) to another (used as a heading). Such references are known as *see* references (e.g., "International Business Machines *see* IBM"; "De Gaulle, Charles *see* Gaulle, Charles de"; "Holy Bible *see* Bible").

The second type of reference is a reference from one name or title used as an access point to another name or title used as an access point, and vice versa. Such references are known as *see also* references (and also as *cross*-references, a term that is accurate in this case though it is commonly and inaccurately used to include *see* references). *See also* references are made, for example, to link the headings for a person using pseudonyms (e.g., "Holt, Victoria *see also* Plaidy, Jean"; "Plaidy, Jean *see also* Holt, Victoria"); to link the headings for a body that has changed its name ("Hendon Birders *see also* Hendon Ornithological Society"; "Hendon Ornithological Society *see also* Hendon Birders") and to link related works (e.g., "Eliot, T.S. Old Possum's book of practical cats, *see also* Lloyd-Webber, Andres. Cats!"; "Lloyd-Webber, Andrew. Cats!, *see also* Eliot, T.S. Old Possum's book of practical cats").

In some cases a reference requires more detail than a simple *see* or *see also* instruction; such a reference is known as an explanatory reference (e.g., "Tolkien, J.R.R. Lord of the Rings. For the separately published parts of this work, see Tolkien, J.R.R. Fellowship of the ring" [etc.]).

It is evident that the traditional reference structure was devised for premachine catalogues. The ideas that underlie references have been taken over in machine systems and incorporated into the notion of authority files.[13] An authority file consists, very simply, of the approved form of access point for a person, body, or title, together with the references to that approved form and links to other related authority records (the latter being the computer equivalent of a *see also* reference). We have already seen that, in the computer catalogue environment, the distinction between a *main* and *added* entry access point no longer has meaning. The authority record takes this progress a step further. It, in effect, abolishes the distinction between an access point and a reference. To take an example, if either "WHO" or "World Health Organization" will get the system user to relevant bibliographic records with equal speed, what does it matter which is the access point and which the reference? In other words, two of the basic assumptions of traditional cataloguing codes—the main entry and the distinction between a heading and a reference—have been subverted. It is a pity that the standards we use in descriptive cataloguing—*AACR2* and MARC—show little or no sign of adapting to accommodate this great change.

MARC AND THE FUTURE OF
DESCRIPTIVE CATALOGUING

MARC is a near-acronym standing for *MA*chine *R*eadable *C*ataloguing. The MARC format (or, to be more accurate, the MARC formats) has been a major influence for good and ill on descriptive cataloguing for more than twenty years. MARC was developed in the Library of Congress in the 1960s, initially as a means of mechanizing the production of LC catalogue cards. In this genesis lies the fatal flaw that hinders descriptive cataloguing to this day and will hinder it for years to come. The MARC format is not and never was a rethinking of the nature of bibliographic data. It embodies none of the ideas concerning the linkage of bibliographic descriptions and authority records prefigured earlier in this chapter. The order, nature, and analysis of bibliographic data in MARC II (the first operational manifestation of MARC) sedulously followed the order, nature, and analysis of bibliographic data current in the Library of Congress in the mid-1960s. As has been seen, that cataloguing practice was traditional and book oriented. In the years that followed MARC II, the Library of Congress issued MARC formats for serials, maps, music, and so on, and other countries issued MARC formats for their own materials (UKMARC, CANMARC, etc.). An international exchange format called UNIMARC was issued in the late 1970s. It, naturally, represents the lowest common denominator of the various national MARC formats. All these MARC formats were based on MARC II which, in turn, was based on a completely discredited approach to descriptive cataloguing.

The irony is that we have a vehicle that has allowed an unprecedented level of international and national exchange of bibliographic data (there are now many millions of MARC records and the MARC format is a keystone of the operations of OCLC and other lesser networks) but that vehicle bears the same relationship to a true computer-based bibliographic format as a Model T does to a Concorde. Moreover, the very success of MARC has created an inert mass that becomes daily more resistant to change. Supposing we were to rethink MARC radically, what would happen to those twenty or so million old MARC records? Who would redesign OCLC? How would all the system vendors with MARC-based systems retool their products? Because there are so many people (from LC down) who have a vested interest in resisting even necessary change to MARC, it would take a Herculean effort of will and imagination to accomplish the necessary change. Unfortunately it appears that neither the will nor the imagination are available at present.

A MARC record, apart from some machine-readable information that has nothing to do with bibliographic data, is divided into a number of *fields* (distinct clusters of characters set off one from the other). In a MARC record one finds a series of fixed length fields that contain coded data and a series of variable length fields that contain bibliographic data of various kinds. The fixed length fields (commonly though wrongly called *fixed fields*) are an addition to traditional bibliographic practice. They contain, among other things, information about the type of material being catalogued, its date of publication, language, and so on, and its intellectual level. Two important innovations are the provision of codes indicating the geographic area with which the item is concerned and, if an item is a translation, both the original language and the language of the translation. The variable length bibliographic fields contain free-form data (headings, titles, publication details, series, notes, etc.) derived from the application of descriptive and subject cataloguing rules, codes, and standards. Each variable length field is identified by a three-numeral "tag," and within a field, in addition to the bibliographic data, one finds up to two numerals (indicators) with meanings that vary from field to field, and single-letter codes accompanied by a symbol that is represented at input by a dollar sign ($) that indicate the beginning of a section of a field (a subfield). Note that the *fields* and *subfield* of the MARC formats correspond closely to the *areas* and *elements* of the ISBDs.

Here is an example of a MARC variable length field:

245 14 $a The spoils of Poynton $b / by Henry James ; edited by C.S. Sproule ; illustrated by Felicia Donnelly#

In this example "245" identifies the title and statement of responsibility field. The first indicator ("1") means that an added entry is to be made under the title. The second indicator ("4") indicates that there are four characters (t h e space) to be ignored in filing. The first subfield code ("$a") indicates that what follows is the title proper. The second subfield code ("$b") indicates that what follows is what LC calls "remainder of title page transcription" (a term rooted in pre-*ISBD* practice and a good example of how MARC has fossilized outdated ideas and terminology). At the end of the field is an end-of-field indicator (shown here as "#"). Note that the *ISBD* punctuation is given even when it corresponds exactly to the subfield code. Much excess keying (and potential for error) could be avoided if the punctuation were to be supplied by program at output.

In the future, as in the past, descriptive cataloguing will be concerned with the recording of descriptive data and with the provision of access to that data. However, the structures within which description and access are accomplished may be very different. The MARC formats are the key to change. If they remain more or less as they are, it is hard to see how the cataloguing rules for access points can change. If those rules do not change, it is hard to see how the standard description plus authority records concept can be assimilated fully into descriptive cataloguing theory and practice.

Just before his death (in 1903), Charles Ammi Cutter lamented that the golden age of cataloguing was over. He thought that the spread of the use of LC cards had killed that golden age. It would be easy to think that MARC is killing the "silver age" of cataloguing, but I am optimistic enough to believe that technology, intelligently applied, can bring us a second golden age of cataloguing almost a century after Cutter proclaimed the death of the first.

NOTES

[1]Panizzi, Anthony. Rules for compiling the catalogue of printed books, maps, and music in the British Museum. Rev. ed. London: The Museum, 1936

[2]ISBD(G): general International Standard Bibliographic Description: annotated text. London: IFLA International Office for UBC, 1977; ISBD(M): International Standard Bibliographic Description for monographic publications. 1st standard ed., rev. London: IFLA International Office for UBC, 1978; and other ISBDs for serials, computer software, music, AV materials, etc.; Gorman, Michael and Paul W. Winkler, *eds*. Anglo-American cataloguing rules. 2nd ed., 1988 revision/ prepared under the direction of the Joint Steering Committee for the Revision of AACR. Chicago: ALA, 1988; MARC formats for bibliographic data. Washington, DC: Automated Systems Office, Library of Congress, 1980- . Looseleaf with quarterly updates

[3]Panizzi, Anthony. *Op cit.*; Jewett, Charles C. Smithsonian report on the construction of catalogues of libraries. 2nd ed., reprinted. Ann Arbor, MI: University Microfilms, 1961; Cutter, Charles Ammi. Rules for a dictionary catalog. 4th ed., rewritten. Washington, DC: Government Printing Office, 1904 (special report on public libraries/ U.S. Bureau of Education; part II)

[4]Catalog rules: author and title entries/ comp. by committees of the American Library Association and the (British) Library Association. American ed. Chicago: ALA Publishing Board, 1908

[5]Library of Congress. Rules for descriptive cataloging (adopted by the American Library Association). Washington, DC: LC Descriptive Cataloging Division, 1949

[6]Anglo-American cataloging rules. North American text/ prepared by the American Library Association. Chicago: ALA, 1967

[7]International Conference on Cataloguing Principles, 1961, Paris. Statement of principles. Annotated ed./ with commentary and examples by Eva Verona *et al.* London: IFLA Committee on Cataloguing, 1971

[8]ISBD(M). *Op. cit.*

[9]ISBD(G). *Op. cit.*

[10]Gorman and Winkler. *Op. cit.*

[11]Kaltwasser, Franz Georg. Universal bibliographic control. *UNESCO library bulletin* 25:252-259 (Sept. 1971)

[12]Verona, Eva. Corporate headings: their use in library catalogues and national bibliographies. London: IFLA Committee on Cataloguing, 1975

[13]Burger, Robert H. Authority work. Littleton, CO: Libraries Unlimited, 1985

FURTHER READINGS

Beetle, Clara, *ed.* A.L.A. cataloging rules for author and title entry. 2nd ed. Chicago: ALA, 1949

Dunkin, Paul. Cataloging U.S.A. Chicago: ALA, 1969

Gorman, Michael. Cataloging and the new technologies. *In* The nature and future of the catalog/ ed. by Maurice J. Freedman and S. Michael Malinconico. Phoenix, AZ: Oryx Press, 1979, pp. 127-152

Gorman, Michael. The concise AACR2, 1988 revision : being a rewritten and simplified version of the Anglo-American cataloguing rules, second edition, 1988 revision. Chicago: ALA, 1989

Gorman, Michael and Paul W. Winkler, *eds.* Anglo-American cataloguing rules. 2nd ed. Chicago: American Library Association, 1978

Hagler, Ronald and Peter Simmons. The bibliographic record and information technology. Chicago: ALA, 1982

Lubetzky, Seymour. Cataloging rules and principles: a critique of the ALA rules for entry and a proposed design for their revision. Washington, DC: Library of Congress, 1953

Osborn, Andrew D. The crisis in cataloging. *Library quarterly* 11, no. 4:393-411 (Oct. 1941)

SUBJECT CATALOGUING AND CLASSIFICATION:
The Late 1980s and Beyond

LOIS MAI CHAN and THEODORA HODGES

As online catalogues replace card catalogues in American libraries, the library profession must re-examine many of the functions and operations of the library catalogue. Among these are methods of subject analysis and representation of library materials which have traditionally been accomplished by means of subject cataloguing and classification. The standard subject heading lists used in subject cataloguing of general collections are, first, *Library of Congress subject headings (LCSH)*, used primarily in large libraries; and, second, *Sears list of subject headings (Sears)*, which is favored for smaller collections, particularly those in public and school libraries. The two classification schemes in general use are the Library of Congress classification (LCC) and the Dewey Decimal classification (DDC).

For almost a century, subject headings assigned to individual catalogue records have served as the main subject retrieval tool in library catalogues (card or book catalogues). These traditional forms of the catalogue impose certain limitations on the application and use of subject headings. In a manual catalogue, the access to each subject heading requires a separate cataloguing record filed under the initial word of the subject heading. There is only one access point for each cataloguing record. For the sake of economy, subject headings have not been assigned liberally to individual bibliographic items, because more access points would result in increasing the bulk of the card or book catalogue. The dearth of headings per record has been noted by many critics and documented in a study published in 1979.[1] References were designed to provide additional access points through terms not used as headings (*see* references) or broader terms (*see also* references), but unfortunately, because of their labor-intensiveness and the need for local maintenance, references have not always been properly maintained in local library catalogues.

Both *LCSH* and *Sears* were designed for the card catalogue, and many of their features were developed to cater to its idiosyncrasies. One notable example is the fact that, in both lists, many phrase headings are in inverted order so that the most "significant" word will be in filing position as the access point. *LCSH* was developed at the turn of the century and first published in 1914; *Sears*, based on the same principles as *LCSH*, first appeared in 1920. Over the years, *LCSH* evolved according to LC policies but without the guidance of a subject cataloguing code comparable to the one that has developed and continued to evolve for descriptive cataloguing. Although the *LCSH* list has grown considerably since its inception, the principles guiding its development have not changed appreciably. They are basically the principles of the dictionary catalogue, or alphabetical subject catalogue, set forth by Charles A. Cutter and articulated as Library of Congress policies by David Judson Haykin.[2] These "fundamental concepts" consist of, in Haykin's words, "The reader as the focus," "Unity" (i.e., uniform heading), "Usage," and "Specificity." *Sears* has also adopted these principles in its development and maintenance over the years.

Classification also serves as a device for representing the subject content of library materials. It can be a powerful tool for subject access, because giving a work a class number not only groups it with similar works but gives it a place in a systematic array of related subjects. Until the late 1800s, many library catalogues in North America were "classed catalogues" with multifaceted subject access based on classificatory structures. Not many classed catalogues survive in North America, however, and, since the turn of the century, classification has been used primarily as a device for determining the order of books on the shelves in American libraries. It contributes to subject access only through shelf browsing by the user and in those rare circumstances when libraries open their shelflists for public use. Of the two most widely used systems in American libraries, the Library of Congress classification was designed, and continues to be maintained solely, as a shelf location and browsing device, nothing more. The policies governing its continuing development and maintenance reflect this basic orientation. While continuing attempts are made to provide for new subjects and to represent new alignment or realignment of disciplines or patterns of scholarly pursuit, there have been few structural changes over the years. Stability has been the basic consideration. On the other hand, the Dewey Decimal classification, in its attempt to remain both a shelf location device and a bibliographic tool for classed catalogues (primarily in libraries outside North America), has faced certain problems, among which are the long numbers and drastic changes—relocations and "phoenix" schedules—which necessitate continuous reclassification in order to maintain the integrity of the classified arrangement. While these characteristics increase the effectiveness of the system as a bibliographic or subject retrieval tool, they undermine its effectiveness as a shelf location device in a library.

As American libraries move further into the online age, it is appropriate to pause to ponder the traditional methods of subject analysis and access and to assess their potentials and limitations in terms of their usefulness in online systems. In such an assessment, we take into consideration both the basic characteristics of subject cataloguing and classification and the features and capabilities of online information retrieval mechanisms.

SUBJECT CATALOGUING

With computer application to bibliographic control and information retrieval, traditional subject headings systems have begun to assume a different role. When American libraries, particularly the Library of Congress, began to establish the MARC (*Ma*chine *R*eadable *C*ataloguing) system and create MARC records, they continued to apply the same cataloguing and indexing systems that have been in use in the card catalogue for the last 100 years. For subject representation of documents on MARC records, the same systems of subject headings and classification developed for the manual catalogue continue to be used in online catalogues.

By virtue of the presence of Library of Congress subject headings on millions of MARC records already created, *LCSH* has become an online retrieval tool by default. There have been sporadic suggestions that the Library of Congress's subject apparatus be replaced by a completely new system, one that would be designed to take full advantage of the power of automated systems. These suggestions have so far come to naught, undoubtedly because of the enormous cost of starting afresh. Any change is costly; developing a new system is very expensive, and so is retraining librarians, staff, and library users. Under the current circumstances, libraries would also be faced with remaking twenty years of subject cataloguing.

Since replacing *LCSH* with a new system is not a viable alternative, recent efforts have been concentrated on finding ways to improve the current system as an online retrieval tool. LC MARC records, which carry Library of Congress subject headings, are available for retrieval in online catalogues, particularly in academic and large public libraries across the United States. Within this context, the application of LC subject headings is virtually universal. In 1982, the Council on Library Resources sponsored a subject access meeting in Dublin, Ohio. One of the basic assumptions for discussion at this meeting was that "Library of Congress subject headings will be the basis for the controlled vocabulary in online access catalogs."[3] With its recent conversion into the automated Subject Authority File, the future of *LCSH* as the major online subject retrieval tool in library catalogues appears to be ensured.

Outside the library context, the LC MARC database is available for retrieval in a large number of commercial information retrieval systems (e.g., DIALOG, SDC's ORBIT, and WILSONLINE) as well as being the largest part of the databases of library bibliographic networks such as OCLC and RLIN — although the former does not yet offer retrieval by subject. Furthermore, the use of *LCSH* as the controlled vocabulary is not limited to library cataloguing records. Currently, at least twenty commercial online databases use it (some with augmentation or modification) as their indexing vocabulary; these include *Business Index, Cumulative Book Index, Education Index, Magazine Index, National Newspaper Index*, and *Social Sciences Index*.

In light of the above, the question that comes to mind immediately is, How well can *LCSH* be expected to work in the online environment? Even as a subject retrieval tool in the card catalogue, a function for which it was originally designed, *LCSH* has come under heavy fire over the years. Some of the most common criticisms are outdated terminology, inconsistent and unpredictable forms, and the dearth of subject headings per record. (On the last, it should be pointed out that the number of headings per record is not a function of the system itself, but of the policies governing how the system is applied.) These are the factors that exert a negative impact on subject retrieval by hampering the successful matching of the users' input terms with the controlled vocabulary. A summary of critical literature on *LCSH* was prepared by Pauline A. Cochrane and Monika Kirtland.[4] In the late 1970s and throughout the early 1980s in the wake of the second edition of *Anglo-American Cataloguing Rules (AACR2)*, *LCSH* has become the most discussed topic in the literature concerning bibliographic control. Numerous studies of, or related to, subject access in online catalogues were conducted, and many articles were published on the shortcomings and insufficiencies of *LCSH* in this regard.[5] Many suggestions have been made for its improvement. Most of these concern aspects of the vocabulary: its currency, its entry vocabulary, and the enrichment or enhancement of the subject headings assigned to individual records.

In view of the deficiencies of *LCSH* in the manual catalogue, a valid question is whether its recognized shortcomings will continue to hamper its effectiveness in online retrieval. Alternatively, is it possible that online features can go some way toward making up for the many deficiencies that surface when *LCSH* is used as the indexing vocabulary for a catalogue on cards? Are there feasible changes that could be made in *LCSH* that would increase its usefulness as an online retrieval tool? To answer these questions, we should take into consideration the capabilities of online retrieval systems, particularly those features that are not present in manual systems. These capabilities include (1) keyword or component word searching (including truncation), (2) Boolean operations (including word proximity or word adjacency), (3) limiting, (4) automatic switching (synonym operation), and (5) subject browsing.

There are probably few online library catalogues that offer all these features now. Each of them is, however, available in at least one commercial system, and more and more of them are being implemented in various online library catalogues as time goes on. None is so sophisticated, so far away from likely implementation in online library catalogues in the near future, that it can be ignored. It is appropriate, therefore, to look at the significance of each in turn.

Keyword Searching

The capability of keyword or component word searching has a bearing on subject retrieval in a system indexed by *LCSH* in at least two ways. The first relates to terminology. Keyword or free-text searching over subject-indicative fields (e.g., titles, series, class numbers, and notes) supplements and complements controlled vocabulary searching because it provides access to the authors' own terminology. The authors' terminology is often different from that used in subject headings, and in subjects in which term usage changes rapidly, is often more up-to-date. Thus, the ability to search by keywords overcomes much of the terminological disadvantage that has been attributed to controlled vocabulary. The second is that keyword or component word searching on subject headings means that searchers no longer have to know the first word of a heading in order to find it. Any word in a heading, even those in subdivisions, becomes an access point. All the old arguments on the most effective word order in a subject heading thus become moot. In systems that allow truncation, the chances of the user's input term matching the indexed terms are further enhanced.

Boolean Operations

The capability of Boolean operators in online systems, the most common being AND, OR, and NOT, is probably the most distinctive feature of online information retrieval. The ability to combine and exclude sets of terms in a search can only be achieved laboriously, if at all, in a manual system, but can be easily accomplished in an online system. It is this feature that makes the postcoordinate approach in information retrieval feasible and effective. On records indexed by *LCSH*, a complex subject is often represented by several headings, each of which is broader than the subject in question. In a manual catalogue, this often results in retrieving records that are too broad for the user's purpose. With Boolean operations, subject headings representing individual concepts may be postcoordinated (i.e., assembled *during* the search rather than preassembled) to achieve precision. The more sophisticated capability of word proximity or word adjacency further improves the precision of keyword or component word searching by operating on combinations of words defined by proximity and/or order.

Limiting

The ability to limit a set of retrieved records by certain criteria (the most common being year of publication, document type, language, and geographic area) can be used to refine searching by subject headings in order to achieve the best results in retrieval. Much of the potential of the limiting capacity comes not from *LCSH* itself but from the structure of the MARC system. The MARC format includes many fixed-field codes that allow efficient representation of factors such as publication dates(s), type of material, language, and geographic area covered. A search that is limited by one or another of these coded factors is much faster than when the same limit is achieved using the Boolean NOT operator. Furthermore, coding for the factors just mentioned is much more extensive and consistent than is representation of the same information in subject headings.

Automatic Switching (Synonym Operation)

Synonym operation substitutes valid subject headings for "nonpreferred" input terms and thus acts as a hidden *see* reference system. Online catalogue studies have revealed that users have difficulty in matching their input terms to subject headings. The synonym operator, when available, alleviates this problem to a large extent. Although many online catalogues do not yet have this capability, the technique is available. For example, in many of the databases in the WILSONLINE system, each time a user enters a nonpreferred term in searching, the system switches to a valid term and displays the postings.

Subject Browsing

There are two ways of allowing online catalogue users to scan headings before inputting their search terms. One is to display the headings that are already in the system, in alphabetical and/or keyword order. Some systems already do this, at least for the alphabetical display. The other is to display potential headings, in other words, to include *LCSH* (the Library of Congress subject authority file) in an online thesaurus display. Although not many library catalogues include *LCSH* online, online thesaurus display in other indexing systems such as ERIC (Educational Resources Information Center) and MeSH (National Library of Medicine's medical subject headings) gives an indication of what is possible and feasible in the online environment. With *LCSH* now in online form, more and more online library catalogues will display it in the near future.

Improvements

Given the current status of *LCSH* and the online capabilities discussed above, the next question should be, Which changes in *LCSH* will improve its efficiency and usefulness for online retrieval? Many writers have attempted to answer this question. A number of suggestions and recommendations follow.

1. Adopt natural word order for phrase headings.

2. Eliminate duplicate entries that were made in the past to bring various elements in a heading into the filing position (e.g., "United States — Foreign relations — China" and "China — Foreign relations — United States").

3. Rely more heavily on postcoordination for complex subjects by establishing various elements in a compound or complex heading as separate headings; for example, the two headings — "Federal aid; Health maintenance organizations" — in place of the current heading — "Federal aid to health maintenance organizations." This should not be done, however, in cases in which the meaning of the heading would be affected by the separation, as in the case of "Children in pornography." Precoordination could be reserved for cases where it is needed because citation order of linking words affects the meaning of the heading.

4. Adopt consistent patterns of citation order between topic and place.

5. Adopt direct geographic subdivision at all levels of place headings and subheadings.

6. Eliminate subdivisions the functions of which can be fulfilled by information given in other fields of the MARC record. These include major form subdivisions representing document types, period subdivisions for imprint dates, and subdivisions indicating the language of the document.

CLASSIFICATION

In North American libraries, even though online catalogues are becoming the main bibliographic tool, classification continues to function as a shelf location device. With the capability of online searching by class number or call number, the role of classification as a bibliographic tool has begun to re-emerge. The classed catalogue has all but disappeared from North American libraries over the last century. The shelflist is sometimes viewed as a classed catalogue, but there are a number of important differences between them. A true classed catalogue offers multiple access at a quite sophisticated level. Furthermore, few libraries make their shelflists accessible to the public. The online catalogue, on the other hand, offers both easy shelflist access and, potentially, many of the advantages of the true classed catalogue. It is, in some ways, tantamount to the reintroduction of the classed catalogue to North American libraries.

Recognizing the potentials of online classification access, scholars and researchers in the field have begun making feasibility and retrieval-effectiveness studies of classification as an online tool. Studies by Robert R. Freeman and Pauline Atherton [Cochrane][6] were among the early experiments. One of the more interesting, in terms of potential, is the recent study conducted by Markey during 1984-85 under the joint auspices of OCLC, Forest Press, and the Council on Library Resources.[7] The purpose of the study was to explore the effectiveness of the Dewey Decimal classification as a searcher's tool for online subject access. Two test catalogues were prepared for the project: one offered access to subject headings, keywords in titles, series, and notes and call numbers; the other offered access through various features of DDC in addition to the keyword approach. Two categories of user carried out searches in both catalogues: regular library users who pursued their own queries, and librarians who searched on assigned topics. Test results for the DDC-enhanced test catalogue were revealing, particularly in terms of how many unique subject-rich terms were generated. The study as a whole indicates that incorporating a classification scheme into the online catalogue can provide avenues of subject access that are not possible through the alphabetical approach.

The results of the DDC Online Project suggest three areas in which classification schemes could affect online searching: classification schemes as enhanced vocabulary, online subject browsing, and class number or call number searching. The following sections discuss the potentials and limitations of DDC and LCC with regard to these three aspects. Comments on DDC are largely based on the results of the DDC Online Project; those on LCC, for lack of any experimental data, must therefore be based on the authors' understanding and observations of the system.

Classification Schemes as Enhanced Vocabulary

The DDC Online Project demonstrated that entry vocabulary would be enhanced considerably if the captions in the DDC schedules and the entries in its Relative Index were incorporated into the catalogue. Terms from these sources are often, indeed usually, different in terminology and grammatical form from subject headings or keywords in titles. In the DDC Online Project, with some overlap, different records were retrieved using classification-based terms from those retrieved using keyword or alphabetical subject approaches. No such experiment has yet been performed on LCC, but there are indications that there is great potential here also. In an earlier study of the vocabulary used in the LC subject headings and classification systems, John Philip Immroth deplored the diversity of the sets of vocabulary: "There is the vocabulary of the classification schedules, a different vocabulary of the subject headings, and even a third vocabulary of the classification index."[8] As a benefit to cataloguers and indexers, Immroth suggested merging the different vocabularies to achieve consistency and uniformity. In the online environment, however, it is the very diversity of the *LCSH* and *LCC* vocabulary that holds promise as a source for enhanced entry terms.

One of the reasons for the diversity of vocabulary in LCC results from the fact that the indexes include many proper names—particularly personal, corporate, and geographic names—in addition to subject terms. Another factor here is the different syntax of index entries and captions from that of subject headings or keywords. The main different is that individual entries in classification schedules and indexes contain implicitly or explicitly broader terms in addition to terms that denote the specific topic at issue, while subject headings and keywords name the specific subject directly, for example, "Geysers (Groundwater)" [*LCC* index entry] and "GEYSERS" [*LCSH*]. Online catalogue studies have repeatedly found that users often enter terms that are broader than the subject they have in mind.[9] The bilevel entries in classification systems may be just what is needed to help such users.

A study carried out by Phyllis A. Richmond in 1974 is also relevant here. She selected terms related to *computer* and *computers* from *LCSH* and from the indexes and schedule captions of both LCC and DDC, and found "surprisingly little overlap among the various sources."[10] If such a large diversity existed in 1974 for a relatively new and unambiguous topic like computers, the range must be considerably greater for older and less well defined areas.

The reports on almost all recent online catalogue studies have noted a great need for more subject access points. A frequently proposed method for enhancing entry vocabularies is to assign additional subject terms to individual bibliographic records. Another is to increase the number of references. Linking class numbers on bibliographic records to terms from classification index entries and from classification captions and notes may also be a viable approach. Indeed it could even prove to be cost-effective in the long run because the class numbers already exist in bibliographic records and no additional work with individual records will be required.

Classification in Online Subject Browsing

Many online retrieval systems offer users the opportunity for subject browsing through online thesaurus (or subject heading list) display. With the LC Subject Authority File now available in machine-readable form, online browsing of *LCSH* is becoming a reality. This browsing, however, allows only alphabetical scanning and limited pointers to related topics. By incorporating classification schedules online, users will have access to hierarchical browsing of related subjects collocated in ways different from the subject headings list. However, the cost-effectiveness of such an approach has not been studied. The DDC Online Project explored the technical possibility of incorporating DDC schedules online, but the economic ramifications have yet to be determined. LCC is an even more remote possibility in this respect because of the technical difficulty of converting into machine-readable form an enumerative system with a nonhierarchical notation.

Class Number or Call Number Searching

Shelf-order browsing can be considered a variant of full-schedule browsing. It is already possible in any online system that can display bibliographic records in call number order. Most current systems can do so. Class number ordering collocated material in ways that are often different from what one can find using subject headings. The classification approach can therefore supplement the alphabetical approach, with the combination delivering better results than does either approach used alone. In addition, one can move up or down a list that is displayed in call number order, to broaden or narrow a search. Because of its hierarchical notation, DDC is much more effective than LCC in expanding or refining searches. On the other hand, LCC is particularly effective in known-item searching because LC call numbers are unique to particular items and are also fairly uniform across databases or in union catalogues.

Furthermore, class numbers can be used effectively in retrieving large sets of related records. For example, by using a broad DDC number with truncation or by using a range of DDC or LCC numbers, one could retrieve all the records dealing with the laws of Kentucky or all the records relating to 19th-century America drama. To do the same thing on the basis of subject headings or keywords one would have to input a very large number of search terms — assuming that it would be possible in the first place to determine all the headings or keywords that would be needed. Among library users, the need for broad searches is probably not very high. However, for SDI (Selective Dissemination of Information) services and in downloading subsets of large databases, it is helpful to be able to retrieve a large number of records efficiently. For those purposes, class number search may be much more efficient than either keyword or subject heading searches. In online catalogues or databases that carry both DDC and LCC numbers and perhaps numbers from other classification systems as well, searchers have a wide choice of search parameters. They may use any one of them, or more than one in combination or complementary to each other, according to their individual search requirements.

CONCLUSION

The advent of the online catalogue has necessitated a rethinking of bibliographic control in libraries. It is intriguing to consider what could be gained if a new, zero-based, bibliographical control system could be developed with the full potentials of online searching capabilities in mind. However, economic imperatives have forced us to make the best of what we already have. As a result, our traditional systems for subject access — the LC and Sears subject headings lists, the LC and Dewey classification systems — have been transported to the online catalogue environment. They seem to be working better than was originally expected: online capabilities go a long way toward mitigating shortcomings that tend to cripple searches in the manual environment. Why, then, the need for rethinking? The need comes from the fact that study after study of online catalogue use shows that users are not faring very well in their subject searches. We must not relax our efforts to improve what we offer. The good things that can be said about our traditional access provisions when mounted in online catalogues do no more than indicate that those provisions are viable in the new environment — they provide a sound base for incremental steady improvement. One road to improvement leads to efforts to load features of classification schemes into our online catalogues. This is at least a three-lane highway:

1. When mapped onto class numbers, schedule captions and index entries from classification schemes provide alternate routes to postings, without the need to touch the records themselves.

2. The same captions and index entries are a rich source of terms on which to base a systematic program of updating and enhancing our indexing vocabulary, for both authorized headings and for lead-in terms.

3. Classification schedules and their indexes provide a map of how topics are related that is not only different from that available through the syndetic structure of the subject heading system but that is also much more extensive.

A second road leads to changes in *LCSH*, in the system itself and in the policies that govern its use in indexing. Many of the features that make *LCSH* so complex, so difficult to use to best advantage either in indexing or in searching, are the result of efforts to make it maximally effective in the manual environment. We suggested earlier several changes that would move *LCSH* in the direction of simplicity, each of which can be implemented incrementally, without first tearing down in order to rebuild. The simpler *LCSH* can become in structure, the more efficient and effective it can be expected to be all around and the more readily it will be able to adapt to future changes in the library environment. Effectiveness and adaptability are both important for survival.

The important fact that has surfaced in recent years, as library catalogues have moved into the online age, is that needed changes are within our reach.

NOTES

[1]O'Neill, Edward T. and Rao Aluri. Research report on subject heading patterns in OCLC monographic records. Columbus, OH: OCLC, Research and Development Division (OCLC research report series, OCLC/RDD/RR-79/1)

[2]Cutter, Charles A. Rules for a dictionary catalog. 4th ed. Washington, DC: Government Printing Office, 1904; Haykin, David Judson. Subject headings: a practical guide. Washington, DC: Government Printing Office, 1951

[3]Russell, Keith W. Subject access: report of a meeting sponsored by the Council on Library Resources. Washington, DC: Council on Library Resources, 1982

[4]Cochrane, Pauline A. and Monika Kirtland. 1. Critical views of *LCSH* — the Library of Congress subject headings; a bibliographic and bibliometric essay. 2. Analysis of vocabulary control in the Library of Congress list of subject headings (*LCSH*). Syracuse, NY: ERIC Clearinghouse on information resources, 1981

[5]Markey, Karen. Subject searching in library catalogs before and after the introduction of online catalogs. *OCLC library, information, and computer science series* 4 (1984); Mandel, Carol A. and Judith Herschman. Subject access in the online catalog: report prepared for the Council on Library Resources. Washington, DC: Council on Library Resources, 1981

[6]Freeman, Robert R. and Pauline Atherton. File organization and search strategy using the Universal Decimal Classification in mechanical retrieval systems. *In* Mechanized information storage, retrieval, and dissemination: proceedings of the FID/IFIP joint conference/ ed. by Kjell Samuelson. Amsterdam: North-Holland Publishing, 1968. pp. 122-152

[7]Markey, Karen and Ann Demeyer. Dewey Decimal Classification online project: evaluation of a library schedule and index integrated into the subject searching capabilities of an online catalog: final report to the Council on Library Resources. Dublin, OH: OCLC Online Computer Library Center, 1986 (report no. OCLC/OPR/RR-86/1)

[8]Immroth, John Phillip. Analysis of vocabulary control in Library of Congress classification and subject headings. Littleton, CO: Libraries Unlimited, 1971

[9]Markey. *Op cit.*

[10]Richmond, Phyllis A. Subject access: report of a meeting sponsored by the Council on Library Resources. Washington, DC: Council on Library Resources, 1974

FURTHER READINGS

Cochrane, Pauline A. Modern subject access in the online age. *American libraries* 15:80-83, 145-150, 250-255, 336-339, 438-442 (1984)

Cochrane, Pauline A. and Karen Markey. Preparing for the use of classification in online cataloging systems and in online catalogs. *Information technology and libraries* 4, no. 2:91-111 (1985)

Gorman, Michael. Fate, time, occasion, chance, and change: or, How the machine may yet save LCSH. *American libraries* 11:557-558 (1980)

Gorman, Michael. New rules for new systems. *American libraries* 13:241-242 (1982)

LaMontagne, Leo E. American library classification: with special reference to the Library of Congress. Hamden, CT: Shoe String Press, 1961

Library of Congress, Subject Cataloging Division. Subject cataloging manual: subject headings. Rev. ed. Washington, DC: Library of Congress, 1985

Miksa, Francis. The subject in the dictionary catalog from Cutter to the present. Chicago: American Library Association

O'Neill, Edward T. and Rao Aluri. Library of Congress subject heading patterns in OCLC monographic records. *Library resources and technical services* 25, no. 1:63-80 (1981)

Svenonius, Elaine. Use of classification in online retrieval. *Library resources and technical services* 27, no. 1:76-80 (1983)

AUTHORITY WORK, AUTHORITY RECORDS, AND AUTHORITY FILES

ARNOLD S. WAJENBERG

The basic purpose of authority work has remained unchanged since the time of Cutter.[1] Optimum use of a catalogue requires that the name of a person or corporate body that serves as an access point appear in a single form. Otherwise, records for the various works identified with a person or organization will be scattered in the catalogue under varying names or forms of name, and the user will not only have to search under all these variants but also will never be sure whether a search is unsuccessful because the library does not have the item sought or because it is listed under a heading different from those that he or she thought to use.[2] References lead from variant forms of name to the form established as standard and also connect headings for related entities (e.g., earlier and later names of a corporate body, the real name of an author and a pseudonym used by the same person). They, therefore, provide an essential aid to searching.[3] Topical subject headings and place name headings require the same kind of authority control, as do titles such as uniform titles and series titles that appear in several items in various forms.[4]

THE NEED FOR AUTHORITY WORK

The advent of library automation has introduced some new factors into authority work, giving rise to the databases shared by networks of libraries and to online catalogues in many of those libraries. The networks (OCLC, RLIN, UTLAS, and WLN) originated to make it possible for libraries to share cataloguing and, thus, reduce the cost of cataloguing for all participants. Those networks have gradually expanded into other areas (e.g., acquisitions, interlibrary loan, circulation, serial control, and preservation) without ever losing their original function.[5] However, participation in networks complicates authority work. Authority control, necessary for the optimum use of the catalogue of a single

library, is equally desirable in a shared database. Also, the use of shared cataloguing is much more efficient if the headings established by contributing libraries do not have to be changed by the libraries that use the contributed records in
their own catalogues. This requires adherence to standards that are agreed to by
all participants in the network.[6] In addition, cataloguers now must establish
headings both for their own catalogues and for the shared network database.

In the United States, the Library of Congress name authority file (LC NAF)
is almost always followed as the standard for name, title, and series headings.[7]
The file is available through all the major networks and can be purchased by an
individual library either in machine-readable form or on microfiche. The
machine-readable version (for networks or individual purchase) is updated regularly (the networks receive weekly updates). The microfiche is updated quarterly.[8]
By using the headings that they find in this file, cataloguers benefit from the work
already done by LC and also provide the users of their catalogue with what
Runkle calls "cross-catalog consistency."[9] That is, the users will find the same
person, corporate body, or uniform title, or series under the same heading in each
catalogue that they consult.

Although participation in a network using the LC NAF facilitates authority
work, it also complicates it. A cataloguer needing to use a personal, corporate, or
uniform title heading is relieved of the necessity of establishing the heading if it is
already in the NAF. However, it is still necessary to determine if the name of the
person, body, or work has already been used as a heading in the local catalogue.
If so, and if the heading is different from that found in the NAF, the cataloguer
must either change the heading in the local catalogue or alter the heading established by the Library of Congress to conform to local practice. In the long run,
the latter course is almost always self-defeating. Participants in a network such as
OCLC are *obliged* to use the headings found in the LC NAF in records that they
add to the shared database. Also, if the NAF form is not adopted as soon as it is
encountered, it may have to be altered repeatedly over many years, whenever new
materials that require the use of the conflicting heading are catalogued. This
creates the distinct possibility that the discrepancy will sometimes be missed, and
that the name or title will go into the local catalogue in two or more different
forms. Moreover, the users of that local catalogue will be denied the advantages
of cross-catalogue consistency referred to above. Ultimately, it is better to change
the headings in the local catalogue to conform to national standards, even though
such changes are, in the short term, time-consuming. Sometimes, of course, the
heading that is needed has not yet been established in the LC NAF. The cataloguer would then seem to be free to use the heading found in the local catalogue,
or, if it is new to the local catalogue, to follow his or her own best judgment in
following the cataloguing rules to create the heading. However, there is a strong
probability that the Library of Congress will eventually establish the heading.
Usually, therefore, cataloguers are expected to follow the Library of Congress
Rule Interpretations (*RIs*) closely, in the hope that the heading established locally
will agree with the heading that is eventually added to the LC NAF. Second-guess-
ing Library of Congress cataloguers perforce becomes the most common indoor
sport of American cataloguers.

COOPERATIVE AUTHORITY WORK

Recently, the Library of Congress has added a new dimension to that game by inviting selected libraries to share with it in the work of adding new headings to the LC NAF and of correcting and augmenting authority records already in the file. The project is called NACO (Name Authority COoperative project). The records that it produces are to be distributed via the Linked Systems Project.[10] NACO began in 1977, when the Government Printing Office was authorized to create the Library of Congress headings for U.S. government agencies. It was expanded gradually to other libraries, until there were thirty-five participants in 1985. Cataloguers from participating libraries undergo rigorous training and review by Library of Congress staff so that the authority records they add to LC NAF will conform to the national standards established by the Library of Congress.[11] As a result, LC NAF is gradually being transformed from the authority file of a single library—the Library of Congress—into a truly national authority file. It grows more rapidly, and headings enter the file more quickly, as a result of the participation of many libraries in its creation.

AUTHORITY WORK IN ONLINE CATALOGUES

In addition to giving rise to networks using online databases, automation has made it possible for individual libraries to create their own online catalogues. The change from manual, card catalogues to online catalogues is quite fundamental, and librarians are only beginning to explore the impact of this change on various library operations. The problems are further complicated by the great differences among the various online catalogues—greater by far than the differences among card catalogues. These differences tend to increase as new capabilities are developed. The differences are of various kinds, two of which have great impact on authority work: differences in the way online catalogues are searched, and differences in the way online catalogues process and store headings.

Some significant differences in searching capabilities involve the level of specificity required and permitted, the capability of keyword searching and truncation, and elements within the MARC record that are searched. Some systems permit searches that do not indicate the type of heading sought, whereas other systems require that every search command include an indication of type of heading (e.g., "find author," "find title," "find subject," and "find series"). Systems also vary in the level of specificity that *may* be given and that *must* be given. In the online catalogue of the University of Illinois at Urbana-Champaign, a search of the authority file must specify one of the categories listed above. It may be further refined, so that a name/title search is limited to personal name, corporate name, or uniform title. Subject headings may be specified as topical, geographic, personal name, corporate name, or uniform title.

The extent to which keyword searching is available varies greatly among different catalogues. In MELVYL, the system developed for the University of California, searches are automatically keyword searches. This sometimes results in the retrieval of an unacceptably large number of records. As a result, ORION, the system based on MELVYL that was developed for the University of California, Los Angeles, has recently introduced the capability of suppressing the keyword aspects of searches. As a result, if a search retrieves too many records, and the searcher is reasonably sure of the exact heading, she or he can specify an exact search.

Systems also vary as to the elements in a MARC record that are searchable. In catalogues based on Western Library Network (WLN) programs, for example, author, subject, and series searches are carried out above the subfield level. This permits a user of the catalogue to search for an author without being required to supply dates or titles (i.e., data in subfields *c* and *d* of the 100 field). It also means that a search for a subject such as "Danish poetry" will retrieve records with such subjects as "Danish poetry—History and criticism," "Danish poetry—Bibliography," and "Danish poetry—Translations into French," since the subdivisions go in separate subfields in the MARC record. It also permits searches for these subdivisions. A user can enter a request such as "find subject: translations into Danish" and retrieve records with such headings as "English drama—Translations into Danish," "Sonnets, French—Translations into Danish," and "Spanish fiction—Translations into Danish."

The ways in which a catalogue can be searched have a profound effect on the kind of authority work (i.e., the establishment of headings and references) that is appropriate for the catalogue. The current *Anglo-American Cataloguing Rules, Second Edition,* presupposes a manual catalogue (book, microform, or card) with entries arranged in alphabetical order. A few investigations have explored the question of whether consistent forms of headings need to be established in online catalogues. Arlene Taylor concludes from studies that she and two of her students carried out that consistent forms of headings are necessary to achieve collocation in online catalogues just as much as in manual catalogues.

THE USE OF REFERENCES IN
ONLINE CATALOGUES

Rather more studies have investigated whether, and to what extent, references are needed in online catalogues. These studies usually presuppose a catalogue with keyword searching and right-hand truncation (i.e., the ability to enter, say, "John#" and, thus retrieve "Johnson," "Johnston," etc.). Watson and Taylor studied a random sample of 400 personal name records and 400 corporate name records from the LC NAF. They found that 68.3 percent of personal name records and 25.5 percent of corporate name records contained no references. They also found that 41.5 percent of personal name references and 21.9 percent of corporate name references would be unnecessary in a system with keyword searching, right-hand truncation, and automatic elimination of embedded punctuation. They found that 14.5 percent of personal name records and 8.5 percent of corporate name records contained only such "unnecessary" references.[12]

Thomas carried out a similar study of *see* references in the manual authority file of the University of California, San Diego, to see if they would be necessary in an online catalogue using UC's MELVYL. MELVYL allows keyword searching, and provides automatic right-hand truncation after all initials in personal name headings (e.g., a search for "Fisher K H" would retrieve a heading such as "Fisher, Kenneth Harold." Given these searching capabilities, references from shorter forms of headings, inverted and variant forms, and different entry elements are not necessary. Thomas found that, in an online catalogue with MELVYL searching capability, 48 percent of personal name references and 44 percent of corporate name references (or 47 percent of all references) were unnecessary. Furthermore, 43 percent of the necessary personal name references were from more complete forms to shorter forms in established headings.[13]

Jamieson and colleagues carried out a slightly different kind of investigation. They studied 341 monographic bibliographic records taken from a tape of cataloguing at Western Ontario University Library. They searched for the authority records for each name and subject heading in the bibliographic records, and recorded all of the *see* references found in the authority records. A total of 1,189 *see* references were found. The bibliographic records were then examined to see if keyword searching of all fields in the bibliographic records would duplicate the information in the references. They found that 53.7 percent of name references, 73.5 percent of name subject references, and 69.6 percent of topical subjects (or, overall, 67.6 percent of the references) were not duplicated by keyword searching of bibliographic records.[14] They conclude that keyword searching and truncation are not a satisfactory substitute for *see* references. It seems apparent, however, that such searching capabilities provide a satisfactory substitute for some *see* references.

Taylor carried out an interesting study of 682 failed searches in the Northwestern University online catalogue based on NOTIS. She endeavored to discover whether *see* references from the LC NAF, or constructed according to Library of Congress cataloguing practice, would have allowed the searches to succeed. She found that the searching capabilities found in MELVYL (i.e., keyword searching, automatic right-hand truncation, and automatic truncation after each initial in a personal name heading) would be far more useful than references as now constructed.[15]

Taylor and Thomas both suggest that the cataloguing rules for *see* references should be revised for online catalogues in order to eliminate references rendered unnecessary by the searching capabilities of those catalogues.[16] The data in these studies would also seem to justify changes in rules for form of heading. The present cataloguing rules, which are designed for manual catalogues such as card catalogues, quite rightly direct the cataloguer to choose as the heading for persons and corporate bodies the form of name that is best known. In online catalogues, it would be better to use the most complete form of name, provided that form included the best-known form. Then keyword searching and truncation would permit retrieval of the best-known form, but also other more complete forms. For example, under the present rules, the heading for Mozart is "Mozart, Wolfgang Amadeus." In an online catalogue with keyword searching and right-hand truncation, a more useful heading would employ the complete name: "Mozart, Johann Chrysostom Wolfgang Amadeus." A user could retrieve the heading by requesting any combination of the words in this name, (e.g., "Mozart, Wolfgang Amadeus"; "Mozart, W. A."; "Mozart, J. C."; "Mozart, Chrysostom").

A similar change to the rules for corporate headings would make sense for online catalogues with keyword searching capability. The present rules for the treatment of subordinate bodies give preference to entering subordinate bodies directly under their own names.[17] When they must be entered as subdivisions of a parent body, the rules lead to the omission of intervening bodies as much as possible. However, for an online catalogue with keyword searching, the most useful heading would be the most complete heading. An example will show the difference. "Bureau of Health Manpower" is the name of a U.S. government agency. Its heading in the LC NAF, in coded form, is "110 10 United States. #b Health Resources Administration. #b Bureau of Health Manpower." The suggested online catalogue heading would be "110 10 United States. #b Department of Health and Human Services. #b Public Health Service. #b Health Resources Administration. #b Bureau of Health Manpower." It is unlikely that any searcher would key in the entire heading. However, she or he would be free to use any words in the heading that assist in identifying the specific corporate body being sought. If "Bureau of Health Manpower" retrieves more than one corporate body, the searcher could narrow the search by adding any words from any of the parent bodies' names.

Before the profession rushes to revise the rules, one essential prerequisite must be met. There must be sufficient standardization of searching techniques in online catalogues to guarantee that they all provide keyword searching, right-hand truncation, and the elimination of embedded punctuation. Although agreement on such matters is slowly developing, different online catalogues are still searched in quite different ways. The changes recommended above would work reasonably well in catalogues such as MELVYL and ORION, but would not be as useful in catalogues based on WLN programs, since such catalogues lack keyword searching of personal name, series title, and subject headings.

CATALOGUE MAINTENANCE

Catalogue maintenance is an activity closely related to authority work. Inevitably, cataloguers find it necessary to change headings from time to time in order to correct errors, resolve conflicts, or conform to changes in cataloguing rules and lists of subject headings. Such change can be extremely burdensome or, in some cases, impossible in manual catalogues. A large research library may easily have several thousand cards with headings such as "Clemens, Samuel Langhorne," "Negroes," or "Illinois, University of Illinois at Urbana-Champaign"—all headings that have been changed in recent years.

Such change is usually easier and faster in online catalogues, depending on the structure of the catalogue and the sophistication of the programs used for making changes. Online catalogues are often structured in such a way that each heading is stored only once, and linked to bibliographic records by numerical pointers. In such a system, an indefinite number of bibliographic records can be linked to a heading. If it is necessary to change the heading, a single change corrects all of the bibliographic records connected to the heading. The process is called global change.[18]

However, there may be limitations to the extent to which global changes are truly global. In most online catalogues, each combination of MARC subfields creates a new heading. For example, "Underdeveloped areas" is one subject heading. "Underdeveloped areas #x Bibliography," to take but one example, is another, separate subject heading. When the Library of Congress changed "Underdeveloped areas" to "Developing countries," the online catalogue of the University of Illinois at Urbana-Champaign was found to have more than 800 headings that began with "Underdeveloped areas," each of which had to be changed separately. Fortunately, some systems have been developed that can carry out changes of headings at the subfield level. Such capability permits truly global change.[19] Progress has also been made in writing microcomputer programs that can assist with online catalogue maintenance.[20] Unfortunately, as with searching, a survey of online authority maintenance found great variation in such features as validation of MARC coding, global updating features, hierarchical checks of headings with multiple subfields, and reciprocity checks (i.e., check to determine if a *see also* reference leads to an actual existing heading).[21]

The purpose of authority work remains unchanged since the time of Cutter, and it is now seen to be as essential for online catalogues as for manual files. However, the online environment, and online networks, have greatly changed the way in which authority work is done, sometimes making it easier and sometimes making it more complex.

NOTES

[1]Burger, Robert H. Authority work: the creation, use, maintenance, and evaluation of authority records and files. Littleton, CO: Libraries Unlimited, 1985. pp. 4, 9; Rochefort, A. Le controle d'autorité: implications pour les reseaux de catalogue. *Documentation et bibliothèques* 31:151 (1985)

[2]Oddy, Pat. Name authority files. *Catalogue & index* 82:1-4 (1986); Clack, Doris H. Authority control: issues and answers. *Technical services quarterly* 3:130 (1985)

[3]Burger. *Op cit.* p. 19; Runkle, Martin. Authority control: a library director's view. *Journal of academic librarianship*, 12:145 (1986)

[4]Burger. *Op cit.* pp. 18-19; Smith, B. G. Online series control in the integrated library system. *Technicalities* 6:3 (1986); Wilson, Mary Dabney. Back to the concept: perspectives on series authorities. *Information technology and libraries* 7:79-80 (1988)

[5]Rochefort. *Op cit.* p. 153

[6]*Ibid.*

[7]Burger. *Op cit.* p. 21; Runkle. *Op cit.* pp. 145-146; Franklin, L. F. Preparing for automated authority control: a projection of name headings verified. *Journal of academic librarianship* 13:206 (1987)

[8]Burger. *Op cit.* p. 21

[9]Runkle. *Op cit.* p. 146

[10]Avram, Henriette D. The Linked Systems Project: its implications for resource sharing. *Library resources and technical services* 30:36-46 (1986); McCallum, Sally H. Linked Systems Project in the United States. *IFLA journal* 11:313-324;

McCoy, R. W. The Linked Systems Project: progress, promise, realities. *Library journal* 1:33-39 (October 1986)

[11]Burger, Robert H. NACO at the University of Illinois at U-C: a narrative case study. *Cataloging and classification quarterly* 2:19-28 (1986)

[12]Watson, M. R. and Arlene G. Taylor. Implications of current reference structure for authority work in online environments. *Information technology and libraries* 6:10-19 (1987)

[13]Thomas, Catharine M. Authority control in manual versus online catalogs: an examination of "see" references. *Information technology and libraries* 3:393-398 (1984)

[14]Jamieson, Alexis *et al.* Keyword searching vs. authority control in an online catalog. *Journal of academic librarianship* 12:277-283 (1986)

[15]Taylor, Arlene G. Authority files in online catalogs: an investigation of their value. *Cataloging and classification quarterly* 4:15-16 (1984)

[16]Taylor. *Op cit.* p. 16; Thomas. *Op cit.* pp. 395-397

[17]Gorman, Michael and Paul W. Winkler, *eds.* Anglo-American cataloguing rules. 2nd ed. Chicago: American Library Association, 1978. rules 24.11-24.14 and 24.17-24.19

[18]Romero, Nancy and Arnold Wajenberg. Authority records and authority work in the online catalogue. *Information technology and libraries* 4:320 (1985)

[19]Miller, D. Authority control in the retrospective conversion process. *In* Improving LCSH for use in online catalogs/ ed. by P. Cochrane. Littleton, CO: Libraries Unlimited, 1986. p. 274

[20]Clark, Sharon E. and Winnie Chan. Maintenance of an online catalogue. *Information technology and libraries* 4:333 (1985)

[21]Grady, Agnes M. Online maintenance features of authority files: a survey of vendors and in-house systems. *Information technology and libraries* 7:51-55 (1988)

FURTHER READINGS

Di Lauro, Anne and Maureen Sly. Guidelines for the building of authority files in development-information systems. (Recommended methods for development-information systems; vol. 2). Ottawa, Canada: International Development Research Centre, 1985

Epstein, Susan B. Automated authority control: a hidden timebomb? *Library journal* 110:36-37 (1 Nov. 1985); 111:55-56 (Jan. 1986)

Hunn, Nancy O. and Jean Acker Wright. The implementation of ACORN authority control at Vanderbilt University Library. *Cataloging and classification quarterly* 8:79-91 (1987)

Udoh, D. J. E. and M. R. Aderibigbe. The problems of development, maintenance, and automation of authority files in Nigeria. *Cataloging and classification quarterly* 8:93-103 (1987)

COPY CATALOGUING AND THE BIBLIOGRAPHIC NETWORKS

LESLIE A. BLEIL and CHARLENE RENNER

Copy cataloguing, shared cataloguing, fast cataloguing, cooperative cataloguing — all mean the same thing, the use of a cataloguing record created somewhere other than in one's own library. In other words, one is copying someone else's work.

To have the ability to use another's work, one must be able to get to it. In cataloguing today, most libraries share records through bibliographic networks (which are also referred to as bibliographic utilities). Most networks are based on computer systems and operate on a database that includes both catalogue records created by the national libraries (notably the Library of Congress) and original catalogue records contributed by members of the network. The resulting database is shared by all members of the network.

In order for libraries to share cataloguing through a bibliographic network it is necessary for the records to be in a standard format. The most common such format is known as MARC (*Ma*chine *R*eadable *C*ataloguing). Although MARC was developed in the United States there are several national and regional variants on the MARC format in other countries. The MARC formats used by the Library of Congress and the bibliographic networks are called USMARC. Within USMARC there are variant formats for different types of material (books, serials, music, etc.), though work on a single integrated USMARC format is at an advanced stage. The uniformity of MARC makes bibliographic information more easily transferable. Through the Linked Systems Project (LSP), which began in 1979, the bibliographic networks have begun to share records with each other. At the present time, LSP is used mainly to transfer and exchange authority records.

There are three levels of cataloguing. The first is original cataloguing, which means creating a new record for an item. The second is a form of copy cataloguing in which a library uses another library's cataloguing, but modifies it to meet its own real or perceived cataloguing requirements. The third is true copy cataloguing — that is, making a catalogue record that is an exact copy of the originating library's work.

HISTORICAL PERSPECTIVE

Cooperative cataloguing began when libraries started looking for less-expensive and faster ways to process material. Librarians in a number of countries have had an interest in this topic since as long ago as the middle of the 19th century. In 1901, the Library of Congress began supplying printed cards and developing a union catalogue. In 1903, the *Bibliography of Co-operative Cataloguing and Printing of Catalogue Cards with Incidental References to International Bibliography and the Universal Catalogue (1850-1902)* was published.[1] In 1946, the Library of Congress started publishing the *Union Catalog*. It consisted of copies, reduced in size, of printed catalogue cards created by the Library of Congress and other participating libraries. In 1948, to reflect the idea of collective cataloguing better, the *Union Catalog* was renamed the *National Union Catalog*.

The real growth in shared cataloguing came in the 1960s with the development of OCLC, a resource-sharing consortium of Ohio academic and college libraries which was then called the Ohio College Library Center. OCLC grew from a state organization to a national/international organization as more libraries began realizing the potential of resource sharing. It is now the largest and most successful network in the world with approximately 6,000 member libraries.

It is important to remember that, while cooperative sharing of bibliographic data has become very sophisticated via the use of computer networks, libraries that cannot afford to be members of a network still rely on more traditional forms of sharing. The *National Union Catalog* is one of these. Libraries that do not wish to, or cannot, expend any effort on original or modified cataloguing rely on full-service vendors such as Gaylord, BNA, Brodart, and Baker & Taylor. These companies will send catalogue card sets with the item when purchased.

NETWORKS

The four major online networks in North America are OCLC (Online Cooperative Library Center), RLIN (Research Libraries Information Network), UTLAS (University of Toronto Library Automated Systems), and WLN (Western Library Network). They have had a most significant impact on the development of shared cataloguing. With their advent, participants could call upon large (and ever-growing) databases of already completed cataloguing records, and manipulate those records to meet their institutional variations. It should be noted that there are some significant differences between these four networks and the way in which they affect cooperative cataloguing.

The oldest and largest of the networks is OCLC. Its database currently contains more than 18 million bibliographic records. OCLC works with its participating members through regional networks. OCLC is a nonintegrated (or nonlinked) system in which the bibliographic files (containing MARC records) and authority files (containing records of the forms of name, title, and subject access points) are separate. This means that manipulation of the authority files does not change the bibliographic files that are related to them. The authority file contains Library of Congress name/title and subject files. However, it does not include all access points used in the bibliographic file of MARC records. While OCLC relies on its members to create and maintain the bibliographic file, it has little or no control over the LC-originated authority file, since the Library maintains strict control over its authority database.

RLIN has another nonintegrated database, though they have plans to integrate it. RLIN began as the local online system (then known as BALLOTS) of Stanford University Library and was developed by RLG (Research Libraries Group) to become their network system. RLIN also uses LC authority files, and RLIN members may add their records to the OCLC database.

One important problem with these nonintegrated database systems is that they have little control over uniformity or duplication. This occurs in part because access points used in catalogue records may not be consistent, thus affecting, to some extent, the indexing or searching capabilities of the database. Many users search by name or name/title access points. If the form of a name is not consistent, not all entries may be found by a searcher or duplicate records may appear. One library may not find a record for an item input by another library because they interpret the form of an access point differently. Duplication, in turn, causes problems for cooperative cataloguing units that have to make a decision about which record to use. OCLC publishes standard criteria stating which records are preferable for use and what to do about duplicates. The bottom line, is, however, that the record that best suits the library (or the cataloguer) is the one that will be chosen. In attempts to ameliorate these problems, OCLC has developed the following practices:

- They have done periodic "flips" of the database, that is, checking all headings in the bibliographic file against the authority file.

- They helped to develop the CONSER (*Co*operative *On*line *Ser*ials) project.

- They developed reporting forms (called Change Request forms) whereby contributing members may report duplicate or erroneous data to OCLC.

- They developed the Enhance program.

The Enhance program began in 1984 with twenty participating OCLC members. These libraries can edit and replace records in the database in most nonserial formats. The CONSER project is the serials equivalent to the Enhance program. The idea behind this program is to improve the usefulness and quality of records in the database and to decrease the number of Change Request forms that OCLC must process, thus allowing OCLC to focus on problems other than quality control. This program has proved to be successful, and today has approximately sixty-seven participating members.

In a system with an integrated database, in which bibliographic records and authority records are linked, access points (name, subject, uniform title, and series) can be checked as they are being input into the database by means of identifiable "tagged" fields (a *tag* is the three digit number that identifies a *field* — a major part of a MARC record). Also, global changes (i.e., simultaneous changes to all records with a common access point) can be made when the authorized form of an access point has been newly established or changed. With systems with nonintegrated databases, such work becomes the responsibility of the (computerized or not) local system.

Integrated systems have an advantage in cooperative cataloguing for the reasons described above. UTLAS, a major Canadian utility, is becoming popular in the United States. WLN is a much smaller network based in the Pacific Northwest. Both networks are integrated systems, with interactive bibliographic and authority files.

QUALITY CONTROL

Quality control is a contentious subject because the definition of *quality* in cooperative cataloguing is difficult. Each library has its own concept of what constitutes a high-quality catalogue record. These ideas of quality are affected by factors such as management philosophy, budget constraints, and user needs and may differ widely from library to library. There are three important aspects of quality control that matter to all libraries. They are standards, bibliographic content, and authority control.

There are three levels of standardization in cooperative cataloguing. The broadest level is national and international—as in the *Anglo-American Cataloguing Rules, Second Edition (AACR2)*, the International Standard Bibliographic Description (ISBD), and the MARC formats. These provide a framework for the building of all cataloguing records. The second level is that of the standards of the bibliographic networks. For example, libraries that use OCLC follow *AACR2*, but must also input according to rules set by OCLC. Certain bibliographic information is mandatory in OCLC records (e.g., name access points [when applicable], title, publisher) whereas other data (e.g., contents notes) are optional. The third level is that of the standards of the individual library, and it is there the most variation occurs.

Individual library standards affect both the records that a library contributes to a network, and the use of records that library derives from a network. In other words, an individual library's standards directly affect the amount of work another library may have to do in using its records, and the amount of work they themselves have to do in using someone else's records. Some of these manipulations may be done by computers changing data in the catalogue records. This applies to changes in the descriptive fields in particular, but not to areas subject to human interpretation. They save both time and money by taking away nit-picking work (e.g., correcting punctuation or deleting certain unnecessary data) from staff members. Awareness of all three levels of standards is a necessary element in the use of cooperative cataloguing.

The second area of quality control, bibliographic content, is an intellectual aspect. Certain decisions in cooperative cataloguing, such as assignment of headings, cannot be dealt with by machine. This is also an area that will differ from library to library. One has the option of accepting another library's intellectual content (here defined as classification and access points), or replacing or modifying it. If cooperative cataloguing is to be effective, the intellectual judgment of other libraries must be accepted.

The trust factor relates to who trusts whom in a bibliographic network. All members are given identifying symbols that are attached to the bibliographic records they create and add to a database. Through this identification, libraries may scrutinize each other's work. For example, the Library of Congress's symbol on OCLC is DLC. Since LC cataloguing is considered the best available, most libraries will make a point of looking for a DLC record when searching the database.

Libraries need to realize that developing complete cataloguing records originally is the most efficient and cost-effective way to use cooperative cataloguing and make trust universal. While it is expensive to do original cataloguing and to do it thoroughly, for most libraries the percentage of original cataloguing in relation to overall cataloguing statistics is very low. If all libraries were to take the time and accept the expense of inputting complete records into their database, they would save time and money in the long run because everyone would have to manipulate fewer records. While it is true that many libraries today take cooperative cataloguing "as is" (i.e., without significant modification), there is vast room for improvement in the quality and completeness of many of the records found in today's databases.

The third aspect of quality control, and the most troublesome one in the current atmosphere of developing computer systems, is authority control. Verification of access points is the most time-consuming aspect of cooperative cataloguing today. Since consistency of access points is necessary for best access and use, all must be examined, either by machine, or by human eye. This is a problem for true copy cataloguing. Even library systems that are totally automated can only use their computers to cross-check access points against those that already exist in their authority file (be it an LC or local file). If a heading is unverifiable, or causes a conflict in the system, it must be checked by hand.

There can be no complete solution to this problem as there will always be new names appearing that must be authenticated, and other names that will change from their verified form to another. There will always be a need for human intervention in authority work, though whether a library chooses to invest time and money in authority work will be a matter of individual philosophy. Access points should be authenticated by the Library of Congress (almost everyone accepts their authority) or by the library using the record.

ECONOMIC REALITIES

Shared cataloguing is cheaper than original cataloguing in most cases. Sometimes, however, other important factors are sacrificed for the sake of economics. Technical services activities in libraries are currently facing times of economic difficulty. Because processing is not perceived as being directly service oriented, and because it usually takes a large portion of the budget, libraries are always looking for ways to decrease processing costs. Also, because cataloguing is quantifiable, increased efficiency can always be sought. In the case of shared cataloguing, one must weigh the factors of economics against quality. This is not to say there are no libraries producing high-quality cataloguing; there are. However, the quality standards and/or needs of one library may not be the same as those of another. For example, an academic research library will usually want a bibliographic record of great depth and detail to aid their scholarly users, but the same record would probably not be suitable for a public or school library. The depth and detail is not necessary and such a library probably could not afford to do cataloguing at that level. Granted, there are differences between the material found in an academic research library and materials found in other types of libraries but, since there are also overlaps, the problem exists. True copy cataloguing (with no changes and, hence, at a lesser cost) is more attainable where collections are similar. The answer to this problem is not to have different libraries making up individual records for a specific item, but in editing records already developed to suit the needs of the individual library. However, the concept of immediate and economical cataloguing by calling up a record on a bibliographic database and pushing a button to produce cards or tapes is a reality, whether cataloguers like it or not.

If exact duplication of preexisting cataloguing is not the best answer, then why use it? Because it is still less expensive to use someone else's work than to create one's own, even if the catalogue records must be manipulated or double checked. A study done at the Washington State University Libraries determined that the per-item cost of original cataloguing is five times the cost of using cooperative cataloguing.[2]

If cooperative cataloguing is to be used, who will do the work? This is where a library may save on costs. It does not take an original cataloguer (i.e., a librarian) to edit existing bibliographic copy, unless classification or subject headings need to be assigned, or the authority of an access point is in question. Well-trained technicians can handle cooperative cataloguing and reconcile conflicts between bibliographic and authority records. The supposition here is that existing bibliographic records are of a high quality and include all necessary information.

Many libraries get around using inadequate existing copy by waiting for the Library of Congress to catalogue the item (of course, LC is infallible!). If there is no copy at all, they wait until someone else catalogues the item. Many potentially useful items wait for years, collecting dust in someone's backlog, for lack of copy or of LC copy. Just because no one has catalogued a book does not mean it has no value. Its rarity alone might make it a valuable addition to the working collection. While it is true that the Library of Congress does catalogue a high percentage of published works (at Western Michigan University, LC copy is used for over 80 percent of books catalogued), it does not catalogue everything that exists. This means that cooperative cataloguing can be most successful if contributing libraries make the effort to do good original cataloguing in a timely manner.

One of the problems with this idea is that all libraries cannot afford to do good original cataloguing, or simply do not want to do it. Many libraries are cutting down on the number of their cataloguers in favor of technicians and clerical staff, as the latter are less expensive. Does this mean that professional original cataloguers will no longer be needed? This seems unlikely. New catalogue records for others to use will not appear magically; unique skills and knowledge are necessary to create catalogue records that are worth copying. Again, the problem is cost. While the Library of Congress will dutifully keep on providing catalogue records, trends indicate that many libraries are giving up on original cataloguing and waiting for other institutions to provide them with copy.

ROLE OF THE LIBRARY OF CONGRESS

The stated primary role of the Library is as the library for Congress, but it is also our national library. As such, one of the responsibilities it has is to facilitate resource sharing. It works diligently with the U.S. and foreign library community to promote cooperation and is good about sharing its own resources. The Library of Congress has helped promote cooperative cataloguing in many ways. It began resource sharing by distribution of its printed cards. This progressed to the development of the *National Union Catalog*, which contains not only LC catalogue records, but also those of other contributing libraries (now numbering over 1,200). The *NUC* continues to be an important contributor to shared cataloguing.

More recently, the Library of Congress developed "Cataloging in Publication" (CIP). CIP began in 1971, and by 1986 was providing more than 35,000 records. The CIP division of the Library works with over 2,500 publishers. Using prepublication proof copies of new publication, its CIP provides a basic catalogue record that is printed on the verso of the title leaf of the published book. Although CIP is useful, there is much controversy concerning the accuracy of the information given. A study done by Arlene G. Taylor and Charles W. Simpson shows that only 49.7 percent of CIP is error free, compared to 57.8 percent of regular LC copy.[3] While this is a significant difference in accuracy, it is up to each individual library to weigh the lesser cost and the greater ease of use against the reduced quality of the resulting catalogue records.

The Library of Congress also distributes its cataloguing records in MARC format to networks and libraries alike. An enormous amount of data for sharing is thus distributed in an efficient manner. However, a problem with this is that, since the Library uses very little cooperative cataloguing for its own database, it does a lot of duplicative work. New projects such as the National Coordinated Cataloging Program (NCCP) in which the Library accepts cataloguing from other institutions are steps in the right direction.

The Library of Congress has recently made great strides in serial cooperative cataloguing. Their publication of *New Serials Titles (NST)* gives libraries without online capabilities the opportunity to share cataloguing. The development of standards is assisted by the National Serials Data Program (NSDP) which assigns International Standard Serial Numbers (ISSNs) and key titles to serial records, thus giving each serial a unique identifier. Most important was the development of the CONSER program, a collaborative effort by the Library of Congress and a select group of participating libraries (about twenty four), working with OCLC to produce standardized and high-quality serial cataloguing records.

Another aspect of LC support of cooperation is the distribution of its authority file. Many libraries base their authority control on LC authority records. Through National Coordinated Cataloguing Operations (NCCO), an organization that creates and distributes authority records, the Library of Congress is expanding the size of its authority database.

Historically, the Library of Congress can be considered a catalyst for cooperative cataloguing. Many libraries want to use LC catalogue records when they are available and to emulate the LC level of cataloguing when they are not. Though in the past the Library was a law unto itself, in recent times it has made a great effort to participate in the development of national uniform codes and standards.

FUTURE TRENDS

Library technical services will look more toward resource sharing as library budgets decrease and the sophistication of computer systems increases. The consequences of such sharing will be evident in the following trends.

The first is a paradox. Although most libraries are moving away from "perfect" cataloguing because it is too expensive and time-consuming, at the same time they want the cataloguing of others, which they will use, to be of a high quality. One of the main problems for cooperative cataloguing in the future will be in maintaining good databases while still maintaining economy.

The second trend is toward using copy cataloguing to the extent of abandoning original cataloguing. This will affect the acquisitions of libraries that will not order items unless they have already been catalogued. What are the ramifications of this? How will such a "selection policy" affect the needs of the library user? Gary Charbonneau of Indiana University Libraries concludes that "there is little or no difference in the rates at which patrons use materials that have received original and copy cataloguing."[4] In other words, using more copy cataloguing will get the books out faster with no significant change in the usage rate by patrons and thus will not affect the quality of the collection, as perceived by the patrons. However, Charbonneau also warns that "any library that wishes to take the seemingly radical step of modifying its collection pattern based on the availability or non-availability of acceptable cataloguing copy would be advised to proceed — but with caution."[5] This, of course, does not address the problem of the materials that the patrons cannot use — those that were not purchased because cataloguing copy was unavailable.

An effect of the trend toward more copy cataloguing will be to produce an increase in the number of cataloguing technicians relative to the number of original cataloguers. Despite the fact that editing or completing existing records will be done by clerical staff and computers, original cataloguers will continue to flourish. They will be taking on more responsibility for the management and supervision of cataloguing technicians and database systems. With this shift in workload will come an overall decrease in the number of technical service people, as computers manage workloads more efficiently.

A third trend will be toward shared programs. An example can be found within the Research Libraries Group. RLG libraries have started a program in which they are dividing up responsibility for original cataloguing of monographs within a selected group of series.[6] Other programs like this predate the RLG experiment and more will be developed.

Finally, linked network systems will become more popular as computer systems and databases become more sophisticated, and data sharing more economical. The problems posed by dissimilar hardware and software will no longer deter communications between networks, allowing more sharing and cooperative cataloguing to take place. Eventually, this will lead to a national network.

There are also several challenges that will have to be met in the future. The first is the issue of performance standards. Both quantity and quality standards must be maintained in cooperative cataloguing. Quality standards are not being widely addressed at this time. In a survey taken of Resources and Technical Services Division/CCS Copy Cataloguing Discussion Group members on copy cataloguing activities, twenty of twenty-eight libraries reported having quantity standards, while only six of twenty-eight monitor error rates (i.e., check for quality of cataloguing).[7]

Another challenge lies in the proliferation of local online systems. Local cataloguing will become more popular, as more libraries acquire these systems. Many of the records that result from that local cataloguing may not be added to the databases of the bibliographic networks. Even those records that are added may not meet national standards. The net result will be a diminution of resource-sharing capability.

It is possible that in the future there will be complete text searching online, making traditional cataloguing unnecessary. By entering raw data such as title page information, bibliographic references, index, and, perhaps, introduction, the use of concepts such as main entry will become obsolete.

The overall picture of the future for cooperative cataloguing is one of growth. Economic demands will make the major issue the need for greater efficiency and better quality control, especially in authority work. Through even greater use of computer networks, the standardization and sharing of bibliographic data will be done worldwide, to the advantage of all libraries.

NOTES

[1]Jahr, Torstein Knutson Torstenaen. Bibliography of cooperative cataloguing and the printing of catalogue cards with incidental references to international bibliography and the universal catalogue (1850-1902). Washington, DC: Government Printing Office, 1903

[2]Drushel, Joselyn. Cost analysis of an automated and manual book processing system. *Journal of library automation* 14:32-34 (1981)

[3]Taylor, Arlene G. and Charles W. Simpson. Accuracy of LC copy: a comparison of copy that began as CIP and other LC cataloging. *Library resources and technical services* 30:375-387 (1986)

[4]Charbonneau, Gary. A comparison of rates of patron utilization of library materials receiving original cataloging and materials receiving copy cataloging. *Collection management* 8:25-32 (1986)

[5]*Ibid.*

[6]Mandel, Carol A. and Susan F. Rhee. Shared cataloging: some remaining issues. *Cataloging and classification quarterly* 7:29-38 (1986)

[7]Hudson, Judith. Copy cataloging activities: report of a survey. *Cataloging and classification quarterly* 7:63-67 (1986)

FURTHER READINGS

Avram, Henriette D. Current issues in networking. *Journal of academic librarianship* 12:205-209 (1986)

_____. The Linked Systems Project: its implications for resource sharing. *Library resources and technical services* 30:36-46 (1986)

Boll, John J. Professional literature on cataloging — then and now. *Library resources and technical services* 29:226-238 (1985)

Brandehoff, Susan E. The catalogerless society. *American libraries* 14:730 (1983)

Carpenter, Michael and Elaine Svenonius, *eds.* Foundations of cataloging: a sourcebook. Littleton, CO: Libraries Unlimited, 1985

Freedman, Maurice J. and S. Michael Malinconico, *eds.* The nature and future of the catalog. Phoenix, AZ: Oryx Press, 1979

Gislason, Thora. CIP: how it's being used. *Canadian library journal* 43:413-416 (1986)

Hafter, Ruth. Born-again cataloging in the online networks. *College and research libraries* 47:360-364 (1986)

Holley, Robert P. The future of catalogers and cataloging. *Journal of academic librarianship* 7:90-93 (1981)

Horney, Karen L. Minimal-level cataloging: a look at the issues: a symposium. *Journal of academic librarianship* 11:332-342 (1986)

_____. New turns for a new century: library services in the information era. *Library resources and technical services* 31:6-11 (1987)

Hunter, Eric J. Cataloguing: a guidebook. Hamden, CT: Linnet Books, 1975

Malinconico, S. Michael. Catalogs and cataloging: innocent pleasures and enduring controversies. *Library journal* 109:1210-1213 (1984)

Martin, Susan K. Library networks, 1986-87. White Plains, NY: Knowledge Industry, 1986

McBride, Ruth. Copy cataloging of serials: proceedings of the ALA/RTSD/CCS Copy Cataloging Discussion Group meeting, July 10, 1982, in Philadelphia. *Serials librarian* 8:23-47 (1983)

Reid, Marion T. and Norma H. Martin. Non-MARC and MLC records—to upgrade or not? *RTSD newsletter* 13:1-3 (1988)

Saylor, V. Louise. Cooperative cataloging quality control in the OCLC Pacific Network. *Information technology and libraries* 5:235-239 (1986)

Schoenung, James Gerald. The quality of the member-input monographic records in the OCLC On-Line Union Catalog. PhD dissertation, Drexel University, 1981

Share, Donald S. Waiting for cataloging. *Technical services quarterly* 4:19-24 (1986)

Taylor, Arlene G. Cataloging with copy. 2nd ed. Littleton, CO: Libraries Unlimited, 1987

Truett, Carol. Is cataloging a passé skill in today's technological society? *Library resources and technical services* 28:268-275 (1984)

Special Topics

PRESERVATION IN THE RESEARCH LIBRARY:
Its Past, Present Status, and Encouraging Future

NORMAN B. BROWN

In reviewing the literature on preservation, it seems only proper to return to two early contributions. Adams's classic reproof of "librarians as enemies of books" and Barr's concern with the inadequate attention paid to the binding and maintenance of library materials reminded colleagues of their curatorial responsibilities, only one of the many concerns of the modern preservationist.[1] Even though neatly bound and properly shelved, the Adams and Barr pages were torn, smudged from the use of many readers, and rapidly approaching embrittlement, only two of the countless volumes now known to contain "the acidic seeds of their own destruction."[2] As reiterated in professional literature and now occasionally in the public press, collection deterioration to the point of disintegration, mainly because of the high acidic content of book paper in use since the 1850s, but also due to improper maintenance and storage and heavy use, imperils humankind's intellectual and cultural heritage.[3] Understandably alarmed by the crisis and committed to the preservation of priceless records, libraries (especially research libraries) in increasing numbers are marshaling current resources and implementing new strategies to expand their preservation responsibilities. These are now understood to include the restoration and repair of those materials which should and can be saved, the reformatting (microfilming) of those so embrittled as to be beyond repair, the replacement of important items still available, the surveillance and necessary repair of new acquisitions, and the proper maintenance of all collections in a secure, clean, and atmospherically controlled environment.[4]

While the general maintenance of library collections has always been a matter of concern, the causes and dimensions of collection deterioration were unknown until organizational strategies and the technology for combatting massive deterioration arose in the 1960s and 1970s. Deterioration tended to be ignored or minimized by all but a few research libraries for several years. They also had other pressing priorities in the 1950s and 1960s. Supported by unprecedented financial resources, research libraries amassed huge collections in a variety of formats and in almost every known subject area, all to meet the increasing demands of scholars whose research interests had become international in scope. To provide accessibility and minimize duplication, research libraries then devoted their energies to the development and refinement of automated bibliographic databases. When university budgets and, therefore, funding for library acquisitions declined in the early 1970s while research demands and the cost of materials continued to escalate, there was further incentive for individual institutions to share their resources through consortia and national and regional arrangements. An increasing number of research libraries have come to recognize preservation as a critical institutional priority, a major component of sound collection management, and a shared responsibility.

PRESERVATION'S AMERICAN PAST

Preservation is a subject of major interest to all cultural institutions, but it is here examined only as a critical concern of American research libraries. It is important to mention another limitation. This essay discusses the preservation of paper-based materials only, while fully recognizing that the rescue of nonpaper formats is of equal importance. It is appropriate to mention at least a few of the many research institutions and organizations which have played major roles. Chief among them are the Council on Library Resources (CLR)[5]; the Association of Research Libraries (ARL), acting usually through its Committee on the Preservation of Research Library Materials and in recent years its Office of Management Services; the Library of Congress; the American Library Association (ALA), especially the Resources and Technical Services Division's Preservation of Library Materials and Reproduction of Library Materials Sections and the Preservation Microfilming Committee; and the Research Libraries Group (RLG). Of several nonlibrary funding organizations, the most important are the National Endowment of the Humanities (NEH) and the Andrew W. Mellon Foundation. The American Institute for Conservation, the Society of American Archivists, the Library Binding Institute, and the National Institute for the Conservation of Cultural Property have also contributed extensively.

THE REORGANIZATION OF
RESEARCH LIBRARIES

Research libraries have been somewhat slow in integrating the many aspects of sound preservation programs with other institutional priorities. However, their growing understanding of preservation problems is clearly reflected by comparing the subjects discussed in the 1956 "conservation" issue in *Library Trends* with those presented at the 1969 conference of the University of Chicago's Graduate Library School.[6] Concerns of the mid-1950s included the care of old and rare books, binding problems, commercial and in-house binding, stacks maintenance, and personnel. Focusing national professional attention on several of today's preoccupations, the 1969 Chicago conference reviewed collection deterioration and the need for preservation, the acidic nature of modern book paper, environmental factors affecting paper permanence, the promise of alkaline paper, the importance of sound binding practice, and the need for overall institutional preservation programs.

Prior to the mid-1960s, most libraries had some form of basic repair unit, a section responsible for commercial binding, and a stack maintenance group, but each of these functions was normally separate from the others, and staff acted without the knowledge of archival methods and materials that the library community now possesses. Until the Newberry Library began its conservation program under Paul Banks in 1964, there were literally no comprehensive preservation programs at the local level. Most deteriorated materials were either ignored or discarded.[7] The Newberry Library set standards for others to follow. The Library of Congress appointed its first preservation officer in 1967 and organized its preservation activities shortly thereafter. A few other institutional programs were established in the early 1970s. By 1988, a Library of Congress survey "discovered fifty-four institutions where there are either designated preservation departments or staff persons, and where a noticeable level of preservation activity is occurring."[8] There were only six in 1978.

The Collection Analysis Project of ARL's Office of Management Services (OMS) in the late 1970s included a preservation component, emphasizing its importance in sound collection management.[9] OMS published the first edition of its self-study guide, *Preservation Planning Program* and accompanying *Resources Notebook* in 1982, with a second edition in 1987 which announced that its predecessor has been used in some fashion by over 300 libraries.[10] This guide includes chapters on environmental conditions, the physical conditions of the collections, organization, disaster control, preservation resources, and two new chapters on staff and user education.[11] Two OMS SPEC kits on preservation education in ARL libraries and organizing for preservation activities were issued in 1985.[12] During this period ARL also published its guidelines for minimal preservation efforts and surveyed the preservation activities and expenditures of its membership.[13]

It soon became obvious that there was an urgent need for preservation education at all levels. There are three significant instructional manuals of the late 1960s and early 1970s, and several later manuals.[14] There are also guides on a variety of special problems, notably on the prevention and handling of collection disasters.[15] A few library schools began offering formal courses on preservation in the 1970s. Today twenty-three American and four Canadian library schools offer one or more such courses.[16] The most important is Columbia's Rare Book School which offers formal training programs for conservators and preservation administrators. Until this time, conservators learned professional techniques through private study, self-training, and in the conservation units of hand binderies and the more advanced research libraries. Today, conservation education on several levels is currently available through internships and special programs offered at the Library of Congress, the New York Public Library, and at several university libraries; in articles, books, manuals, and videocassettes; and at conferences and other meetings. One of the best of the recent conferences was a series of three, for the administrator, middle manager, and the materials repair staff, sponsored by the Library of Congress.[17] Many educational opportunities are announced in *The Abbey Newsletter, Conservation Administration News*, and *National Preservation News.*[18]

THE PAPER PROBLEM: ITS NATURE, DIMENSIONS, AND RESOLUTION

The resolution of the problems inherent in unstable paper has been the major preoccupation of the preservation movement and the prime factor in motivating libraries to attend to other preservation issues. It was a prominent theme in the first twenty-five years of the movement (from 1956 to 1980).[19] The high points of the search for a solution to the paper problem include the impact of William J. Barrow's paper research; the introduction of alkaline-based, acid-free paper and encouragement of its use; the initiation of institutional and collaborative reformatting projects; the development of mass deacidification systems; the formulation of strategies designed to meet the problem of the brittle book; and growing public recognition that preservation is a national problem in urgent need of massive private and public financial support. During this period libraries learned that basic preventive measures prolong the life of paper-based materials. They also learned that the ultimate solution to the paper problem is to be found in the use of permanent or acid-free paper, the reformatting of embrittled book paper, and the deacidification of imperiled book paper.

The identification of the high acid content of the book paper in widespread use since the 1850s as the major cause of paper deterioration grew out of the investigations of William J. Barrow. An early Barrow study indicated that probably "most library books printed in the first half of the 20th century will be in unusable condition in the next century.[20] A few years later Edwin Williams found that almost 60 percent of the monographs recorded in the *National Union Catalog* in 1961 were probably printed on deteriorating paper.[21] The alarming dimensions of collection deterioration have since been made abundantly clear. A 1984 survey of the 13 million volumes in the Library of Congress's general and law collections indicated that 25 percent are embrittled, another 10 percent approaching embrittlement, and 36 percent of only moderate strength.[22] The recent Yale collection condition survey, which sets standards and guidelines that other institutions are encouraged to follow, shows the extent of deterioration in another major research library. In an examination of over 36,500 volumes it was found that "37.1 percent of the books sampled overall had brittle paper ... and that 82.6 percent of the books overall had acidic paper (i.e., a pH of below 5.4)."[23] It has been estimated that

> American research library collections contain 300,000,000 books, and almost half of the books in some of these libraries cannot be used. The lowest estimates of brittle books in research library collections average about 9 percent, the highest estimates average almost 50 percent. At an overall average of 30 percent, 90 million books standing on the shelves of American research libraries cannot be used because their leaves have become so brittle as a result of acid attack.[24]

Before Barrow it was generally assumed that collection deterioration was due mainly to heavy use. Barrow and others established that the sources of acid in book paper are lignin in wood pulp, alum used in rosin sizing, residual bleaching chemicals, almost all modern ink, sulfur dioxide in polluted air, and migration from other materials such as acidic chemicals used in the manufacture of some leather bindings.[25] It was also found that light, higher temperatures, high humidity, and polluted air accelerated deterioration. These discoveries prompted Barrow's further study of older paper which, because of its high alkaline content, showed minimal or no signs of deterioration and was resistant to aging. In 1960 he introduced the first permanent/durable paper made from chemically treated wood pulp with a high alkaline content.[26] The new paper was clearly a significant achievement; it was handsome, dependable, economically produced, and proved that paper need not have a high rag content.[27]

The use of acid-free or permanent/durable paper has increased but its use has been limited mainly to the monographic publishing of private and university presses and to special editions of commercial publishers.[28] Since the use of permanent paper would virtually eliminate future problems, ARL, CLR, ALA, and other members of the research community encourage its production and use for the several categories of research materials meriting permanent retention in research libraries.[29] Production and use have increased, but the paper industry has generally been reluctant, arguing that permanent paper is more expensive to produce and not economically advantageous because only about 5 percent of the 11 million tons of paper sold annually is used for books and serials. Advocates of alkaline paper insist that the percentage of use is much higher, that it may not be as expensive to produce as projected, and that conversion to the alkaline process produces a cleaner environment.[30]

The Reformatting of Embrittled Materials

Silver halide microfilm is currently accepted as the perferable and least expensive medium for the reformatting of embrittled paper materials to preserve their intellectual content.[31] Microfilm is easy to produce, durable if production and storage standards are observed, inexpensively copied, and easily reproduced should another medium, such as the optical laser disk, prove superior.[32] Since the 1950s it has been considered a most satisfactory replacement for materials which cannot be lent and for newspapers and other publications issued on paper of poor quality or difficult to store. It has also been used in commercial ventures, making unique and rarely held materials available, preserving original materials, and ensuring accessibility of copies in the process. Other examples of its early and continued use by libraries include the CRL Foreign Newspaper Microfilming Project, Africana, Southeast Asian, Latin American, and South Asian microfilming projects, and the extensive microfilming programs of the Library of Congress and the New York Public Library. Since the early 1980s, NEH has sponsored the U.S. Newspaper Project, awarding grants to many institutions and states to identify and prepare bibliographic records for American newspapers prior to their eventual microfilming. The American Theological Library Association, which had been microfilming theological serials for years, recently expanded its program to include monographs issued between 1860 and 1929, and the American Philological Association continues its project of preserving classical studies materials published between 1815 and 1918.

The RLG Cooperative Preservation Microfilming Project (CPMP) is recognized as a model collaborative program, well planned and successfully implemented. Eight important libraries filmed approximately 30,000 American imprints and Americana in specific subject areas published between 1876 and

1900 from their collections. In addition to a service copy for each title, there are two master negatives, one for the owning institution and one in a storage vault in a renovated limestone mine in Boyers, Pennsylvania. To avoid duplication by other libraries and assure accessibility, each title appears in the Research Libraries Information Network (RLIN) database and in a microfiche listing. The RLIN records are expected to be added to the OCLC database.[33] The detailed procedures developed for the project are available in the second edition of the *RLG Preservation Manual*.[34]

Preservation microfilming is very expensive and to a large extent has depended on supplemental funding by private and public agencies. It is also a fact that the extensive production of archival quality microfilm cannot easily be undertaken by most research libraries because they lack the necessary expertise, equipment, and space. Nor is it always efficient and cost-effective.[35] Thus the special importance of two nonprofit and mainly self-supporting regional centers, the Northeast Document Conservation Center (NEDCC), organized in 1973 at Andover, Massachusetts, and the Mid-Atlantic Preservation Service (MAPS), established at Lehigh University, Bethlehem, Pennsylvania, in early 1987. NEDCC's continuing primary interest has been the provision of expert conservation and consultation services and educational programs for libraries with limited or no facilities, mainly those in the New England states, New York, and New Jersey. It began its preservation microfilming service in 1979 and in recent years expanded it to handle part of RLG's Cooperative Microfilming Project.[36] MAPS, which was known as the Mid-Atlantic States Cooperative Preservation Service when it was established in 1985 at Princeton, has concentrated on archival quality microfilming, a service which has expanded considerably in a very short time.[37]

Since item-specific bibliographic access is crucial to the success of all reformatting projects, it is important to mention the retrospective conversion of the Library of Congress's master file of some 460,000 monographic records reported to the *National Register of Microform Masters* (*NRMM*) between 1965 and 1983. The project will provide machine-readable records which will be available via the MARC Cataloging Distribution Service. While many master negatives are not recorded in *NRMM* and the quality of some *NRMM* records has been questioned, the new file clearly makes it easier to determine the existence of a record, now a tedious and labor-intensive process.[38]

Mass Deacidification Systems

Mass deacidification technology is still in a developmental stage. When operational, a system must be an effective, fast, and economical method of deacidifying and buffering a large amount of endangered, but not yet embrittled, paper at one time. Three processes are currently receiving attention: the Wei T'o System, the Library of Congress's Diethylzinc Process (DEZ) now under arduous testing, and the recent and relatively unknown Bookkeeper Process initially developed in 1981 by the Koppers Chemical Company of Pittsburgh.

The Wei T'o Nonaqueous Book Deacidification System, in successful operation at the National Library and Public Archives of Canada since 1980, is the oldest of the three processes. Volumes are first dehydrated in a vacuum drier, then transferred to a vacuum chamber in which they are deacidified by magnesium carbonate applied as a liquid gas, and after removal from the treatment chamber allowed to regain their original moisture content. A bench-top version is used in several research libraries. The DEZ Process, under development since 1973, was under public scrutiny in the mid-1980s because of two fires caused by inappropriate equipment and inadequate safety and testing procedures. It is now being tested in a pilot deacidification facility, in Houston, Texas. Volumes placed in a vacuum chamber are dehydrated, deacidified through the permeation of DEZ vapors, and rehydrated. The Library of Congress's continued confidence in the process by which it plans to deacidify 1 million volumes annually, at an estimated average cost of $3.50 to $5.00 per volume, has greatly encouraged research libraries, which depend on the national library for leadership and guidance. The Bookkeeper Process is now owned by Richard Spatz who, after his retirement from the Koppers Chemical Company, purchased the patent from the company. Koppers personnel continue research on the process under a contract with Spatz. The system treats volumes requiring no predrying in a processing tank filled with particles of magnesium oxide suspended in a nonaqueous solution of other chemicals; moisture is later removed in an air dryer. Unlike the Wei T'o and DEZ processes, books are deacidified over the course of time, as acids migrate and react to the magnesium oxide particles implanted in the paper. While considered an effective system, its development lags behind that of the DEZ and Wei T'o processes.

Descriptions of these systems are available in the literature, but only recently have there been substantive evaluations.[39] Cunha describes and compares Wei T'o and DEZ.[40] The final report of the Office of Technology Assessment's (OTA) study is a thorough examination of the DEZ program and process, with a comparison of Wei T'o and Bookkeeper.[41] Cunha concludes that both DEZ and Wei T'o are effective, each having certain advantages and some shortcomings,[42] and meet established criteria for acceptable systems. He has little to say about Bookkeeper because the Koppers Company abruptly terminated its further development at the time of his study, a decision Cunha terms "unfortunate" because it has "great merit." OTA reports frankly and, on the whole, favorably on DEZ but also says that Wei T'o and Bookkeeper may well be feasible alternatives. All three systems, each at a different level of development with ultimate production capabilities and costs unknown, require time and further research before valid evaluations and comparisons are possible.

Research libraries are anxious to establish mass deacidification facilities as soon as evaluations are available and sustained funding is guaranteed. The choice of the process and the configuration of facilities are matters of conjecture. One fact, however is inescapable. Both Wei T'o and Bookkeeper can be established in any existing building and safely operated by personnel with some, but not extensive, training. The DEZ system must be installed in a separate building and it must be operated and monitored by a licensed chemical engineer and supervised by chemical technicians. Since a mass deacidification installation is beyond the financial resources of most, if not all, institutions, it is likely that any DEZ facility will be financed through regional agreements or by consortia. A few of the larger commercial binderies have also shown interest in adding deacidification services if their clientele guarantee continued use at a level that is attractive economically. A recent development may well have a major impact. The OTA report recommended that the Library of Congress abandon its long-standing plan to establish and operate its own facility and reach an agreement with a private firm willing to assume all responsibility. Congress has approved the LC request to award such a contract to a chemical company willing to build and operate a facility and guarantee an average cost of $4 to $5 per volume.[43] Privatization may have advantages, but there may be some objection to licensing a process developed at national expense to a private company. Whatever the answer to this and other questions about mass deacidification, its promise of rescuing large collections of endangered materials quickly and safely may soon become a reality.

THE SEARCH FOR A NATIONAL PRESERVATION STRATEGY

The ambitious program of the new Commission on Preservation and Access is the third national preservation plan. The first was described by Williams in a 1964 report.[44] After noting the pervasiveness of deterioration, the problem of selecting items to be preserved, the cost of restoration and microfilming, and the necessity for bibliographic control, the report recommended that the nation's libraries deposit the best copies of significant materials in a federally supported library as national preservation copies, provide microfilm copies for use, preserve microfilm masters, provide bibliographic control of all deposited materials through the *National Union Catalog*, and coordinate institutional and national preservation activities. This plan never happened, for although the Library of Congress was willing to accept responsibility it soon found that the magnitude of its own preservation problems prevented it from serving as the national preservation library. The second call for collective effort, in 1972, is a major contribution to preservation literature.[45] The report first reviewed the preservation problem and preservation activities and the financial and organizational problems which inhibited progress. It then urged further research on the causes of paper deterioration, on the techniques of preservation and restoration, and on the best approaches to textual preservation; enhanced education of librarians and users; and the establishment of comprehensive programs in individual research libraries for the preservation of their significant resources. Its major recommendation was the organization of a "preservation consortium" of the nation's major research libraries which would establish standards and procedures, facilitating "the creation of a national library corporation as a base for collective action in the full range of activities in the inter-related areas of preservation and resource development."[46] Initial consortium programs would include "the creation of prototype preservation collections at the local level, the formulation of preservation priorities, and the preparation of plans to establish, maintain, and finance a national collection of negative microfilm."[47] The report envisaged "the creation of a coordinated system of collections in a national plan, each with a distinctive and specific research orientation or, in certain cases, a format orientation.[48] While other technologies for textual preservation might eventually prove superior, consortium libraries should "consider the concept of a planned program of microfilming, including collective ownership of master negatives produced as part of any text preservation project.[49] The report thus provided general guidelines for the current national preservation strategy, as well as for collection development and resource sharing.

Research libraries have reason to be cautiously optimistic that the third national plan, promoted by the new Commission on Preservation and Access, supported by its National Advisory Council on Preservation, will be successful in coping with the most critical aspect of the preservation problem — brittle books. The commission was established in 1986 and is funded for its first three years by CLR, the H. W. Wilson Foundation, and twenty major university and other research libraries. Its mission and functions are explained in the committee's report on *Brittle Books* and in a pamphlet issued by CLR in 1987.[50] The first issue of the new commission's occasional newsletter appeared in June 1988, "intended to inform members of the university community about activities of the [c]ommission and information related to the national brittle books program."[51]

Recognizing that the increased use of alkaline paper, deacidification, and conservation all have important roles in meeting preservation objectives, the committee concluded that "for the greatest portion of books that are already brittle, reproduction of content is the only realistic course of action; otherwise, an important segment of the record will be lost forever."[52] In the commission's view, the success of the brittle book plan depends upon meeting basic requirements: widespread understanding of the preservation problem to generate financial and institutional support; the use of the most effective technology, which at this time is microfilming following archival standards; an efficient bibliographic system to assure access and to track activity; and systematic collaboration among all participating institutions. The goal is to create a national collection of microfilmed materials dispersed among participating libraries which guarantee their production and permanent preservation under archival standards and their access through bibliographic networks. The commission reaffirms: since not everything can or should be preserved, selection demands the "thoughtful involvement" of a large number of individuals; the ultimate success of the plan is dependent on the performance of each institution. It depends also on the commission's success in developing funding programs, establishing policies and procedures for preservation work, promoting further development of a preservation information service by LC, encouraging research, establishing a monitoring system to provide data on all aspects of preservation activity, monitoring the performance of a bibliographic system, assuring access to preserved materials, and maintaining effective communication with key organizations. The National Advisory Council's responsibilities are to serve as a liaison between the commission and other organizations, assist in developing outside funding, and promote preservation and conservation interests internationally.[53]

It is well understood that the commission's primary responsibility is to locate the sustained financial support needed to coordinate cooperative preservation microfilming of brittle books at an unprecedented level. The commission advised Congress in 1987 and 1988 of the continued need for federal support through NEH and has reason to believe that Congress is sympathetic.[54] Considerably enhanced nonfederal support is also essential. "Slow Fires," an excellent, widely viewed film, is an initial effort to increase public awareness of preservation as a national emergency and generate nonfederal support.

The commission will rely on recent CLR sponsored research: Kantor's study of the cost of preservation microfilming; Hayes' study of the magnitude, costs, and benefits of preservation in research libraries; and Cummings' survey of preservation research in the three national libraries and the National Archives.[55]

The commission itself has asked MAPS to work on the development of archival standards for microfiche. The commission's president has proposed

> a model for a national cooperative microfilming program. A goal of filming 150,000 volumes a year would require 20 institutions to commit to filming 7,500 volumes each. At the 150,000 annual rate, it would take about 20 years to film 3 million volumes—the estimated number of volumes it would be important to save in order to preserve a representative portion of the 10 million or more volumes that will turn to dust by that time.[56]

This model shows "that the brittle book preservation problem has quantifiable objectives, and is not just an 'insurmountable problem'."[57]

Those confident of the profession's capacity to resolve the problem of brittle books have expressed their confidence in the new national strategy. While in agreement that the time is right and all elements are in place, they also share a familiar and sobering concern that "until there is reasonable assurance of funding in sufficient amounts and over a period long enough to do this specific job, little more will happen."[58]

PRESERVATION TODAY AND TOMORROW

The preservation activities and concerns of today's research libraries, suggested in part by the foregoing survey, are well detailed in a vast literature. It is very clear, however, that much needs to be done and there is a need for expanded and intensified effort. It is true that much of the data derived from ARL's 1984-1985 survey of the level of preservation activity among its members is impressive, but it is a fact that sixty-three of the ninety-seven respondents were seen as lacking well established programs.[59] However, an analysis of the forty-eight "detailed, thoughtful replies" in a follow-up survey of these sixty-three libraries indicated their special interest in implementing them, even if it also suggests that "respondents were not uniformly aware of the resources already available to them" to assist in their planning.[60] Nevertheless, it is evident that throughout the 1980s an increasing number of research libraries are devoting institutional energies to the implementation of comprehensive internal programs.

The Institutional Preservation Program

ARL's 1984 recommendations on preservation within the research library establish minimal goals "to which all ARL libraries should aspire in the course of this decade." Based on the tenet that "individual research libraries bear responsibility for preserving their collections as part of the collective resources of the research libraries of North America,"[61] the guidelines call for (1) a comprehensive internal preservation program; (2) a document defining goals and objectives; (3) the annual compilation of statistical data on staff and preservation expenditures and the number of items bound, deacidified, and reformatted; (4) attention to the proper maintenance of all materials, especially unique and otherwise special items; (5) annual expenditures equal to 10 percent of expenditures for library materials or 4 percent of total library expenditures; and (6) the coordination of preservation activities with other institutions. The guidelines are recognized as sound and prudent; but their implementation is far from easy. The 10 percent or 4 percent expenditure goal alone is a major challenge for most libraries.

By now, research libraries have assembled a corpus of general principles:

1. Advanced planning is essential to assure the participation of key administrators, consistency with general library policies, and maximum return from financial resources.

2. Since internal preservation needs are many and the cost of meeting them great, it is agreed that not everything can or should be saved.

3. Assuming that self-interest has been, and will continue to be, a major motivating force in research library development, the institution's preservation program should place the highest priority on meeting its own needs first.

4. A sound, institution-oriented program, documented in a manual and summarized in a general and widely disseminated statement of goals and objectives, encourages philosophical commitment within the library and beyond and is also a powerful factor in attracting additional financial support.

5. Considering the high cost of other preservation alternatives, preventive measures are the most cost-effective and in many cases can be implemented at minimal expense.

6. The lack of major funding for capital improvements and major projects should not impede the implementation of other preservation measures.

7. While new and sustained funding for staff, equipment, and projects is clearly essential for a comprehensive and effective preservation program, reallocation of a portion of the library materials and personnel budgets, however wrenching, is necessary and a clear demonstration of the library's commitment.

8. The institutional program must emphasize that local preservation problems are national too and require cooperative participation with other institutions in mutually advantageous preservation projects and in the pursuit of supplemental funding from external governmental and private sources.

Internal organization for preservation has been facilitated by the information provided in the 1982 and 1987 editions of ARL's *Preservation Planning Program*, in the published reports of institutions participating formally in ARL's self-study program, and in two OMS SPEC kits.[62] An ARL analysis of organizational structures in several research libraries indicates that separate preservation units are now quite common. They may be part of technical services, collection development, or report directly to the librarian. "Several libraries have no separate departments, and handle preservation/conservation issues through a committee, or through several departments according to a decentralized system." The technical service relationship is sometimes an extension of binding and repair responsibilities. "Those advocating aligning preservation with collection development cite the integral relationship between collection development and collection maintenance, and the close alliance that the preservation officer needs to have with bibliographers and other selection officers in deciding on preservation priorities, policies, and procedures." There is no one organizational model, and each of the existing arrangements can be justified.[63] Whenever possible, research libraries are appointing professional conservators either to administer or to develop their programs. These positions are not easily filled since conservators are so scarce.

Preservation in a research library should need no justification, but it does require explanation. It is important that there be a statement of program goals and objectives, adapted from a comprehensive manual explaining the program in detail. The manual must insist on and provide for (1) the integration of preservation priorities and procedures with all other library policies and procedures; (2) the education of all members of the staff so that they are well informed on all preservation matters and on their respective roles in the formulation and implementation of sound collections management procedures; (3) the protection of all library materials; (4) the systematic repair, restoration, or replacement of deteriorating materials; (5) the handling of collection emergencies; (6) participation in useful cooperative preservation programs at all levels; and (7) the education of users and the general public on the proper handling of library materials, the magnitude of the preservation problem, and the steps necessary to combat it.[64]

Selection

Some of the many issues that the preservation program must address merit special mention. Not the least among them is the determination of where general and specific preservation decisions are made and by whom. The identification of goals, expansion of facilities, and participation in cooperative programs are the responsibility of the institution's administration, but it is prudent to have the support of subject specialists, curators, and bibliographers. It is important also that decision makers share a common perception of the research collections and that they agree on selection criteria and appropriate preservation alternatives. The recognition that not everything can be saved must be reconciled with the principle that the research library is committed by tradition and policy to retain, preserve, and make available for use at least one copy of each item of research and/or intrinsic value acquired for its collections. Since *research value* is a subjective determination and judgments vary with time and with selectors, the term should be broadly interpreted, and whenever there is a question, emphasis be placed on retention and preservation rather than on withdrawal. *Intrinsic value* is more easily determined and obvious in many cases.

Recent literature has placed the traditional concept of the research library's collections in a preservation context. Preservation priorities and decisions may well be facilitated if the research library's collections are divided into three equally important and not always discrete segments or classes.[65] Class 1 consists of research materials having intrinsic or economic value to the institution. These are rare books and manuscripts, unique or otherwise special items, and significant subject or author collections whose comprehensiveness gives them research value beyond that of the individual items. All are usually shelved in rare book collections. The primary method of preservation is restoration, but reformatting may be appropriate to preserve the original yet provide access to materials frequently used.[66] The funds to do this should come primarily from the library, but outside financial support may indeed be necessary, especially in the care of extensive nationally known collections. Class 2 includes higher-use items, in demand for instructional and research purposes; they are frequently recent imprints. The need for preservation often results from overuse but may also be based on projected use. The principal method of preservation is by replacement, or by photocopies or microforms if copies or reprint editions are unavailable and copyright law permits. Funds for their preservation should also be provided by the library. Class 3 consists mainly of little-used research materials in subject collections built carefully over the years to assure that, as far as it is humanly possible, divergent viewpoints are represented. These have become known as *collections of record*. They are often well known by subject specialists and in some cases can be identified through collection-location sources such as the RLG conspectus and Ash's *Subject Collections*.[67] The intellectual content of these collections is best preserved through microfilming. The size, number, and wide distribution of collections of record, many of which are embrittled, make them worthy candidates for cooperative microfilming projects.

Prevention

Considering the high cost of restoration, deacidification, reformatting and replacement, it is worth repeating that prevention is the most cost-effective preservation method. This is not to suggest that a comprehensive preventive program is inexpensive. If fully implemented, it may well require major expenditures for space, air conditioning, and special equipment; in most libraries it entails additional personnel as well as the revision of current staffing responsibilities. Ideally, newly acquired materials should be examined and repaired upon receipt, a procedure which may conflict with institutional insistence upon rapid accessibility. All library materials should be repaired, restored, and otherwise protected and then shelved in secure, uncrowded, air-conditioned, systematically cleaned, and properly lighted stacks and reading rooms. Most research libraries do not enjoy this preservationist's utopia. However, they must not allow the lack of funding for capital and other improvements to deter the implementation of less-expensive preventive measures. One of the most important of these is the education of staff and patrons on the proper handling of materials and identification of endangered items. Workshops for staff and informal presentations for patrons are inexpensive, well received, and effective.[68] Since disasters are inevitable, an easily readable and practical disaster manual covering both prevention and control is an absolute necessity. It must address recovery from calamities caused by water, fire, and smoke, but must also include measures to prevent them and precautions that assure the security of the collections from theft and mutilation.[69]

A sound binding program, with contract binding as its major component, is usually the research library's largest annual preservation expenditure and the most important of all preventive measures. The commercial binder's adherence to the specifications detailed in the library's own binding contract, based on Library Binding Institute standards, must be monitored.[70] Among other considerations are the type of paper, margins, width, value, and known or anticipated use (all factors in determining the type of binding used); some materials may not need to be bound at all; reformatting in many instances may be preferable to commercial binding; and simple repairs and boxing are done far more economically and expeditiously within the library.[71]

The capability of internal repair/restoration facilities usually depends upon the size and nature of the research library's collection and, the library's funding. There is no question that local basic repair, pamphlet binding, and containerization are essential parts of a research library's program. They are practical, convenient, and far less expensive than work done commercially. Several libraries, often through special grants and private donations, have expanded modest repair facilities to full-fledged conservation units in recent years. It must be understood that it is very expensive to equip the ideal conservation laboratory, that its continued support must be guaranteed, and that almost all conservation work is labor-intensive and costly.[72] There are, however, decided advantages. The laboratory addresses more pressing conservation needs through fumigation, deacidification, binding restoration, and encapsulation and makes it possible to reformat at least some materials by photoduplication and microfilming. In addition to work being done more economically and perhaps better than in hand and commercial binderies, the internal facility provides faster service, minimizes security problems and recordkeeping, and enhances the visibility of the research library's entire preservation program.[73]

In the future, there may be another alternative. Since commercial binderies concentrate on binding restoration and only a few of them work on paper deacidification and restoration,[74] and the full range of conservation services offered by hand binderies is understandably expensive and very slow, there is an obvious advantage in the cooperatively supported conservation facility. The great success of NEDCC has encouraged libraries to explore the possibility of establishing similar regional facilities.

Preservation Microfilming

With the exception of a few institutions, research libraries have much to learn about preservation microfilming. Their current interest in some cases may stem from a need to establish modest facilities or enhance existing ones so that they go beyond the occasional reformatting of a few items to a level which meets at least some of their internal needs, thus reducing expenditures for contract microfilming. In most cases heightened interest is due to general awareness of the institutional and financial advantages to be found in cooperative microfilming projects, especially those attractive to funding agencies. Whether filming is done locally or by contract, libraries recognize the need for archival quality preservation microfilming and that money would be better spent on establishing regional cooperative facilities modeled on NEDCC and MAPS. They are also aware of another alternative, the interest of major commercial microform publishers in the contract microfilming of marketable institutional collections, assuring their preservation and promising some financial return to libraries.

The implementation of a local preservation microfilming program, in many instances, has been possible only through special, usually noninstitutional, funding. Each step in planning and implementation is discussed in detail in *Preservation Microfilming*.[75] RLG's *Preservation Manual* is also most helpful.[76] Both make it clear that the production of archival quality microfilm requires extensive professional and technical staff involvement. The intensive work of any project is indicated by the twelve procedures set out in a study of the costs incurred by seven libraries participating in RLG's 1876-1900 American imprints preservation project: "(1) identification of titles within the scope of the project, (2) retrieval of the materials, (3) preparation of circulation records, (4) searching for extant microforms, (5) curatorial reviews to select titles to be microfilmed, (6) recording intent to microfilm, (7) physical preparation of the items for filming, (8) preparation of targets, (9) filming, (10) inspection of film, (11) cataloging of microform editions, and (12) storage of master negative."[77] The most intensive work includes the searching of *NRMM* and other sources to verify that acceptable microforms, or perhaps reprint editions, do not exist; page-by-page collation; the repair of torn and procurement of missing pages; the inspection of volumes for brittleness; the creation and updating of a variety of internal records; systematic inspection of completed microfilm; and *AACR2* cataloguing or *recon standard* cataloguing (i.e., based on existing records rather than on the materials themselves). It is essential that research libraries understand that preservation microfilming is a commitment to keep microfilm permanently accessible and easily identifiable through item-specific reporting to national bibliographic databases.

Experience in preservation microfilming has produced any number of practical guidelines.

1. A volume is considered embrittled if a corner of one or more of its pages "cannot withstand two or three double corner folds without breaking off."[78]

2. Candidates for preservation microfilming are often identified through transactions and by surveys of specific segments of a collection, but microfilming without inspection of all volumes in a limited collection is justified if brittleness has been established through random sampling.

3. Since patrons usually prefer to use materials in their original format, they should be returned to the collections whenever possible.

4. While $50 for a "typical" 300-page monograph is an accepted and useful figure for preliminary planning purposes, "costs vary significantly from item to item, project to project, and institution to institution."[79] For example, a study of 1984 RLG costs, which exclude overhead, administrative, and certain RLIN costs, found that average costs among the seven institutions "ranged from $25.81 to $71.80, with $48.20 representing the median cost."[80] Late in 1987 ten members of CIC estimated that preservation microfilming costs range from $48.64 to $83.55, excluding

most overhead costs. The 1987 Hayes study estimated a sobering average cost of $100 per volume when all overhead is included.[81]

5. Whatever the actual cost, research libraries participating in cooperative projects supported by funding agencies must be prepared to absorb a portion of overhead costs.

Mass Deacidification

Research libraries await viable mass deacidification systems. The manual systems used today are normally reserved for rare items.[82] They are expensive, time-consuming, and painstaking, and require skilled technicians who must first detemine that the paper will not be damaged and then treat one page at a time by the use of a solution or a spray containing one or more alkaline compounds.[83] The attraction of a mass system is clear; it promises to save the millions of volumes at risk at an average cost currently estimated at about $5, before embrittlement requires reformatting at an average cost of perhaps $100.

Bookkeeper may eventually be developed to the level of Wei T'o and DEZ, but only these latter two have been found to meet the criteria for an effective system. As summarized from Cunha's study, paper must be uniformly neutralized and buffered with an alkaline reserve to prevent acidic attack over a long period of time. The treatment must be cost-effective and economical. It must work quickly, penetrate masses of books at one time, and accommodate materials of all sizes. It must be unharmful to all components of the book, be safe to use and nontoxic, and create no new problems.[84]

A number of research libraries may find Wei T'o well suited to their needs since it can be installed and operated safely in any library. Lacking adequate institutional funding for installation, operating, and other expenses, regional or consortium libraries may well be interested in enjoying its benefits by sharing its costs. Larger commercial binderies might find Wei T'o equally attractive if guaranteed continued support. On the other hand, one can easily envision privately operated DEZ installations strategically located throughout the country, serving a large number of libraries. Whatever the outcome, research libraries must recognize other realities. They must guarantee continued support on budgets which have been severely strained for years. In addition to deacidification costs they must also meet inescapable expenditures for the selection, preparation, and packing of materials to be deacidified, the maintenance of dispatch and return records, transportation, the processing of deacidified materials, and reshelving them in quarters segregated from other collections.

Preservation Priorities

There is no question that research libraries are fully aware of the critical importance of preserving the materials entrusted to them and that they are increasing their internal efforts to meet this commitment. They now recognize also that institutional preservation problems are part of a national problem and that the resolution of both depends to a very large extent upon cooperation. It is also clear that, however strong this institutional and national commitment, the future of all preservation effort depends upon sustained large-scale financial support.

The Commission on Preservation and Access has defined the attraction of additional sources of financial support as one of its primary objectives, but it is imperative that research libraries redouble their efforts also. On the broadest level this means convincing the general public that the preservation of its endangered intellectual and cultural heritage is a national problem and that its resolution depends upon financial support from every level. This was one of the major themes of a forum held in Chicago in 1987 and is made very clear in "Slow Fires."[85] Similar initiatives must be encouraged.

In the academic world the search for funding often means the allocation of a larger portion of the materials budget to preservation, easier if it is "new" money, but difficult if it means reallocation. It also requires an intensified effort to convince colleagues, university administrators, library patrons, and other benefactors of the need for increased and sustained funding. A sound and well-publicized preservation program, reinforced by one or more surveys of alarming collection conditions, is an effective first step. Lectures which include the showing of "Slow Fires" and videocassettes for library benefactors and patrons are also productive. Benefactors are known to be especially responsive to specific preservation proposals.[86] Initiatives may well be limited only by institutional imagination.

Cooperation with other institutions and agencies to attract financial support is also essential. A number of the foundations have done so much, and they continue to respond generously to proposals supported by research libraries, their consortia, learned societies, and other organizations. While several states increasingly support preservation of needs, they should be encouraged to follow the example of New York, the first state government to provide substantial and continued financial support for preservation.[87] Despite a prevalent notion that the private sector should do more and federal agencies somewhat less, it is only realistic to observe that increased federal support is absolutely essential. The number of NEH grants for preservation, especially preservation microfilming, has increased dramatically over the last few years.[88] Its special interest must be sustained through the continued submission of nationally significant cooperative proposals and through the influence of the Commission on Preservation and Access. If Congress should approve the NEH preservation capabilities budget which describes what could be done if NEH funding is incrementally increased from the present $4.5 million to $12.5 million in 1989 and to $20.3 million in 1993, preservation's immediate future will brighten considerably.[89]

Other necessities must also be addressed. Only about half of ARL's 118 members have significant preservation programs. Others must be encouraged to establish them, for their own benefit and that of other institutions. Progress in preservation should continue to be monitored regularly. Clearly the number of cooperative preservation projects must be increased. However, much more work needs to be done in areas which facilitate this. These would include the identification of significant but unknown collections, especially those which are endangered; improved access to information on preservation projects under consideration, in progress, and completed; and the establishment of additional cooperatively supported conservation/preservation facilities as well as the expansion of local institutional capabilities.

There are obvious needs. Educational opportunities at the graduate level for the training of conservators and preservation technicians must be increased to relieve a critical shortage. There is also a clear need for continuing educational programs for everyone involved with preservation. Research on preservation technologies, notably on mass deacidification systems and on the media for information storage, and on the varied problems emerging from all preservation strategies must be increased and the results of this research disseminated rapidly. Indeed, there is a special need for improved communication on the international as well as on the national level. As the Vienna conference on preservation clearly documented, preservation is truly an international cause and a responsibility more easily faced through the sharing of information on research, strategies, and current projects.[90]

The Commission on Preservation and Access will undoubtedly play an important role in addressing many of these needs and in encouraging continuing commitment. Perhaps its most important role is in the coordination of the diverse individual and cooperative efforts of American research libraries and all others responsible for preservation's progress to its present encouraging state.

NOTES

[1]Adams, Randolph G. Librarians as enemies of books. *Library quarterly* 7:317-331 (July 1937); Barr, Pelham. Book conservation and university library administration. *College and research libraries* 7:214-219 (July 1946)

[2]This apt phrase apparently originated in the "Report on book paper" in Book longevity: reports of the committee on production guidelines for book longevity. Washington, DC: Council on Library Resources, 1982. p. 7

[3]Darling, Pamela W. and Sherelyn Ogden. From problems perceived to programs in practice: The preservation of library resources in the U.S.A., 1956-1980. *Library resources and technical services* 25:9-29 (Jan./Mar. 1981); Fox, Lisa L. A two-year perspective on library preservation: an annotated bibliography. *Library resources and technical services* 30:290-318 (July/Sept. 1986); Montori, Carla J. Library preservation in 1986: annotated bibliography. *Library resources and technical services* 31:365-385 (Oct./Dec. 1987); Merrill-Oldham, Jan and Merrily Smith, *eds.* "Library preservation: its scope, history, and importance" in The library preservation program: models, priorities, possibilities. Chicago: American Library Association, 1985. pp. 7-18; Stanage, Eric. Millions of books are turning to dust—can they be saved? *New York times book review* 92, no. 13:3, 38 (Mar 29, 1987)

[4]The term *preservation* includes *all* of the techniques which extend the life of library materials or their intellectual content. *Conservation* refers exclusively to any of the restorative treatments applied to individual items.

[5]Gwinn, Nancy F. CLR and preservation, *College and research libraries* 42:104-126 (Mar. 1981)

⁶Tauber, Maurice F., *ed*. Conservation of library materials. *Library trends* 4:215-334 (Jan. 1956); Winger, Howard W. and Richard D. Smith, *eds*. Deterioration and preservation of library materials; the thirty-fourth Annual Conference of the Graduate Library School, Aug. 3-6, 1969. Chicago: University of Chicago Press, 1970

⁷Rogers, Rutherford D. Library preservation: its scope, history, and importance. *In* The library preservation program: models, priorities, possibilities. Chicago: ALA, 1985. p. 10

⁸Increase in number of libraries with preservation programs. *Commission on preservation and access newsletter* 1:2 (June 1988)

⁹Association of Research Libraries. The collection analysis project: operating manual for an assisted self-study for the review and analysis of the collection development functions in academic and research libraries. Washington, DC: ARL, Office of Management Studies, 1977

¹⁰Association of Research Libraries. Preservation planning program: an assisted self-study manual for libraries and resource notebook. Washington, DC: ARL, OMS, 1982

¹¹Association of Research Libraries. Preservation planning program: an assisted self-study manual for libraries. expanded 1987 edition and resource notebook. Washington, DC: ARL, OMS, 1987

¹²Association of Research Libraries. Preservation education in ARL Libraries: SPEC Kit 113. Washington, DC: ARL, OMS, 1985; Association of Research Libraries. Organizing for preservation in ARL libraries: SPEC kit 116. Washington, DC: ARL, OMS, 1985

¹³Association of Research Libraries. Guidelines for minimal preservation efforts in ARL libraries. Washington, DC: ARL, 1984; Heynen, Jeffrey and Margaret McConnel. Pilot preservation statistics survey, 1984-1985: a compilation of statistics from a one-year pilot survey of the members of the Association of Research Libraries. Washington, DC: Association of Research Libraries, 1986

¹⁴Cunha, George M. and Dorothy G. Cunha. Conservation of library materials: a manual and bibliography on the care, repair and restoration of library materials. Metuchen, NJ: Scarecrow Press, 1967; Horton, Carolyn. Cleaning and preserving bindings and related materials. Chicago: American Library Association, Library Technology Project, 1967 (2nd ed. 1969); Tauber, Maurice F., *ed*. Library binding manual: a handbook of useful procedures for the maintenance of library volumes. Boston: Library Binding Institute, 1972; Morrow, Carolyn C. and Carole Dyal. Conservation treatment procedures: a manual of step-by-step procedures for the maintenance and repair of library materials. 2nd ed. Littleton, CO: Libraries Unlimited, 1986

[15]Barton, John P. and Johanna G. Wellheiser. An ounce of prevention: a handbook on disaster contingency planning for archives, libraries and record centres. Toronto: Toronto Area Archivists Group Education Foundation, 1985; Morris, John. The library disaster preparedness handbook. Chicago: American Library Association, 1986; Waters, Peter. Procedures for salvage of water-damaged library materials. 2nd ed. Washington, DC: Library of Congress, 1979

[16]Where preservation is taught. *The Abbey newsletter* 11:3 (Jan. 1987)

[17]The papers delivered at the first of these conferences, held at the Library of Congress, April 29, 1983, have been published in The library preservation program: models, priorities, possibilities. Chicago: ALA, 1985. pp. 7-18

[18]The Abbey newsletter: bookbinding and conservation. Provo, UT: Preservation Department, Harold B. Lee Library, Brigham Young University, Aug. 1975- ; Conservation administration news. Laramie, WY: University of Wyoming Libraries, July 1979- ; National preservation news. Washington, DC: National Preservation Program Office, Library of Congress, July 1985-

[19]Darling and Ogden. *Op. cit.*

[20]Quoted in Gwinn. Op. cit. p. 106 The Barrow studies have been published in Permanence/durability of the book. Richmond, VA: W. J. Barrow Research Laboratory, 1963-1974 (7 vols.)

[21]Williams, Edwin E. Magnitude of the paper deterioration problem as measured by a national union catalog sample. *College and research libraries* 23:449, 543 (Nov. 1962)

[22]Survey of book condition at the Library of Congress. *National preservation news* 1:8-9 (July 1985)

[23]Walker, Gay *et al.* The Yale survey: a large-scale study of book deterioration in the Yale University Library. *College and research libraries* 46:111-132 (Mar. 1985), pp. 111, 124; Buchberg, Karl. Paper: manuscripts, documents, printed sheets and works of art. *In* Conservation in the library: a handbook of use and care of traditional and nontraditional materials/ ed. by Susan G. Swartzburg. Westport, CT: Greenwood Press, 1983. p. 37

[24]Smith, Richard D. Mass deacidification: the Wei T'o understanding. *College and research libraries news* 48:2-10 (Jan. 1987), p. 3

[25]Cunha, George M. and Dorothy C. Cunha. Conservation of library materials: a manual and bibliography on the care, repair and restoration of library materials. 2nd ed. Metuchen, NJ: Scarecrow Press, 1971. vol. 1, pp. 87-93

[26]*Permanent* refers to the degree to which paper resists chemical action resulting from impurities in paper or agents from the environment, *durability* to the degree to which paper retains its original qualities under continued usage.

[27]Clapp, Verner W. The story of permanent/durable book paper, 1115-1970, *Scholarly publishing* 2:107-24, 229-45, 353-67 (Jan., Apr., July 1971)

[28]Book longevity: reports of the committee on production guidelines for book longevity. Washington, DC: Council on Library Resources, 1982

[29]The caɩegories are primary printed sources, important works of fiction and non-fiction, collected editions, bibliographies, guides to collections, yearbooks, gazetteers, scholarly periodicals and monographs, dictionaries, encyclopedias, and other reference books. See Book longevity. *Op. cit.* p. 8

[30]These and other facts are reported in the *Alkaline paper advocate* (Provo, UT: Abbey Publications) an occasional newsletter which began publication in January 1988

[31]Gwinn, Nancy E. The rise and fall and rise of cooperative projects. *Library resources and technical services* 29:80-86 (Jan./Mar. 1985); Child, Margaret S. The future of cooperative preservation microfilming. *Library resources and technical services* 29:94-101 (Jan./Mar. 1985)

[32]Progress on the Library of Congress's study of optical disk technology is reported regularly in the *National preservation news.*

[33]McClung, Patricia A. Costs associated with preservation microfilming: results of the research libraries group study. *Library resources and technical services* 30:363-374 (Oct./Dec. 1986)

[34]RLG preservation manual. 2nd ed. Palo Alto, CA: Research Libraries Group, 1986

[35]Kantor, Paul B. Cost of preservation microfilming at research libraries: a study of four institutions. Washington, DC: Council on Library Resources, Inc., 1986

[36]Zipkowitz, Fay. Saving paper treasures: the Northeast Document Conservation Center. *Library and archival security* 7:15-20 (Summer 1985); Russell, Ann. If you need to ask what it costs. *In* The library preservation program: models, priorities, possibilities. Chicago: ALA, 1985. pp. 84-87

[37]MAPS is described in Mid-atlantic preservation group receives Exxon grants, *Association of research libraries newsletter* 131:8 (Aug. 29, 1986); A new place to have brittle books filmed. *The Abbey newsletter* 11:32 (Mar. 1987)

[38]Since 1984 all reports of microform masters for monographs are included in the National union catalog, books, and microform masters for serials in New serial titles.

[39]Smith, Richard D. Mass deacidification: the Wei T'o way. *College and research libraries news* 45:588-593 (Dec. 1984); The Koppers deacidification patent. *The Abbey newsletter* 10:85-86, 88 (Dec. 1986)

[40]Cunha, George M. Mass deacidification for libraries. *Library technology reports* 23:361-472 (May-June 1987).

[41]U.S. Congress, Office of Technology Assessment. Book preservation technologies, OTA-0-395. Washington, DC: Government Printing Office, May 1988

[42]Cunha. *Op. cit.*

[43]LC proposes new approach for development of DEZ facility, *Association of Research Libraries newsletter* 139:5 (March 31, 1988)

[44]Williams, Gordon R. The preservation of deteriorating books: an examination of the problem with recommendations for a solution. Washington, DC: Association of Research Libraries, 1964

[45]Haas, Warren J. Preparation of detailed specifications for a national system for the preservation of library materials. Washington, DC: Association of Research Libraries, 1972

[46]*Ibid.* p. 18

[47]*Ibid.* p. 20

[48]*Ibid.* p. 21

[49]*Ibid.* p. 25

[50]Brittle books: reports of the Commission on Preservation and Access. Washington, DC: Council on Library Resources, 1986; The Commission on Preservation and Access. Washington, DC: Council on Library Resources, 1987

[51]Commission on Preservation and Access newsletter. Washington, DC: Commission, Jan. 1988-

[52]Brittle books. *Op. cit.* p. 8

[53]The Commission on Preservation and Access. *Op. cit.*

[54]At the request of a congressional subcommittee NEH "produced alternative capability budgets showing NEH's Office of Preservation budget increasing from $4.5 million to $12.5 million for the coming fiscal year (FY 89), with continuing increases for the following four years to a level of $20.3 million." See *Commission on Preservation and Access newsletter* 1:1 (June 1988).

[55]Kantor. *Op. cit.*; The Hayes and Cummings studies have not as yet been published.

[56]*Commission on Preservation and Access newsletter* 1:1 (June 1988)

[57]*Ibid.*

[58]Hearing on brittle books March 3, 1987, before the U.S. House of Representatives Subcommittee on postsecondary education: statement of Warren J. Haas, President, Council on library resources. Washington, DC: Commission on Preervation and Access, Council on Library Resources, 1987. p. 3

[59]Heynen and McConnel. *Op. cit.*

[60]ARL committee surveys preservation needs. *Association of Research Libraries newsletter* 135:10-12 (June 12, 1987), p. 10

[61]Guidelines for minimum preservation efforts in ARL libraries. Washington, DC: Association of Research Libraries, 1984. p. 1

[62]Association of Research Libraries. Preservation planning program. *Op. cit.* 1982, 1987; McCrady, Ellen. Nine preservation self-studies. *The Abbey newsletter* 12, no. 2:32-35 (Feb. 1988); Association of Research Libraries, Organizing for preservation in ARL Libraries: SPEC kit 116. *Op. cit.* Also, its preservation guidelines in ARL libraries: SPEC Kit 137, 1987.

[63]Association of Research Libraries. Organizing for preservation in ARL libraries: SPEC Flyer 116:1-2 (July-Aug. 1985), p. 1

[64]These matters are discussed in ARL's preservation planning program. *Op. cit.* Also in SPEC kits 116 and 137. *Op. cit.*

[65]Atkinson, Ross W. Selection for preservation: a materialistic approach. *Library resources and technical services* 30:341-353 (Oct./Dec. 1986); Child, Margaret S. Further thoughts on selection for preservation: a materialistic approach. *Library resources and technical services* 30:354-362 (Oct./Dec. 1986)

[66]Walker, Gay. The book as object. *The Abbey newsletter* 11, no. 1:4 (Jan. 1987)

[67]Gwinn, Nancy E. and Paul H. Mosher. Coordinating collection development: the RLG conspectus. *College and research libraries* 44:128-140 (Mar. 1983); Ash, Lee, *comp.* Subject collections: a guide to special book collections and subject emphases, as reported by university, college, public, and special libraries. 6th ed. New York: R. R. Bowker, 1986

[68]The "staff and user education" chapter in ARL's preservation planning program. *Op. cit.* its SPEC Kit 113, preservation education in ARL Libraries. *Op. cit.*

[69]Morris, John. The library disaster preparedness handbook. Chicago: American Library Association, 1986; Barton, John P. and Johanna G. Wellheiser, *eds.* An ounce of prevention: a handbook on disaster contingency planning for archives, libraries and record centres. Toronto: Toronto Area Archivists Group Education Foundation, 1985

[70]Library Binding Institute. Standards for library binding. Rochester, NY: The Institute, 1986

[71]Walker, Gay. Library binding as a conservation measure. *Collection management* 4:55-71 (Spring/Summer 1982)

[72]It is worth noting also that conservators and curators do not always agree. The conservator's professional ethics demand optimal treatment of each item. The curator/subject specialist, mindful of the time and costs involved and of other items equally in need, may find this unacceptable.

[73]Dean, John F. Conservation and collection management. *Journal of library administration* 7:129-141 (Summer/Fall 1986); Peterson, Kenneth G. Preservation at the Morris Library, Southern Illinois University. *In* The library preservation program: models, priorities, possibilities. Chicago: ALA, 1985. pp. 41-50

[74]Certified library binders: binding, special work, services. *New library scene* 6:12-13 (Feb. 1987)

[75]Gwinn, Nancy E., *ed.* Preservation microfilming: a guide for librarians and archivists. Chicago: American Library Association, 1987

[76]RLG Preservation manual. *Op. cit.*

[77]McClung, Patricia A. *Op. cit.* p. 365

[78]Gwinn. Preservation microfilming. *Op. cit.* p. 38.

[79]*Ibid.* p. 150

[80]McClung, Patricia A. *Op. cit.* p. 365

[81]The Robert Hayes study has not been published. The average cost estimate is taken from correspondence.

[82]The manual processes used today, notably those using sprays applied in vacuum chambers, are quite appropriate for the treatment of rare and other special items in a conservation facility where they can be deacidified and restored far more economically than in the conservation units of specialized hand binderies.

[83]U.S. Congress, OTA. *Op. cit.*

[84]Cunha. *Op. cit.* pp. 436-440

[85]For a summary of the issues addressed at the forum, Invest in the American collections: a midwest forum. *National preservation news* 8:1-4 (Oct. 1987)

[86]The University of Illinois Library Friends, for example, raised almost $100,000 in one afternoon to restore the University Library's Audubon's *Birds of America.*

[87]Preservation initiatives in the states. *National preservation news* 6:1-6 (Oct. 1986)

[88]Summaries of NEH grants appear each year in the *Association of Research Libraries newsletter* and *National preservation news.*

[89]Federal developments in preservation of library materials. *Association of Research Libraries newsletter* 140:8 (June 6, 1988)

[90]Preservation of library materials: conference held at the National Library of Austria, Apr. 7-10, 1986. Munich, New York: K. G. Saur, 1987 (2 vols.)

SLAVIC TECHNICAL SERVICES

ROBERT H. BURGER

Many aspects of acquisitions and cataloguing activities in Slavic libraries deserve special examination. This chapter will define and discuss those areas that make this subspecialty of technical services unique: the major activities of Slavic acquisitions and cataloguing, alternative ways of organizing and administering those activities in research libraries, professional groups of Slavic librarians and their influence on the field, special bibliographic projects in the Slavic area, and speculation about the future of these activities.

It is necessary to define what we mean by *Slavic* in the technical services context. The word can be applied legitimately to those ethnic groups that are descended from the historic Slavs, a nomadic people inhabiting an area north of the Carpathian mountains in East Central Europe until the 1st century A.D. In the following centuries the Slavs expanded east, west, and south. As a result, three groups of Slavic languages were formed—the East Slavic languages (Russian, Ukrainian, and White Russian); the South Slavic languages (Bulgarian, Macedonian, Serbo-Croatian, and Slovenian); and the West Slavic languages (Czech, Slovak, Polish, and Wendic). The modern countries in which Slavic languages are found are the USSR, Bulgaria, Yugoslavia, Czechoslovakia, Poland, and East Germany (Wendic is spoken in Lusatia, a province of the DDR). More than 100 languages are spoken in the Soviet Union. In addition to the East Slavic languages, the Slavic specialist must deal with such non-Slavic languages as Latvian, Estonian, Lithuanian, Uzbek, Kazakh, Turkmen, Kirghiz, Azerbaijani, Georgian, and Armenian. This wide range of languages; the use of Roman, Cyrillic, and other scripts; and the bibliographic complexities of this group of countries present special problems for the Slavic and East European area of technical processing. In addition, Hungary, Romania, East Germany, and Greece are often included by libraries in the Slavic and East European area because of their geographic location.

ACQUISITIONS

The basic activities of acquisitions work are selection, ordering, receipt, processing, and precataloguing receipt of all library materials. Of particular relevance to Slavic technical processing are placing of individual and blanket orders for monographs and standing orders for serials; administration of interlibrary exchange agreements; administration of a host of records including check-in records for serials, order and receipt files, vendor files and correspondence, exchange partner files, claims, and financial records; and plans and activities dealing with the preservation and conservation of the collection.

Organization and Administration

There are many ways to organize and administer Slavic acquisitions activities. Only some possibilities will be described here. The first step in the acquisitions process is the selection of materials to be added to the collection. The materials are selected from prepublication announcements, dealers' catalogues, exchange partner offer lists, and other conventional means. This selection is carried out by a bibliographer having both language and subject expertise in the Slavic and East European area. In some libraries bibliographers form a selection unit that deals only with collection development. In other libraries such bibliographers also serve in some capacity as reference librarians for the Slavic and East European collections. In yet other libraries bibliographers are dispersed in subject discipline libraries. Organization of these activities is guided by language expertise as well as by subject expertise. The Slavic bibliographer might select only those materials in the Slavic and East European languages but in all subjects collected by the library, whereas the history librarian, for example, might select English and other Western European language materials dealing with Eastern Europe. There are, perhaps, as many ways of dividing up these tasks as there are libraries performing them.

Once materials are selected, order forms are prepared and sent to the order processing unit. This unit, usually staffed by support staff, selects vendors, assigns prices, encumbers the funds in the accounting system, and keeps a record of the order — usually in an order-and-receipt file. Such a unit may be in the general acquisitions department, staffed by persons with the necessary language skills, or, in larger libraries, in a separate Slavic acquisitions unit.

When items are received they must be processed, at least in part, by persons with language skills. Unless one can read the Cyrillic alphabet, the author and title of, say, a Bulgarian monograph will be indecipherable. Once the item is received, the invoice (bill) must be approved and paid. Many of the financial and currency conversion tasks may be handled by the library's business office. The materials are now catalogued, put into cataloguing backlogs, or, in the case of serial issues, checked in. A discussion of various areas of acquisitions work in which Slavic materials present unique problems follows.

Blanket Orders

Blanket orders are contractual arrangements with vendors that can be very efficient and beneficial to a library. They work in this way. A library determines the type of materials it desires from a particular country. A librarian creates a profile describing the materials in terms of such characteristics as subjects, publishers, dates of publication, formats, and languages. The vendor, if willing and able, agrees to supply the materials that match the profile. In order to control such arrangements further, either a dollar or volume limit is imposed. In the Slavic-speaking countries and in East Europe generally, publications are announced weekly in prepublication announcements and published with a specific print run. Even if the demand exceeds the number of copies available, a new printing is usually not possible because of the publisher's long-term printing plan. In order to obtain books from these countries, it is necessary therefore to order items based on the information given in the prepublication announcements. Books are often sold out as soon as they are published. Major vendors in this area have long-standing arrangements with the book export institutions in the countries of publication. Examples are Les Livres Étrangers and Victor Kamkin, Inc., for publications in the USSR; Kubon & Sagner for publications from the USSR, Bulgaria, Romania, Yugoslavia, Poland, Czechoslovakia, and Hungary; and Kultura for Hungarian publications. Such agents accept dollars for the books they sell and the financial arrangements are fairly straightforward. However, not all books published in Eastern Europe can be obtained in this manner, nor can they always be obtained at the lowest possible price. Exchange agreements are important for such materials.

Exchange Agreements

Libraries in the West take part in exchange agreements with libraries in the USSR and Eastern Europe for two main reasons. First, they can obtain materials that cannot be purchased through commercial channels. Second, exchanged materials are often cheaper than purchased materials. Many libraries in the USSR and Eastern Europe are national depositories for materials published in their countries—much as the Library of Congress is in the United States. Unlike the Library of Congress, these libraries may receive half a dozen copies of each publication. They use the extra copies to exchange for materials published in the West.

There are several steps in setting up an exchange agreement. First, each library must agree to enter into the agreement and to its terms. In some cases, academic libraries in the West receive several copies of books and journals published on their campuses. Thus, one type of agreement can consist of exchanging one series for another, or one volume for another. Another arrangement is based on monetary value. In this case, the libraries agree on a so-called monetary exchange. The library in the West will select monographs or serials from an offer list compiled by the library in the East. In turn, the library in the East uses common Western selection tools, such as *Books in Print* or publishers' catalogues, to select items. Each library then acts, in effect, as a vendor. The library in the East fills the "order" (items requested from the offer list) from the Western library. The library in the West usually sends the requests from the Eastern library to a Western vendor, who sends the materials to the foreign library and bills the Western library. Funds are not paid directly to the foreign library, but to domestic or foreign vendors with whom the Western library has established commercial relations.

The types of exchange arrangement and their administration can vary greatly depending on the libraries involved. To illustrate this point, let me mention an arrangement that exists between the Biblioteka Narodowa in Warsaw and the University of Illinois at Urbana-Champaign (UIUC). The latter has a blanket-order exchange agreement with the Polish library for currently published Polish books. As with all blanket orders, UIUC produced a profile of the kind of Polish books desired along with a *zloty* (Polish currency)/dollar exchange rate that was mutually agreed and a limit on the amount of money to be expended in a given year. In return, UIUC places orders for, and pays for, requests from the Biblioteka Narodowa for books selected from *Books in Print* and other selection tools.

Recordkeeping

All acquisitions activities require extensive recordkeeping. A particular problem in Slavic acquisitions is posed by the use of Roman and Cyrillic scripts as well as other odd scripts such as Georgian and Armenian, and by the various diacritics and modified letters found in those scripts. Records can be kept in the vernacular scripts, but most libraries choose to Romanize (transliterate) all non-Roman scripts so that the records can be integrated in a single file. Not all Slavic library clerical personnel can read non-Roman scripts. For this reason, records in Roman and non-Roman scripts are often separated in the library. For example, the check-in records for Roman alphabet periodicals may be found in a centralized periodical check-in section in the acquisitions department while Cyrillic periodicals are checked in in a Slavic acquisitions section or in a separate file in the main acquisitions department.

Other recordkeeping problems also arise in the Slavic and East European area. Order and receipt files, as well as periodical and continuation check-in records must follow a standardized filing scheme. Since filing is usually done by clerical personnel, or students, from whom a high level of linguistic sophistication is not required, the filing vagaries for the languages involved may present problems. For example, ignoring the initial letter *A* in Hungarian and English, but not in Russian where it is significant, may be difficult, especially if the filer cannot recognize Hungarian. Furthermore, the incorrect transliteration of titles and authors can often separate works that should be filed together (e.g., when the Ukrainian *h* is mistransliterated as *g* resulting not in *heohrafiia* but *geografiia*).

Another problem can occur with claiming of issues of periodicals. Because of the slow delivery and out-of-sequence publishing of some continuations, issues may not be received when expected. This can cause unwarranted claiming of some issues. To compound the problem, it is often impossible to replace a missed issue of a periodical because Soviet and East European publishers do not produce extra copies of periodical issues for over-the-counter stocks or other contingencies. When issues are lost in the mail or otherwise become unobtainable, the issue is considered lost and the publisher does not give monetary credit.

Financial Aspects

Not only are the financial aspects of Slavic and East European acquisitions convoluted, as we saw with the exchange program, but they depend almost exclusively on the value of the U.S. dollar relative to other currencies. One danger inherent in such a dependence is illustrated by the devaluation of the U.S. dollar against most world currencies, especially the West German mark and the French franc, from 1985 to 1987. During this period, American librarians buying French and West German books or, as in the case of Slavic and East European librarians, using French and West German vendors to acquire their materials, saw the U.S. dollar lose one-third of its purchasing power. This devaluation had a devastating effect on foreign acquisitions budgets. For example, if a library were spending $50,000 a year on Slavic and East European serials at the beginning of the period, the cost of the same periodicals would have risen to $75,000 in just two years! As that kind of money is not usually available to libraries, there are only three possible actions in the face of such a crisis: (1) cancel serial subscriptions; (2) shift money earmarked for other uses, such as purchasing monographs, to serial budgets; or (3) a combination of the two. Of course, the opposite can happen and the library can find itself with extra purchasing power if other currencies lose value as compared to the U.S. dollar.

Preservation

The preservation of library materials, an increasingly important problem in the past decade, is acute for Slavic and East European materials. Most of the books received from the USSR and Eastern Europe are printed on high-acid paper. Because of this, much of the major holdings of Slavic and East European materials in the United States are in brittle or near-brittle condition. A recent estimate places about one-third of such collections in brittle condition, one-third in danger of becoming brittle, and one-third safe. As far as pre-World War II materials are concerned, much has already been done to *reformat* (make microform copies of) important serial publications by commercial firms such as IDC or University Microfilms International, by the investment of individual libraries, and as the result of grants from federal agencies and private foundations. Although in the past thirty years the energies of Slavic librarians in this country have focused on collection development and access to the collections, we are now sadly aware of the deterioration of the collections that have been built so painstakingly. The cost of reformatting is now about $65 a volume. A process has been developed, though it is not yet available commercially, that will deacidify books at $5 a volume. However, in the meantime we must focus on currently available technology. The Conference on Access to Slavic Materials in North American Libraries was held in May 1989. Its scope included preservation and retrospective conversion. The conference helped to draw attention to the preservation crisis and initiated moves to bring about a cooperative effort to solve the access and preservation problems with which we are all faced.

CATALOGUING

Slavic cataloguing operations vary from library to library. Despite this, there are three principal areas that are common to all libraries: organization and administration, personnel, and special problems posed by Slavic materials.

Organization and Administration

There are four principal ways of organizing Slavic cataloguing within technical services. To some degree, the type of organization depends on the size of the collection and the amount of Slavic materials received by the library. In most smaller institutions, materials received are in Russian and, possibly, other major Slavic languages such as Polish, Czech, Ukrainian, or Serbo-Croatian. For example, at Trinity College in San Antonio, Texas, some Russian materials are received. The amount requiring cataloguing is not large enough to require a full-time cataloguer. In such institutions, a cataloguer who has knowledge of Russian is assigned to catalogue these and other "unusual" materials.

In larger institutions, three other ways of organizing Slavic cataloguing have emerged. First, a section consisting of one or more cataloguers who deal with Slavic materials is formed within the main catalogue department. In institutions such as this, cataloguing is centralized and Slavic specialists in catalogung and acquisitions will have little contact with each other. Second is a pattern found at the University of Washington. There, one person with Slavic training does both Slavic cataloguing and Slavic acquisitions work. In contrast to the first arrangement, Slavic cataloguing and acquisitions form one unit. Since one librarian deals with both processes, adequate control is maintained. Finally, in large collections within large libraries, such as that of the University of Illinois at Urbana-Champaign (UIUC), the Slavic library incorporates all library functions — reference, cataloguing, and acquisitions. Librarians direct each of these sections and carry out their responsibilities with the assistance of support staff. Each of these three arrangements is the result of historical circumstances, the size of the Slavic collection, and the personnel available.

Personnel

In order to function effectively as a Slavic cataloguer, one must have reading fluency in at least one Slavic language. However, this skill alone is not sufficient. It is not uncommon to find many Slavic cataloguers with master's and doctoral degrees (in Slavic areas) in addition to their MLSs. Cataloguing is a demanding activity for many reasons. It is difficult enough to find librarians with either the requisite language skills or the requisite professional skills. It is even more difficult to find those with both professional and linguistic abilities. Both are needed because the problems commonly encountered in general cataloguing are magnified and made more complex when one is cataloguing specialized materials.

Special Problems

CLASSIFICATION SCHEMES

In an article that appeared in 1980, Andrew Turchyn discussed some deficiencies in the Library of Congress classification schedule with regard to Slavic and East European materials. Many problems of access to Slavic materials can be traced to these deficiencies. For instance, schedules such as D (History) and P (Philology) were initially prepared in the first quarter of this century "when the majority of Slavic peoples were dominated by Austria-Hungary, Germany, Russia, and Turkey, and when the very existence of some Slavic peoples was being denied."[1]

Political considerations aside, the LC classification schedules are the product of the LC collection itself. The schedule is entirely based on the subject content of books added to the LC collection. At the beginning of this century, Slavic holdings in U.S. libraries were scanty. After the Second World War, U.S. Slavic holdings were increased and more libraries, including the Library of Congress, began to collect intensively.[2] With the increase in LC holdings came improvement in, and expansion of, the LC classification schedules. In the mid-1960s, the American Library Association Slavic and East European Section became active in this area and offered many suggestions aimed at improving the schedules. The only major area of the LC classification in which the scheme is still deficient with regard to Slavic studies is Soviet law. There is no schedule at all for this subject, although one is in preparation.

The other classification scheme used for major Slavic collections in the United States is the Dewey Decimal classification (DDC). This scheme presents another set of problems. DDC is a so-called universal scheme, not based on an individual library's collection but upon the realm of knowledge existing at the time of the creation of the current edition of the scheme. When the first edition of DDC was published, more than a century ago, another bias — ethnocentrism — manifested itself. As a result, the early schedules assigned little space and, hence, little room for expansion to the Slavic and East European area. However, because of its capacity for expansion, the present (20th) edition of *DDC* provides adequately for the classification of most materials collected by U.S. Slavic and East European libraries. One exception is Soviet Central Asian linguistics and literature, which is subsumed under Turkic languages (DDC 494.3) and literature (DDC 894.3). At the UIUC library, Harold Leich developed a local expansion of DDC for this area, breaking each of the two DDC numbers into approximately twenty-five subclasses representing the major Soviet Central Asian languages and literatures.

SUBJECT HEADINGS

In recent years, the list of *Library of Congress Subject Headings (LCSH)* has come under fire for its lack of specificity, currency, and neutrality. These flaws are not apparent in dealing with scientific materials. Scientific terms tend to be more denotative and, hence, less subject to the vagaries of interpretation and culture than nonscientific and more connotative terminology. The troublesome aspect of this is that most Slavic collections in major U.S. research libraries consist primarily of materials in the social sciences and the humanities. The latter are areas in which there can be difficulty in matching the *LCSH* terminology to the concepts found in library materials. In addition to the difficulty of all social science and humanities materials, Slavic materials present yet another conceptual problem. In Soviet economics, for example, the subject analyst must not only match an economic concept found in a work to an existing subject heading, but must first translate the communist economic concept into a noncommunist concept before matching it to a subject heading. The absence of scope notes for most terms in *LCSH* further complicates subject heading assignment. Subject heading specialists at the Library of Congress possess a knowledge of the conceptual boundaries of subject headings that has not been put into writing. Since those specialists constantly work with a narrow range of materials and concentrate solely on subject heading assignment the conceptual boundaries, which should be explained in scope notes, are only communicated via an oral tradition and are known at the Library of Congress but not elsewhere. Therefore, other cataloguers cannot apply agreed-upon criteria in assigning subject headings to similar materials. The problem results from the absence of direct communication between LC subject cataloguers and those "in the field." However, the success of any cooperative cataloguing project, such as the new NCCP (see below), rests on the uniform application of subject headings to materials dealing with the same subjects.

DESCRIPTIVE CATALOGUING

The implementation of *International Standard Bibliographic Description (ISBD)* conventions has had a positive effect on international cooperation in cataloguing. The effect on the descriptive cataloguing of Slavic materials, however, has been minimal. In spite of the fact that the USSR does use *ISBD* and has produced machine-readable cataloguing, no full-scale exchange of bibliographic data between the United States and the USSR has taken place. The same can be said of the other East European countries except that in those countries the level of technical sophistication, the extent of the national bibliographic apparatus, and the ability to carry out such cooperation varies widely. The greatest impact of *ISBD* on the descriptive cataloguing of Slavic materials has been on the mutual exchangeability of such records between the United States, Canada, and the United Kingdom. Magnetic tapes prepared at the national libraries of each of these countries are now used and exchanged easily with only a few minor processing problems.

Another set of difficulties in the descriptive cataloguing of Slavic materials relates to specific provisions of the *Anglo-American Cataloguing Rules, Second Edition (AACR2)* and to their interpretation by the Library of Congress. In rule 22.3C2, for example, *AACR2* prescribes the Romanization of Cyrillic names according to the Romanization tables used by the cataloguing agency. However, the Library of Congress has decided to follow an alternative rule set out in *AACR2*. Under these guidelines, a cumbersome procedure must be followed for persons who are "well known" — hardly an objective criterion. The form that such person's names appear in the catalogue depends upon the consistency with which a specific form of name appears in three major encyclopedias. This results in, for example, the Romanized form of the Russian author *Dostoevskii* becoming *Dostoyevsky*. Other less "well known" *Dostoevskiis* will appear in the catalogue as *Dostoevskii*. Several Slavic librarians disputed this decision, but with little effect.

A final problematic area of descriptive cataloguing is *superimposition* — the policy of adopting a new cataloguing code while leaving headings derived from another code unrevised. This practice is described by the Library of Congress in its *Cataloguing Service Bulletin* 6 (Fall 1979) thus: "In assessing *AACR2*, the Library has identified several categories for which needed changes, although desirable, do not significantly affect the filing arrangement and consequently the user's access. Therefore, the Library of Congress, in general, plans to continue to use such headings that already exist."[3] Although many old headings retained under this practice have subsequently been revised because of name conflicts and so on, such a prescription adds just one more layer of complexity to an already complex process. The policy affects both personal and corporate names. Difficulty in assigning subject headings, complexities in descriptive cataloguing, and staff shortages all contribute to another problem — backlogs.

SLAVIC BACKLOGS

Backlogs are collections of library material that have been received by the library but are still not catalogued. Because they are not catalogued, they are not, for the most part, available to library patrons. In larger Slavic collections, which usually have larger backlogs, the problem is national and is not restricted to the institution possessing the backlog. Within those institutions, materials in their backlogs are often unique in North America. Only the larger collections can afford to purchase the less popular and less readily available but valuable items. The major difficulty lies in getting these unique or rare items out of backlogs and onto the shelves and recorded in local catalogues and national databases. The larger collections must also satisfy the institutional demand for the more popular items. Several approaches are possible. Most of them involve cooperative ventures of some kind. At least, the problem has been recognized. Partly as a result of this recognition, the BIRD (Bibliography, Information Retrieval, and Documentation) Committee of ACLIS (American Council of Learned Societies) held the previously mentioned Conference on Access to Slavic Materials in North American Libraries which has led, *inter alia*, to plans for dealing cooperatively with Slavic backlogs and improving cataloguing efficiency in individual institutions. Two projects that are already under way are the creation of authority records through NACO (Name Authority Cooperative Project) and the creation of national level catalogue records through NCCP (National Coordinated Cataloging Program). Each of these programs can help to reduce backlogs, and can also serve to improve the quality and efficiency of Slavic cataloguing throughout the country.

NACO. NACO is a cooperative program between the Library of Congress and approximately forty other libraries. Each of the libraries contributes Name Authority Records (NARs) to the Library of Congress on a regular basis and on forms provided by the national library. Each NACO participant is required initially to send representatives to attend a two-week training session at the Library of Congress at which they learn the various procedures entailed in the completion of a NAR.[4]

Once a NACO member begins submitting authority records, the NARs are checked at the Library of Congress and then input into the MARC database for national distribution. A detailed examination of NACO procedures and their effects at one library has been given by Burger.[5] The creation of this pool of trained personnel outside the Library of Congress has increased the number of NARs over that produced by the Library alone. The availability of reliable authority data has led to more efficient processing and the consequent reduction of some backlogs.

NCCP. Another program carried out by cooperating libraries on a national basis is the National Coordinated Cataloging Program (NCCP). The purpose of this program is to make non-LC-produced but LC-quality cataloguing available nationwide. Before it was renamed, this type of cooperative venture was run under the aegis of NACO. In this incipient stage, the University of Chicago and Harvard University were engaged in converting and updating existing LC cataloguing records to machine-readable form. Records were upgraded to *AACR2* standards and the subject headings changed to conform to current LC subject-heading guidelines.

In the summer of 1985, representatives of the University of Illinois (UIUC) Library and the Library of Congress met to work out procedures for the cooperative cataloguing of currently published Russian-language monographs. This meeting resulted in the UIUC Library agreeing to catalogue monographs from seven Soviet publishers (Kniga, Mysl', Mezh. otosheniia, Politizdat, Finansy i statistika, Ekonomika, and IUrid. lit.) as they were received at Illinois. These publishers were chosen by UIUC primarily because of their subject coverage (social sciences and humanities) in which the UIUC Library has a special interest and experience in processing. For its part, the Library of Congress would upgrade the cataloguing priority of 2,000 Russian books from Level 4 to Level 2. As with the NACO project, UIUC submits cataloguing data on worksheets provided by the Library of Congress.

After UIUC began to submit records, the Library of Congress decided to expand the project to five other libraries (Texas, Yale, Indiana, Michigan, and Berkeley). These libraries focus on materials for which they have the necessary expertise and in which their collections are strong. Some doubts have been raised about the net positive effect of this project on backlogs across the country. As of this writing, Tantalus, Inc., has been given a contract to conduct a cost study to help in evaluating the project.

FUTURE OF SLAVIC TECHNICAL SERVICES

There are three major trends affecting Slavic technical services. In some sense, they are more incipient than actual but can be expected to develop and to grow.

The first trend is national cooperation, exemplified by NACO and NCCP. These programs provide highly visible examples of interlibrary cooperation. One danger inherent in these programs is that the Library of Congress may have a tendency to view the participants not as equals, but rather as outlying units of itself. However, NACO procedures have been relaxed without any diminution in the quality of the records. It remains to be seen whether NCCP will achieve a similar equilibrium.

The second trend is personal and professional cooperation between Slavic librarians across the country. This is not new and can be traced back to the mid-1960s when a Slavic and East European Section was formed within the American Library Association. It was followed by the 1970 Slavic Librarians' Seminar, the creation of a Slavic librarians group within the American Association for the Advancement of Slavic Studies (AAASS), two world congresses for Soviet and East European Studies that included a meeting of Slavic librarians and information specialists, and other less far-ranging cooperative activities.

A third trend, not confined to Slavic librarianship, but beginning to be influential there, is the reliance on personal computers for public and technical services. Existing systems at Berkeley and Harvard, and a system being developed at Illinois for their Slavic Reference Service and Slavic Exchange Program, are examples.

Slavic librarianship is not a growing professional area in the United States in terms of the number of specialized Slavic libraries. In the early 1950s, the U.S. holdings of Slavic materials were small. Only a handful of libraries had collections that even warranted mention. By the end of the 1960s, strengths had increased dramatically, partially as a result of the U.S. response to the launching of *Sputnik* by the USSR in 1957, and partly as a result of the growth in U.S. higher education in that period. By the 1970s, those collections that were already established were fighting hard to maintain their strengths, but were certainly not expanding as they had done in the first ten to fifteen years of their existence. Libraries without Slavic collections are not now establishing them. However, those with strong collections are stable, despite budgetary problems caused by the devaluation of the dollar and bursts of xenophobia.

Finally, one area in which cohesion, if not growth, has taken place is among Slavic librarians themselves. Over the past twenty years, what started out as a small but determined group of Slavic library specialists who formed the ALA Slavic and East European Section in the 1960s now numbers more than 100 such specialists in the United States, Canada, and abroad. The aforementioned international and national conferences of Slavic librarians and information specialists, as well as the annual meetings of the ALA Slavic section and the librarians' group within AAASS, have all served to make this group cohesive. This closely knit group of Slavic librarians will serve to keep this area strong in the future.

NOTES

[1]Aman, Mohammed M., *ed.* Cataloging and classification of non-Western materials: concerns, issues, and practices. Phoenix, AZ: Oryx Press, 1980. p. 312

[2]Ruggles, Melville J. and Vaclav Mostecky. Russian and East European publications in the libraries of the United States. New York: Columbia University Press, 1960 (Columbia University studies in library service; no. 11)

[3]Library of Congress. *Cataloguing service bulletin.* 6 (Fall 1979)

[4]Fenly, Judith G. and Sarah D. Irvine. The Name Authority Co-op (NACO) project at the Library of Congress. *Cataloging and classification quarterly* 7, no. 2:7-18 (Winter 1986)

[5]Burger, Robert H. NACO at the University of Illinois at U-C: a narrative case study. *Cataloging and classification quarterly* 7, no. 2:19-28 (Winter 1986)

FURTHER READINGS

Access to resources in the '80s: proceedings of the first International Conference of Slavic Librarians and Information Specialists. New York: Russica, 1982 ("Russica" bibliography series, no. 2)

Choldin, Marianna Tax, ed. Books, libraries, and information in Slavic and East European Studies: proceedings of the second International Conference of Slavic Librarians and Information Specialists. New York: Russica, 1986 ("Russica" bibliography series; no. 8)

Automation and Technical Services

CIRCULATION SERVICES

MARSHA J. STEVENSON
and PAUL M. ANDERSON

Some may wonder why a book on technical services should include a chapter on circulation, since this operation has been viewed traditionally as a public services activity. Computerization has led many libraries to take a hard look at this structure, however. Functional departments used to be organized around separate physical files (the shelflist, trays of circulation charge cards), but automation is making such files obsolete. Even a relatively unsophisticated stand-alone online circulation system operates from brief item records which include the most essential features of bibliographic description. As Epstein observed, "Even with the limited access points of the early systems, library staff began to see the circulation system as a de facto online catalog with the added benefit of being able to tell where the actual books should be found."[1] In addition to this merger of the functions of the two files, today's integrated library systems require a particularly close coordination between the work of these formerly separate departments. Taken together, these factors have led some libraries to relocate the circulation department administratively in technical services.

Charging (i.e., issuing), renewing, and discharging materials are the major activities of a circulation unit, and comprise the bulk of standard transactions. Two different classes of problem are also part of daily circulation routine—loosely grouped into *not-on-shelf* and *nonreturn* problems.

One not-on-shelf category involves volumes whose locations are known to the library, such as those out to the borrower but desired by another. The typical remedy for this problem is to hold the material upon its return and subsequently notify the person who requested the item. "Recalls" can be employed to hasten the return of these books.

The second group of not-on-shelf problems involves materials the whereabouts of which cannot be ascertained immediately, thus requiring searching on the part of the staff. Frequently, the item in question is available in the library, but the requester failed to locate it, for any of several reasons. At times the inability to find the volume can be due to an error on the part of the staff, such as misshelving; or the material could be in transit after a recent use. At other times, however, the problem lies with the borrower's incomplete understanding of some aspect of the library's operation; this may involve anything from the faulty interpretation of information on the catalogue record to confusion about the collection's physical arrangement. Consequently, some libraries try to search for these "missing" materials immediately—while the requester is still on the premises.

The second large category of circulation problem revolves around the non-return of materials. Some libraries send preoverdue notices to inform people of impending due dates. More commonly, an overdue remainder is generated and mailed to the borrower at some specified period of time after a due date. In some libraries, these notices are sent out for one-quarter or more of their total circulation transactions, so their volume can be substantial. It is common to charge a fine for the late return of materials, though the amounts collected from each individual are generally small.

Libraries either send additional overdue notices to unresponsive borrowers or proceed directly to billing for the replacement of the late materials. Since billing often results in a speedy return of items, some libraries take a shortcut in determining the price to charge, reasoning that the cost of staff time is too high to search *Books in Print* for exact prices when the use of a single flat amount (such as $50) usually achieves the desired effect. It is common to add a service charge to the replacement price of the materials.

Most libraries attract a diverse clientele, and the privileges granted vary widely. Public libraries/library systems will generally offer free service only to residents within their funding boundaries, or within larger areas if reciprocal borrowing arrangements have been made between libraries. Academic libraries often permit borrowing only by people affiliated with their institution, with the length of the loan period being further differentiated by the individual's status; for instance, undergraduates may be allowed to borrow books for one month, while faculty members may retain them for three.

The maintenance of accurate name/address data (the "patron file") is of critical importance to the smooth functioning of a circulation department. This can be a remarkably difficult goal to achieve. The problem is particularly acute in academic libraries, in which the eligible user population is a highly mobile and ever-changing group. Public libraries in locations with large transient populations (e.g., tourist areas) or in cities that are rapidly growing or diminishing in size also experience considerable difficulties in keeping name/address data current. Outdated or otherwise erroneous information in this file exacerbates the problems of overdues, recalls, fining, and billing, which taken together can absorb a considerable amount of staff time.

Libraries generally subscribe to the principle of the confidentiality of circulation records; that is, they do not divulge information about the reading habits of individuals, nor will they provide listings of the borrowers of a particular title. Some librarians have gone to court to defend the privacy of such information, and thirty-eight states now have statutes protecting the confidentiality of circulation data. In actual practice, supervisors may decide to reveal loan records in very unusual circumstances; still, their release is rarely routine procedure and is in violation of ALA policy on confidentiality.

The preceding discussion lists the usual functions and problems of a typical circulation department. In addition, a variety of other responsibilities may be located administratively in this unit. Security functions, such as monitoring and responding to alarms set off by individuals going through theft detection gates, are common. In academic libraries, readings required for classes are often kept on reserve near the main lending desk. Employees responsible for the reshelving of materials frequently report to the circulation supervisor. Interlibrary loan activities, which were usually performed by reference personnel in a preautomated environment, are now handled by circulation staff in some libraries.

MANUAL FILES

Over the years, a variety of methods have been employed to handle the core functions — charging, renewal, and discharging. One common manual method uses descriptive book cards which are kept in the back of each volume. Borrowers sign these cards and turn them in to the library staff, who put them in a file of all items in circulation. Confidentiality is almost impossible to achieve with this method.

Another typical manual method requires library users to fill out forms identifying themselves and the items they are borrowing. The circulation staff keeps these as a record of each transaction. This system resolves the problem of confidentiality, but is very time-consuming for the borrower, especially since a separate form with all identifying information is required for each volume being borrowed.

It goes without saying that manual circulation files demand a great deal of maintenance, since each card must be accurately filed, and all must be sorted through if overdue materials are to be identified. To alleviate this situation, some libraries employ the McBee Key-Sort System, which was developed at Harvard in 1937.[2] This system uses cards ringed with holes, each of which signifies a date or a borrower category. A punch is used to notch each chargeout card, opening up the hole by that item's due date. To identify overdues, a thin rod is inserted through the forms in the transaction file at the punch for a particular date. Any cards which fall back when the "needle" is lifted are, therefore, overdue.

The labor-intensive character of manual files makes them difficult to maintain in good order. Moreover, such systems are decidedly limited in their capabilities. It is, for example, a problem of gargantuan proportions to determine all of the items charged out to a given borrower. Frequent demand for such services, and the desire to increase staff productivity, has led to considerable experimentation with available technologies.

Mechanical devices for circulation transactions were first used at the turn of the century, and refinements of these, such as Brodart's Sysdac Mark III and Gaylord's Model C Book Charger, are still in use today. These machines permit speedy chargeouts, but there is no efficient means of identifying delinquent borrowers, items charged to a patron, or other desirable information, at the circulation desk.

Another type of precomputer technology commonly used in circulation systems has been microfilm. A specially designed camera photographs a surface on which information identifying the book and the borrower is placed, along with a transaction slip giving a due date and a unique number. Checkouts on these systems are quick and easy for both staff and library users, but there is no practical method of determining the whereabouts of a book not found on the shelves. Microfilm reels must be read sequentially to retrieve the book and borrower information necessary for overdues. Freedman describes this as a

> widely accepted but terrible solution.... Libraries rushed to adopt this system because it eliminated the paper files of earlier manual circulation systems, and thus eliminated the labor costs associated with them.... The borrower is poorly served in terms of reserves and overdue notification.[3]

All these systems have some attractive features, but are at the same time limited in the information they can offer. Library automation changed all this and dramatically expanded the capabilities of circulation systems. Circulation was a natural early candidate for automation, since its basic operations are simple, repetitive, and high volume, not unlike the business inventory control for which many early computers were employed.

KEYPUNCH CARDS

The use of keypunch cards for data entry was usual in most early computing applications. A number of libraries designed and implemented batch circulation systems using these ninety-column Hollerith cards, following the University of Texas at Austin's pioneering use in 1936.[4] Some significant advances were achieved in departmental workflow: the computer kept the chargeout file in close to shelflist order, overdue notices were printed and fines calculated automatically, and fairly sophisticated usage statistics (e.g., items charged to a borrower) were readily available. The major drawback of these batch systems was the delay between the occurrence of transactions and their appearance on the circulation file. At best, these systems were updated overnight, so that records of a transaction were never available on the day of the transaction. Another significant problem that occurred regularly was an equipment misreading of the punches on the card, leading to the recording of incorrect data. Today, keypunch is no longer a viable technology, IBM has ceased manufacturing eighty-column cards, and the necessary punch machines and reading equipment have become very rare.

ONLINE SYSTEMS

As computer technology evolved, the capacity to store large amounts of information increased while costs of data storage decreased. This led to the development of online, real-time systems to handle circulation. CL Systems, Inc., (now CLSI) paved the way with the introduction of its LIBS 100 automated circulation system in 1973, and other vendors followed with such similar systems as

Geac and DataPhase. These are referred to as *turnkey*, meaning that the company contracts to provide the hardware, software, installation, and support necessary to run the system. As Fayen observes,

> One of the major reasons that turnkey library systems are so popular [is that] the vendor, who presumably is expert at running large-scale computer systems, assumes all the burden of systems support. The library is thus relieved of the burden of attempting to develop and staff a project that is outside the scope of its normal operations and for which traditional library education has not prepared it very well.[5]

At the other end of the spectrum are nonturnkey systems such as NOTIS, the operation of which requires substantial computer expertise on the part of the local library's staff.

A survey conducted in 1985 polled 300 academic libraries concerning their automation. Nearly one-fifth of the respondents has online circulation systems; over half of these were turnkey operations. The size of the library's collection and the amount of its use were directly related to the presence of such a system, with only 10 percent of those circulating less than 50,000 volumes a year employing online methods, while 75 percent of those issuing more than 500,000 annually were using them. Of the libraries without real-time systems, 65 percent were planning to implement them in the future.[6]

State-of-the-art circulation systems offer both simplified methods of performing basic functions and a host of new features for the convenience of the staff and the library's users. Perhaps the greatest advantages derive from the ability to gain access to the whole of the online file from any terminal or workstation (including, in some cases, remote "dial-up" access from home or office via modem). The availability of an item in a remote location can be ascertained immediately; those materials charged out by a borrower from any branch of a library system can be printed in a single integrated list; all data concerning problem transactions, such as dates of overdue notices or fine payments, are immediately at hand. Sophisticated management information is also available, since a computer can readily provide figures about the use of particular sections of the collection or the reading habits of specified categories of borrowers.

The original concept of the circulation file as a record only of those items currently in use began to change with the advent of online systems. The prospect of typing a volume's identifying information into a computer database each time it circulates is daunting; such transactions would be both slow and prone to error. Instead, online circulation systems are designed to operate using a file of brief records for all or most materials in the collection (an "inventory" system), most or all of which data has been input in advance. This is a very significant change from the character of previous circulation files, which listed only those items with an exceptional (not-on-shelf) status (called an *absence* system).

The data necessary to identify a volume for a circulation transaction are minimal; call number, item or copy number, and brief author and title are all that is important. In the early days of computerization, when the cost of data storage was very high, such brief records were commonly employed by turnkey systems, since it was not economically feasible to build a file with full cataloguing information, nor was such a file essential for circulation purposes.

However, libraries found that labor costs made the development of an database even of short records an expensive proposition. As computer capabilities expanded and the price of data storage dropped, the rationale for creating less-than-full bibliographic descriptions for the sole purpose of issuing materials began to seem less sensible. Libraries realized that if they created a full record once, it could serve the dual needs of cataloguing and circulation, and thereby eliminate duplicate data entry. This is the basic concept behind an integrated system. In the opinion of Richard Boss and Judy McQueen,

> The construction of full bibliographic records is warranted even when a library does not have firm plans to establish an on-line or patron-access catalog. The data base, if properly built, will last for several decades and outlive several computer systems. The data base is analogous to the 100-percent rag catalog cards that libraries have been filing in their card catalogs. The cards are intended to last indefinitely and to be transferred to new card-catalog cabinets when the old cabinets are replaced.[7]

An integrated system is one in which multiple functions are supported by a single bibliographic file. The online catalogue is the base from which other functions, such as circulation, acquisitions, serials, and authority control can operate. The advantages of integrated systems are many; as Boss points out, "Only one input or update needs to be performed to keep the entire data base current for all functions and only one query needs to be made to search the entire data base."[8]

The integrated library system provides an elegant solution to both the public's information needs and the employees' tasks of processing and access. Work done in one function is recorded instantly in others. Staff members and users no longer have to switch from one file (the catalogue) to another (circulation records) to determine the availability of an item. All terminals can display current status information, such as whether an item is checked out or has been recalled. Except for the public access catalogue, which often uses a simplified mode with a limited number of access points, the wording of inquiries and commands to the database is common across functions. The use of integrated systems is growing rapidly; while in John Camp's 1985 study only seventeen libraries had functioning integrated systems installed, over half of the others planned to implement them in the future.[9]

The requirements of an integrated system move the circulation staff into some operations which formerly were considered part of technical services. They, therefore, require some of the same training as is given to support staff in cataloguing and acquisitions; log-on procedures, passwords, and security clearance at various authority levels are necessary. An even more significant crossover from circulation to technical services functions occurs when staff need to input record into the database; this activity is required when ephemeral materials are placed on reserve, and when items not linked to specific piece records in the catalogue are charged out.

Materials put on course reserve have always included items other than books owned by the library. Photocopies of articles are common, and other ephemeral items such as sample course exams are often seen. Sometimes instructors will put their own copies of books on reserve when the library does not own desired volumes. These types of materials are heavily used by students and thus require records in the database so that circulation transactions can be speedily performed. They are, however, not the sort of items which are normally acquired through technical services departments, and it is unlikely that any will become a permanent part of the library's collection. For the time in which they are on reserve, however, records of such items must be available for circulation and so added to the file. These records need to be removed when the materials are no longer required for reserve. The mechanism employed by integrated systems for the addition/deletion of such temporary records to the database varies, but it is clear that this is, in essence, what has always been considered a technical services function.

The other area in which circulation requires the addition of records to the database is for volumes in the collection which are "unlinked"; that is, those for which specific item records do not exist in the catalogue. Unless the library has added every single circulatable piece in its collection to the online file, unlinked items are bound to appear at the circulation desk. The frequency with which this occurs depends on the degree to which the library has been able to enter computerized records for its collection into its catalogue; that is, the amount of retrospective conversion it has been able to perform. Many collections are not fully represented in online files; some of the largest ones have only those materials processed after a specified date (often in the 1970s) included in the database. At times, a basic bibliographic record will exist for a multivolume work such as a journal, but specific item records identifying each separate physical piece are lacking. For circulation transactions, that level of specificity is essential. The library might also own specialized collections, such as pamphlets, maps, and government documents, for which records have not been added to the database.

Online systems have various means of accommodating circulation transactions involving unlinked items, but typically they are slow and cumbersome. The desk staff is generally required to type information identifying the item, thus creating a brief record in the database to be used for the chargeout transaction. This is not a speedy process. When a patron wishes to borrow a large number of such unlinked materials, long lines can form at the circulation desk. Moreover, these brief records are quite literally added "on the fly"—in pressure situations with borrowers waiting. The probability of typographical mistakes is high, and there is no time to perform the usual quality-control checks. Therefore, these records for unlinked materials are not usually considered permanent additions to the main bibliographic database; they reside temporarily in the circulation file. In most cases, they cannot be searched via usual catalogue access points, and are often deleted when the items are returned to the library, meaning that the same process must be performed again for subsequent circulations of that item. In order to avoid this repetitive work, many libraries give high priority to adding permanent records to the database for items charged out via unlinked transactions.

While it is undesirable for circulation staff to add permanent records to the catalogue on the fly, the input of piece information to an existing bibliographic description is a possibility. The creation of a basic record demands considerable care and expertise; the addition of holdings data describing individual physical items is less complex. With the piece in hand, volume and copy information can be speedily added to the catalogue with a fair assurance of accuracy. For this task to be handled properly, circulation staff must be trained by catalogue specialists.

In online systems, the link between the physical piece presented by a borrower and its database record is generally made by using a bar-code label. The unique number on the label is matched by one in the holdings file of the catalogue, which permits the current status of individual items in the collection to be readily determined. Bar codes offer a quick and easy method of inputting these multidigit numbers into the circulation file, thus assuring that each transaction is associated with the correct piece record in the database. Owing to sophisticated check digit calculation, misreading data from a bar-code label is rare.

In order for this link to be established, unique numbers must be attached to each piece represented in the library's holdings file. If such numbers do not already exist, they must be created. Once these are available, a tape can be generated using selected information from the online catalogue; this is usually sent to a commercial vendor for the production of bar codes. In addition to the unique number represented in machine-readable format, each label displays in eye-readable characters the call number of the specific piece matching that number in the online catalogue. Since these bar codes are produced with the numeric link to an individual piece record already made, they are referred to as *smart*.

Bar-code labels can be applied to materials either before the implementation of the online system or at the circulation desk the first time an item is checked out. Each method has advantages and disadvantages. Libraries choosing to bar code in advance produce labels and systematically apply them to all volumes in the stacks before the system is installed, which can be a poor use of staff time if many of the materials are never charged out. Still, advance bar coding saves time at the circulation desk, and serves the added purposes of shelf reading and inventory. Application of labels at the time materials are issued to a borrower ensures that the effort expended in bar coding is valid but causes significant delays in transactions, particularly when the system is first being used. If smart bar codes are opted for, a great many sheets must be leafed through to locate an item's matching label. To avoid this problem, most libraries that bar code during circulation use generic labels, in which the numeric link to a specific item record has not yet been made. The use of these generic or "dumb" labels requires the circulation staff to create the database link on the fly as borrowers wait. It is, therefore, easier for desk attendants to begin working with a new online system when smart bar codes have been applied to materials in advance. Also, the early days of a new system are important ones in the general public's perception of its efficiency, and unnecessary delays in handling routine transactions should be avoided.

For internal library operations, an automated circulation component can be used to track materials in process. The status of an item can be monitored from the time an order is placed to the time it reaches the shelves, with the piece's precise physical location always discernable, and with "overdues" employed to call attention to materials which have not left an area within a specified amount of time. If the circulation system is to be used in this way, technical services staff must be trained in charging and discharging procedures. The people who are responsible for sending materials out for binding will certainly need to become familiar with basic circulation functions.

The statistical capabilities of automated systems are extremely sophisticated, and can be exploited by all areas of the library. The detailed information about collection use available from circulation records can be used by acquisitions and/or selections personnel to identify and order needed duplicate or replacement copies. Budgeting decisions can be made in the light of documented usage patterns, and administrators can determine the borrowing rates of patrons in various categories, including those of people who are not part of the library's primary clientele.

In an academic environment, other computerized databases created for various administrative purposes may already exist. These can serve the library's needs. For instance, an automated file of the institution's students, faculty, and staff may have been developed for the use of registration, payroll, and other management activities. While it makes good sense to avoid duplicate work, achieving an interface between the campus's name/address files and the library's circulation system is not always an easy task. Even if those records are readily available, many libraries issue materials to persons not affiliated with their institutions, so that some means of adding identifying information to the file for those borrowers must be devised. If an academic library's fines and charges are collected by a centralized campus cashier's office, an interface with that system must be created. At most schools all three of the above-mentioned operations are automated, but since the computer systems will have been developed independently, the records may not be immediately compatible. (This is an excellent example of the reason for an integrated system; but those developed for libraries are not designed to support the work of other campus operations.)

Problems

Along with the numerous advantages of online systems come some problems inherent in computerized work. Hardware must be extremely reliable, and backup procedures immediately available. In behind-the-scenes technical services operations, slow response time is a serious annoyance, but it is scarcely as detrimental as in a circulation environment in which lines of borrowers may be kept waiting. During extended downtime, online catalogue work can be postponed but the issuing of materials cannot, a fact which necessitates the availability of a backup to the online system. If a workstation with memory, such as a personal computer with a hard disk, is used for these backup transactions, special software can transfer the data to the main file automatically when the system instability is resolved.

Even assuming that hardware and software are performing perfectly and that interfaces with other campus databases are straightforward, new kinds of problems will confront the circulation staff. Implementation of an integrated library system presents the challenge of handling highly complex tasks made more difficult by their interrelation with other library technical operations. The circulation department manager is confronted in a much more fundamental way with concerns relating to administering computer-mediated work. Issues of ergonomics, job design, and training as they relate to day-to-day operations are very similar to those faced in a technical services environment.

The amount of processing done at a video display terminal (VDT) workstation will increase dramatically with the introduction of an integrated system. Most staff members will spend part of their day in front of a VDT; for some, it may dominate a large percentage of their working time, since transactions and file maintenance previously performed manually will be handled using terminals. The long hours spent before a screen on tasks such as reserve list processing, name/address additions and corrections, and fines updates have important implications for both the ergonomics of the workstation and for job design, although the amount of time spent at a terminal affects people differently; as Horney observes:

> Staff members seem to show wide individual variance in tolerance for and enjoyment of work at VDTs. Some sit enthusiastically at a terminal for most of the day without apparent drop in concentration and accomplishment. Others go glassy-eyed after little more than an hour of complex input work.[10]

Considerable public attention has been focused on the health-related problems of working with VDTs. Concerns fall into three basic areas: dangers from radiation, the contributions of VDTs to visual problems, and muscular/skeletal discomfort. At this time, there do not seem to be significant grounds for concern over radiation emissions. In a number of studies conducted by the National Institute for Occupational Safety and Health (NIOSH), emissions from VDTs were deemed to be below safety threshold standards.[11] In a study at Eastern Washington University, thermoluminescent badges were placed on terminals and worn by library staff. The badges established that emissions were well below conservative maximum allowable exposure levels.[12]

The effects of terminal work on visual and muscular/skeletal health problems are more complex, and relate to both ergonomic and job design considerations. Studies show that physical discomfort is higher among clerical staff working with terminals than with people doing more traditional office work.[13] The ability to adjust the contrast of the screen and to control glare is important in reducing visual fatigue. Extended periods of time spent at any task require that workers have proper postural support and that muscle load be minimized. Chairs providing appropriate lumbar support and having adjustable height and tension controls are essential for comfort. For tasks requiring data entry from hard copy, a document holder will reduce fatigue by eliminating much movement of the neck muscles. Very specific information about what constitutes an ergonomically sound workstation is readily available and should be consulted when setting up new workstations or in evaluating existing equipment and facilities.[14] Knowing the optimal height of work surfaces, methods for controlling glare, the essential features of posturally supportive seating, and how to develop workstations which can be adjusted to the needs of each staff member will help to eliminate problems resulting from poor ergonomic design.

A sudden increase in the level of automation in the workplace can greatly diminish the intellectual content of some jobs, and thus decrease staff members' satisfaction. In some environments, tasks are fragmented and simplified in order to accommodate machine processing better. Repetition of activities does increase efficiency, but also can lead to boredom and fatigue. Workers who are assigned such duties can lose a sense of the relationship of their jobs to the service being provided. It is easy for them to view themselves as operators of a computer system, not as people providing vital service to others. Whenever possible, responsibility for a complete function should be built into a job, since having a variety of tasks to perform will reduce boredom. It also allows the integration of high-content activities with lower-content tasks, so that employees get the opportunity both to be challenged and to take a break from highly demanding jobs. In cases where fragmentation is unavoidable, it is important for supervisors to make clear the importance of each task to the larger function, so that staff members can recognize their contributions to the overall effort. Every library manager has a responsibility to try to build opportunity for satisfaction into employee work assignments.

The degree to which staff interact primarily with a terminal also can have a negative effect on the social fabric of the department. The focus of attention can shift from communication between two people to interaction between a worker and a machine. Wells believes that "computerization will lead to fewer contacts among coworkers, less cohesiveness and cooperative effort and less time for formal or informal interaction in the work place."[15] However, social support is one of the most important elements in controlling or moderating dysfunctional stress at work. Through these networks, individuals obtain emotional support which builds and reaffirms self-esteem, and gain important information through feedback, appraisal, and advice that assists them in making decisions about work. A number of strategies are available to increase social interaction between employees in a department, ranging from the creation of specialized work groups to the coordination of coffee breaks. Supervisors also need to be aware of their staff's individual situations and needs. While managers cannot halt work flow, often they can control the intensity in one individual's job, giving the staff member the assurance that people have some control over computer-related work problems.

Providing adequate training is one of the greatest challenges facing the library manager in the integrated system environment. Reliance on automation and the new interrelation of functions dramatically increases the amount of material which must be mastered by employees. Glogoff observes that "staff training for an ILS (integrated library system) requires far more planning than for single-function automated systems."[16] Lowry emphasizes the importance of continued training *after* the implementation of a new system, because of both staff turnover and the continuing evolution of software.[17] The significant degree to which libraries rely on their support staff makes solid in-house training programs vital. Given the importance of this activity, it seems wise to formalize a training program, beginning with a needs assessment, and to evaluate its effectiveness continually.[18]

Integrated systems have an impact on the level of personnel required in both circulation and other technical operations. As Karen Horney observes, "Since automation has eliminated much of the lower-level or semiskilled work, what remains is frequently paraprofessional. Thus, a higher degree of skill is often required of non-professional staff.... Staff development and actual retraining of longer-term personnel have become necessities."[19] A fairly sophisticated understanding of the software's capabilities is necessary for the larger number of employees, and a significant amount of cross-training will be required if staff are to comprehend fully the operation of the system in an integrated environment. Employees must have a clear view not only of the system's mechanics, but also of how it supports library objectives and policies, so that they can make informed decisions when necessary.

The public service aspect of circulation can become more difficult in the automated environment of an integrated system. The desk worker serves as an intermediary between the borrower and the computer system. While the requirements of hardware and software will demand the staff member's attention, it is vital that a personal touch, a sense of human communication, be maintained with the borrower. As McDonald notes, "A wholesale preoccupation with machines, technique and efficiency ... has resulted in a blindness to 'personal' considerations, however urgent they may be."[20] A desk attendant focusing all attention on data entry can only reinforce the public's impression of system impersonality. This human contact is just as important for the morale of staff members as for the library's clientele. As Cline points out, "Informal communication makes bearable an otherwise tedious job for many circulation attendants; ... and for the user it fosters a perception of the library as a provider of services as opposed to a warehouser of information."[21] Eye contact, a smile, and a personalized greeting will do much for both parties.

Some employees will resist the library's advancing computerization, either overtly or passively. Zuboff suggests that these staff members may see the terminal as an inflexible supervisor, feeling that it will spy on them, track their actions, and report any departure from strictly defined policy. Such an attitude necessarily inhibits the element or risk-taking essential for problem solving and good public service.[22] Management must make it clear to staff that information gathered from the system will be used to improve decision making, not to ensure staff's slavish compliance with rules.

Much has been written about people fearing the loss of their jobs from automation. One way for them to ensure continued employment is to become indispensable; to become the department's only expert in some operation, and then to jealously guard their knowledge. The dangers to an organization of such people are obvious; in fact, one management training course advises supervisors to single out the "indispensable" people and fire them!

Intraorganizational conflict resulting from the introducton of automation may occur because people either resist or support innovation based upon whether it increases or decreases their power. Those whom Rose calls "cosmopolitans" have superior education or generalizable knowledge, and favor new developments because they see increased opportunities for themselves; conversely, the "locals" have a superior understanding of the preautomated environment and fear the loss of status computers could bring. He states,

> Locals obviously tend to resist the change. For a start it threatens to transform the concern as they know and like it. The technical logic of the computer systems may demand an information grid which trespasses over hallowed departmental boundaries.[23]

It is important to note that this process can be cyclical, with the cosmopolitans of today becoming the locals of tomorrow as new technologies are introduced. In a paper presented at a meeting devoted to library automation, Fine observed,

> I would propose that none of us could be described as resistant to technology—as we know it today. But I would venture that if new and radically different technology were to appear on the scene—one that would make the way we work obsolete, devalue our investments of years and resources, leave us without skills and with reduced status, rob us of valued traditions and our valued belief system—then we who are innovators would become the cringers and whiners.[24]

CONCLUSION

The effect of all these changes on the staff is significant, and should not be underestimated. Michael Rose emphasizes that "the fact has to be faced that the computer is likely significantly to alter conventional methods of management and, on most of the evidence, to outmode present organizational patterns."[25] An integrated library system mandates an environment in which intimate interconnections between formerly separate departments are essential, and in which older methods of organization might only impede the fullest use of system capabilities.

NOTES

[1]Epstein, Susan Baerg. Suddenly last decade! automation arrives. *Library journal* 108:183-185 (February 1, 1983)

[2]Kilgour, Frederick S. Historical note: a personalized prehistory of OCLC. *Journal of the American Society for Information Science* 38:381-384 (September 1987)

[3]Freedman, Maurice J. Automation and the future of technical services. *Library journal* 109:1197-1203 (June 15, 1984)

[4]Kilgour. *Op. cit.*

[5]Fayen, Emily Gallup. Automated circulation systems for large libraries. *Library technology reports* 22:385-469 (July-Aug. 1986)

[6]Camp, Joan A. *et al.* Survey of online systems. *College and research libraries* 48:339-350 (July 1987)

[7]Boss, Richard W. and Judy McQueen. Automated circulation control systems. *Library technology reports* 18:125-266 (March-Apr. 1982)

[8]Boss, Richard W. The library manager's guide to automation. 2nd ed. White Plains, NY: Knowledge Industry, 1984

[9]Camp. *Op. cit.*

[10]Horney, Karen L. Quality work, quality control in technical services. *Journal of academic librarianship* 48:528-536 (Nov. 1987)

[11]Smith, Michael J. Ergonomic aspects of health problems in VDT operators. *In* Human aspects of office automation/ ed. by Barbara G. F. Cohen. New York: Elsevier, 1984

[12]Tracy, Joan I. and V. Louise Saylor. Video display terminals in a medium-sized academic library: concerns and responses. *In* Crossroads: proceedings of the first National Conference of the Library and Information Technology Association/ ed. by Michael Gorman. Chicago: American Library Association, 1984

[13]Smith. *Op. cit.*

[14]Tijerina, Louis. Optimizing the VDT workstation: controlling the glare postural problems. Dublin, OH: OCLC Online Computer Library Center, 1983

[15]Wells, James A. Social support strategies for technostress management. *In* Strategic management of technostress in an information society/ ed. by Amarjit S. Sethi, Denis H. J. Caro, and Randall S. Schuler. Lewiston, NY: Hogrefe, 1987

[16]Glogoff, Stuart and James P. Flynn. Developing a systematic in-house training program for integrated library systems. *College and research libraries* 48:528-536 (Nov. 1987)

[17]Lowry, Charles B. Technology in libraries: six rules for management. *Library hi tech* 3, no. 11:27-29 (1985)

[18]Glogoff. *Op. cit.*

[19]Horney. *Op. cit.*

[20]McDonald, Thomas F. Technostress lurks inside every manager. *Data Management* 21:10-14 (Sept. 1983)

[21]Cline, Hugh F. and Loraine T. Sinnott. The electronic library: the impact of automation on academic libraries. Lexington, MA: Lexington Books, 1983

[22]Zuboff, Shoshana. New worlds of computer-mediated work. *Harvard business review* 60:142-152 (Sept.-Oct. 1982)

[23]Rose, Michael. Computers, managers, and society. Baltimore, MD: Penguin, 1969

[24]Fine, Sara. Terminal paralysis, or, Showdown at the interface. *In* Human aspects of library automation/ ed. by Debora Shaw (Clinic on Library Applications of Data Processing, 1985) Urbana, IL: Graduate School of Library and Information Science, University of Illinois at Urbana-Champaign, 1986

[25]Rose. *Op. cit.*

THE EVOLVING ONLINE CATALOGUE
IN ACADEMIC LIBRARIES

WILLIAM GRAY POTTER

THE GENERIC ONLINE CATALOGUE

Online catalogues have been in development in academic libraries for almost twenty years, and today relatively few online catalogues are in place and fully operational. However, though each online catalogue is somewhat different, it is possible to discern what is becoming the generic online catalogue.

There are, of course, the obvious features of an online catalogue—a machine-readable bibliographic database mounted on a computer with a number of terminals providing at least the same searching power and the same points of access as the card catalogue. Most online catalogues go beyond this, however, and include, or intend to include:

- powerful searching capacities including keyword searching and Boolean operators

- links to a circulation system with detailed holdings and status information

- an integrated authority control system with cross-references

- information on titles that are "on-order" or "in-process," either through the integration of files and programs or by linking an automated acquisitions system to the online catalogue

Not all systems now available provide all these functions, but almost all developers of online catalogues are working to include them. If we assume, then, a generic online catalogue providing these functions, it is possible to analyze how such a system can change traditional technical services functions and also to predict how the online catalogue might evolve and add new functions to technical services.

CHANGING TRADITIONAL TECHNICAL SERVICES FUNCTIONS

Change seldom surprises those who are attentive and reflective. Change is usually gradual and, sometimes, in libraries, almost glacial. Although most libraries still do not have online catalogues, enough exist that we may see trends and delineate patterns of change in technical services. An analysis of traditional technical services functions will reveal some of these trends and patterns.

Collection Development and Selection

Although, in many libraries, collection development has become a separate organizational division, its roots are in technical services. Collection development consists of two essential functions — collection analysis and selection. The online catalogue can aid these two functions dramatically. Having the entire collection in a well-indexed computer database can allow collection development officers and subject specialists to generate an almost infinite set of reports on the scope and nature of a library's collection. Other types of reports might analyze the collection by age, type of material, language of publication, and country of publication.[1] These reports can also be generated using OCLC or RLIN tapes, but having an online database permits greater flexibility in generating reports. They can also be updated regularly by making their generation part of the routine maintenance of the system. If the online catalogue is connected to a circulation system, reports can also be generated on those parts of the collection that are used most intensively.

Frequent and intensive analysis of the library's collection, combined with a thorough understanding of the institution's research and instructional needs, can form the foundation for a durable yet elastic collection development policy. Such a policy is the only basis for the other function of collection development — selection. The online catalogue can be an invaluable selection tool for subject specialists because it puts the whole of a library's collection at their fingertips. This is extremely important to branch librarians who otherwise would have to travel to the main card catalogue, or use an infrequently updated microfilm catalogue, or depend upon a central searching staff to verify that a desired item is not already in the collection or "on order." As mentioned above, the online catalogue will be linked to "on-order" and "in-process" files. If these files are current, the subject specialist or selector will be able to determine not only if a title is in the collection, but also if it has been ordered, has been received on approval or blanket order, is at the bindery, or has been claimed, just to name a few possibilities.

Acquisitions

While it is to be hoped that subject specialists will take the time to search a title in an online catalogue before they send an order to acquisitions, acquisitions staff may still be required to search some titles before placing the order. As with selectors, having the collection online along with in-process files will greatly simplify the searching process in acquisitions. Previously, searchers would have to check the catalogue, the on-order file, approval receipts, and possibly serial check-in files. With a well-designed online catalogue, searchers have only one place to look.

There are two approaches to automating acquisitions and incorporating information from an automated acquisitions system into the online catalogue. The first is to integrate fully the acquisitions system and the online catalogue so that both systems run on the same computer using the same set of programs. NOTIS is an example of this approach. The second is to use a separate acquisitions system running on its own computer and set of programs and link this system to the online catalogue so that in-process information is available via the online catalogue. The link usually consists of loading on-order and in-process information into the online catalogue periodically. The Innovacq system from Innovative Interfaces is the most popular such system. The comparative benefits of linking versus integration have been discussed elsewhere.[2] The end result is the same — current information on the status of materials that are in the process of being added to the collection is available through the online catalogue. This includes serial check-in information.

When linking or integration is done well, anyone can determine the status of an item from the time it is ordered. This extends beyond the acquisitions department into the limbo that exists between the point when a book is received in acquisitions and the point when it is catalogued. Most libraries have a backlog of items that have been received but not yet catalogued. Even after an item is catalogued, it may take some time for the catalogue record to appear in the online catalogue. Putting in-process information into the online catalogue provides greater bibliographic control over materials that are not yet catalogued, even if this control is limited to author and title information.

The impact of having in-process information available via the online catalogue has not been fully analyzed. The most obvious benefit, and the one that should always be kept in mind, is that the library's readers have access to more information than they had before. The second benefit is that library staff have more information, thus enabling them to serve the library's readers better.

Cataloguing

Cataloguing today is largely split between copy cataloguing, using the online bibliographic networks OCLC, RLIN, WLN, and UTLAS, and original cataloguing. Some libraries mount the LC MARC tapes on their own system for copy cataloguing or subscribe to a commercial service that provides LC MARC cataloguing on floppy disks or CD-ROM. Copy cataloguing has become a job for paraprofessionals. Professional librarians now concentrate on original cataloguing. The online catalogue alters the way both types of cataloguing are performed.[3] For copy cataloguing, the greatest change is in authority work, as the checking of headings is done when the records are loaded into the online catalogue rather than before the item is catalogued. When records are loaded into the online catalogue, their headings are checked against the authority file that is part of the online catalogue. If an exact match is found, no action is necessary. If the heading matches on a reference, it is flipped to the correct form. If no match is found, the heading can either be printed out or placed into an online file for further verification. Ideally, a library would acquire and mount the full Library of

Congress Authority file and check all incoming headings against it. However, a library may not have the resources needed to mount the full LC file online. Instead, a library might contract with an outside vendor or another library or bibliographic network to run its tapes past the LC authority files before loading them into the online catalogue.

Original cataloguing still must involve authority work before cataloguing to determine the form of headings, although the post-processing matching discussed above serves as a useful second check. Original cataloguing work benefits from the online catalogue because the entire collection is online and integrated with a full authority file, possibly including all available LC authority files. Having the catalogue integrated with the authority file allows the cataloguer to examine the authority record in the context of the catalogue and to see how the library has applied relevant cataloguing rules in the past. Using call number browsing the cataloguer can also determine the classification number and check the shelflist from the same terminal used to consult the authority file.

Catalogue Maintenance

Perhaps the most obvious change that comes with the implementation of an online catalogue is that there are no more cards to file. Instead, bibliographic records are received either on tape (in batches) or electronically (individual records) and loaded into the online catalogue. This should result in a catalogue that is more current and more accurate, because even the most conscientious filer makes mistakes that can bury a card several feet from where it should be filed. Currently, most online catalogues receive their bibliographic records from a tape of current cataloguing generated by one of the bibliographic networks. Some libraries have implemented electronic transfer of records by connecting an OCLC, RLIN, or WLN terminal to the online catalogue, thus transferring records directly.

Catalogue maintenance changes dramatically with the implementation of an online catalogue. Obviously, it is much easier to modify or delete records from an online catalogue because only one physical record is involved as compared to a full card set of seven or eight cards in the card catalog. Also, batch programs can be written to change whole portions of the catalogue. Implementing *AACR2* would have been far more manageable in an online catalogue with an integrated authority file. Theoretically, one master tape for the LC authority file could have been prepared and run against local online catalogues to change the vast majority of headings that needed to be changed.

However, along with the greater maintenance capabilities of the online catalogue comes the fact that cataloguing or typing errors that were inconsequential in the card catalogue become glaring problems in the online catalogue. For example, a human filer could easily recognize that the two headings "Pound, Ezra, 1885-1972" and Pound, Ezra, 1985-1972" refer to the same person and would have either have sent the card with an error to be corrected or, more likely, filed it where it belonged. However, it is impossible given current technology to anticipate all typing errors when loading records into an online catalogue. The result is that any online catalogue will contain significant errors, especially among the more prolific authors and more popular subjects. The only solution is human review of all headings that do not match an existing or verified heading. More sophisticated programming can probably catch many errors and reduce the number of headings that have to be checked. For example, a simple routine could be written to verify that an author's birth date is earlier than his or her death date. However, other errors will creep in that cannot be caught by programs.

Catalogue maintenance staff must also maintain the authority file. The ideal way to do this is to subscribe to the periodic updates issued by the Library of Congress to its authority file. These can be matched against the local online authority file to bring the local file into agreement with the LC file. While the LC file is the best available, it too will contain inconsistencies that must be resolved.

In addition to the online catalogue and authority file, catalogue maintenance staff will have additional tasks after the introduction of an online catalogue. Because the online catalogue is either linked or integrated with other files, including circulation, on-order, in-process, and check-in, all of which will require some reconciliation with the catalogue record, the effort demanded is likely to increase beyond that saved by not having to file cards. For these reasons, staffing in catalogue maintenance will need to grow and might also require a higher level of staffing. A case could be made for putting a professional librarian in charge of an operation that was previously seen as largely clerical.

Summary

The online catalogue can change the traditional technical services functions dramatically. Collection analysis gains access to a broad range of reports, selectors have ready access to the entire collections, acquisitions and in-process files can come out of the back rooms and into the public catalogue, copy cataloguing becomes more efficient as authority work is batched and performed after the act of cataloguing, original cataloguing becomes more efficient because the authority file and shelflist are online and integrated with the catalogue, the addition of records to the catalogue is more current and more accurate, and catalogue maintenance becomes more efficient and also more intensive.

NEW TECHNICAL SERVICES FUNCTIONS

In addition to changing traditional functions, the online catalogue also creates new technical services functions which may more profoundly affect organization and work flow. As the keeper of the online catalogue, technical services will be called upon to assume these new functions, some of which are examined below.

Retrospective Conversion

Converting the entire catalogue to machine-readable form is a task any library contemplating an online catalogue will face. It should only have to be done once. If done well, many problems will be avoided in the future and the lessons learned from the experience will be invaluable in the continuing maintenance of the online catalogue. There are two basic options for retrospective conversion — doing it oneself or contracting with an outside vendor. No matter which way it is done, the library should take care to avoid the common error of using the retrospective conversion project to address other problems such as reclassification or the correction of old cataloguing sins (of omission or commission). The best approach is simply to get the records into machine-readable form so that they can then be manipulated by computer programs.

As part of the conversion, the resulting MARC records should be run against an authority control program to convert old forms to the *AACR2* forms. This can be done by a vendor — Blackwell North America and UTLAS are the most prominent — or it can be done internally if the LC authority file is to be mounted in full.[4] Many incorrect headings can be caught through sophisticated computer processing, but many will slip through and can be cleaned up only by manual correction. Libraries that have prided themselves on their rigorous manual authority control procedures have often been shocked by how dirty their database is revealed to be when converted to machine-readable form. Cleaning the entire database will take years and some judgment must be exercised as to which headings should be tackled first. It might be wise to ensure that the headings for the 100 authors most represented in the database are consistent. It might be even wiser to take a list of faculty and check that their names are treated consistently in the online catalogue.

An advantage of keyword searching is that many variant forms of a heading can be retrieved, for example, "Illinois. University" and "University of Illinois" can both be retrieved with a keyword search on the two words "University" and "Illinois." Ideally, an online catalogue should allow the retrieval of a set of headings and then permit all headings in that set to be changed to the preferred form. In reality, not all systems allow such a "global change" in which case the procedure for editing headings is cumbersome.

Only a small number of libraries have converted all their records to machine-readable form and loaded them into the online catalogue and fewer still, if any, have undertaken a comprehensive project to make all the headings consistent. If any library did complete such a project, it is certain that errors and inconsistencies would begin to creep in with the next set of records added to the database. This is no different from the card catalogue. The difference is that the card catalogue was more forgiving and also buried our worst mistakes where no one would ever find them. The online catalogue is both less tolerant of inconsistencies and capable of retrieving even the most garbled heading through keyword searching.

One might wonder why we should clean up the database if the online catalogue is such a powerful retrieval tool. The answer is obvious to anyone who has ever witnessed the frustration of a library user trying to wade through four screens of various forms of the heading for Mozart.

Enhanced Access

Access points in the card catalogue were restricted to author, title, subject, and a few other headings because it was expensive to produce and file cards and to buy and house catalogue cabinets. Although the online catalogue has some similar restrictions in terms of computing resources, the cost of computer equipment drops every quarter while the cost of labor and materials for the card catalogue rises. Therefore, it is not surprising that the newer online catalogues offer greatly enhanced access, including keyword access to the entire bibliographic record and indexing of fields that were never picked up in the card catalog. The call number provides a little-used point of access that can be expanded and made part of an overlying structure, much as classification theorists have long advocated.[5] Further, there should be no restriction in adding subject headings or, in the future, in including the table of contents or the back of the book index. Technical services will play an important role in determining how the MARC record can be expanded to include new fields.

Remote Access

One of the principal advantages of the online catalog is that it can be used by readers who are not physically in the library. This is usually achieved through dial-up access or through links to a campus computing network. If the online catalogue provides access to the various in-process files, then technical services will enjoy a new visibility as library users begin to request materials in the backlog or at the bindery from remote locations. Meeting these requests graciously may test both patience and fortitude, but it should always be remembered that increased demand upon the library for new services should provide the library administration with solid arguments for increased funding to meet increased demand.

Transaction Monitoring

Unlike the card catalogue, the online catalogue can remember how it has been used. Transaction logs of searches can be prepared that will show the types of search readers perform and even the specific terminology they use. It is possible to capture any search that gets no results and from this determine if the terminology used to index the collection is consistent with the terminology used by the readers. For example, if library patrons continually look for books on the "Strategic Defense Initiative" under the subject "Star Wars" and get no results, then the system will show this and, at the very least, allow the library the opportunity to insert a reference. Another very valuable way to monitor use of the online catalogue is to analyze an individual's session at the terminal. This can be done through a batch report or by direct, simultaneous monitoring of the activity at the terminal. For the designers of a system to watch how real people interpret and respond to that system is both a painful and a beneficial experience. Again, technical services staff need to be involved in the monitoring of the online catalogue so that cataloguing practices can be examined and, if necessary, changed.

Intelligent Workstations

One way to make an online catalogue more responsive to the users, both readers and staff, is to use microcomputers as terminals and provide these microcomputers with interface programs.[6] Programs developed for microcomputers as reader terminals can make the system easier to use and also allow the creation of personalized databases that can be manipulated on the microcomputer thus saving the resources of the central computer. For staff use, microcomputers have been used to make simple functions more convenient and to perform repetitive work.[7]

As microcomputers and personal computers become more powerful, they have even greater potential to assist staff and readers. In technical services, it should be possible to develop an expert system on a microcomputer that would work hand in glove with an individual cataloguer.[8] Such a system would contain the complete current cataloguing code along with local interpretations and would also be able to recall every book the librarian ever catalogued to illustrate how the rules were interpreted. It would be connected to the online catalogue and the bibliographic networks could be consulted on demand. It would also prompt the librarian for information and format and tag the descriptive portion of the catalogue record. Such a system is possible now; however, cataloguers must take an active interest in developing it and keeping it an assistant and not a master.

Additional Files

Library catalogues were originally intended to profile bibliographic access to everything in a library—not just books and journal titles, but also articles in journals, pamphlets in the vertical file, and special collection of photographs, documents, or other material that is no longer included in the main catalogue.[9] One of the most exciting but neglected features of the online catalogue is its ability to contain bibliographic files in addition to the main library catalogue, a step that would allow us to return to an old idea with new vigor. It is certainly in the interest of our readers to have as few places to look as possible and to reduce the obstacles that exist between them and the material they need or desire. To this end, it is possible to mount additional databases on the same computer or the same computer network as the online catalogue and provide access to these databases from the same terminals as the online catalogue. Reducing this a step further, it is preferable that the search routines and commands used to search the online catalogue are the ones used to search these additional databases.

To illustrate, the library user might be presented with a menu listing several files that he or she can search. This menu would list the library catalogue first, followed by, perhaps, a general periodical index, an index to the local newspaper, an index to a collection of photographs in special collections, and other files as permitted by funding, computing resources, and copyright. The reader could select any one of these files or perform a global search of all the files.

As the keeper of the online catalogue, technical services would be heavily involved in acquiring, mounting, and maintaining these additional files.

Gateway

In addition to mounting additional bibliographic files, the online catalogue can be linked to other systems, including databases on other local computers, the online catalogues of other libraries, and commerical and government databases. In each case, the online catalogue can act as a guide enabling the user to gain access to these other databases.

Access to files on other local computers could be gained by linking the online catalogue's computer to other computers through a local telecommunications network. These files might include census data mounted on a computer in the computing center, a list of classes maintained on the campus administrative computer, or even a bibliographic database on a laser disk mounted on a personal computer in the library.

The online catalogues of other libraries could be reached via dial access or dedicated lines if warranted. Without a standard command language for online catalogues, the local online catalogue will have to interpret between the local user and the remote system. Another practical possibility is giving the user the ability to initiate an interlibrary loan request from a terminal. Studies indicate that only when readers are given easy and convenient access to the holdings of other libraries, without having to go through an intermediary, does interlibrary circulation rise to a significant level thus justifying the cost of resource-sharing arrangements.[10]

Access to remote commercial and governmental databases also requires the local online catalogue to guide the reader through the different commands of these other systems. Software now available for microcomputers does an admirable job in establishing search strategies and interpreting results without requiring readers to learn all the various commands required by the remote systems.[11] Dial access can again be used. Further, while it has never been attempted, it might be possible to use the link into the university's accounts receivable system that is currently in place in many automated circulation systems to recover the costs of searching when absolutely necessary.

Given a capacious telecommunications channel and software that can guide the user, the online catalogue can become a gateway to other databases.

Hierarchy of Databases

As discussed above, the online catalogue can be used to mount bibliographic files other than the main catalogue and also to serve as a gateway to outside databases. A possible arrangement or hierarchy of databases would be to mount the main catalogue and the more commonly used indexes and ready reference works on the computer that supports the main online catalogue. These databases would satisfy the majority of requirements. A second level would be satisfied using CD-ROM databases mounted on microcomputers and connected to the same computer network as the online catalogue. This would allow users to query these databases from any terminal that can access the online catalogue. These first two levels should satisfy the great majority of user needs. The third level would be the most specialized and expensive commercial databases the limited use of which would not warrant local acquisition. These could be searched via dial access using the online catalogue as a gateway.

Technical services will be involved in acquiring, mounting, and maintaining the first two levels of this hierarchy. Collection development staff should be involved in selecting which databases will be purchased. Because a physical item, and not just a service, is being acquired, it makes sense to use the acquisitions budget to purchase the databases for the first two levels. It also makes sense for acquisitions to use its considerable purchasing expertise to see that these databases are purchased at the best price. Catalogue maintenance staff would be involved in mounting and updating the databases. Finally, a database as a collection of records should be catalogued and indexed in the main catalogue thus providing a link between the main catalogue and the other databases. Cataloguers are the persons best equipped to develop a record format to establish this link.

Evolution to Full Text

Beyond bibliographic files, it is now possible to mount the full text of some reference materials online. Several libraries have experimented with this, notably the CARL system in Colorado. The idea is intriguing and suggests that the online catalogue could evolve into an online library, a collection of catalogues, indexes, and complete works that can be accessed through a network of terminals. With the online catalogue as the focus for this development, technical services will begin to play a more vital and visible role in the library.

For the near future, it is not likely that online storage and delivery of full text will be available for more than a handful of ready reference works or a select group of scientific journals. However, by using the online catalogue as the vehicle for delivering these works, the library performs a valuable service and prepares itself for the next step in electronic publication, whatever it might be. This approach is not to be advocated merely to ensure the survival of the library as an organization. Rather, it should be advocated because the library alone has the philosophical grounding, the commitment, and the tradition to make new formats of knowledge freely and openly available.

The Online Catalogue and Electronic Publishing

As mentioned before, the online catalogue can be seen to be evolving into an online library with the full text of ready reference works to start and the addition of selected scientific journals in the not-too-distant future. In addition to storing the full text of selected materials, the online catalogue may become the channel for requesting and receiving the full text of a wider range of publications. For example, catalogue records for titles that can be published upon demand might be loaded, much as University Microfilms provides paper copies of dissertations. If a library user finds a title of interest in the online catalogue, he or she could request that it be printed and delivered. Alternatively, he or she might request that a portion of it be retrieved and displayed at a terminal so that he or she can decide the whole publication or part of the publication is wanted, or that it is not wanted at all. It should be possible to provide a printed version of the desired title either on a central printer or on a printer attached to the reader's terminal for a charge that would be comparable to the cost of photocopying an article today and would still provide the publisher with a royalty. Again, the link to accounts payable now in place with many circulation systems could be expanded to handle this billing. Alternatively, the library could purchase the print-out (which it has already catalogued and added to the database), lend it to the reader, and shelve it upon return.

The role of technical services in the above scenario is subtle but important. First, the catalogue record for the title has to be in the database to begin with and, thus, would involve cataloguing and catalogue maintenance. Second, the publisher would have to be paid and this payment would take place through acquisitions. When considering electronic publishing, one is struck by the fact that it has advanced little in the past several years. The technology and the capability are there, but publishers are hesitant to get involved until they see clearly how they will retain their current profits. Only when publishers are convinced that they can make at least the same amount of money with electronic publishing as with print publishing will they really move on this front. Logically, they will look to those channels that now bring them substantial revenues. In the library market, these are book dealers, periodical agencies, and library acquisitions departments. Therefore, acquisitions has a role to play in bringing electronic publishing into the academic library. Anyone who doubts this should simply compare the budget for online searching (the other candidate for the conduit for electronic publishing) to the acquisitions budget in any academic library.

Changes in Staffing and Organization

Several changes in staffing patterns for technical services resulting from the online catalogue were mentioned previously—increased use of paraprofessionals in original cataloguing, and the need for greater professional supervision in catalogue maintenance as the online catalogue evolves and becomes more complex. Other changes can be perceived as well. Nonprofessional staff in technical services will become less clerical and more paraprofessional in all functions as the clerical jobs of typing and filing continue to disappear. With the transfer of the functions of the shelflist and the authority file into the online catalogue, there is less need for technical services to be located in the main library.[12] Another possibility that has not been pursued is that all of technical services could be moved to a remote site thus freeing up valuable reader space in the main library. While this might tend to isolate technical services staff, space could be designed specifically to meet the needs of a modern technical services division, rather than attempting to force computers and terminals into old and inadequately wired buildings.

While an apparent shortage of original cataloguers has been mentioned in the literature there is another possible shortage looming—one of trained acquisitions librarians.[13] Very few entry-level positions have been advertised recently and many acquisitions departments have only one or two professionals. If acquisitions is to play a role in the delivery of electronic publications, younger librarians should be recruited and trained in this field.

CONCLUSION

The online catalogue should be viewed as the focus of change in the library. It is expanding both in terms of what it contains and in terms of how it is used. More information—that is, information not previously contained in the card catalogue—will be added to the online catalogue. Simultaneously, users will be able to use the online catalogue in their dormitories, offices, and homes. Increased coverage coupled with increased access will almost certainly result in increased demand. If handled wisely, this growing demand can be translated into burgeoning support for the library.

The online catalogue as the focus of change will give technical services a higher profile in the library and in the campus community. How technical services handles the limelight will, in many ways, determine how the services provided by the online catalogue are received and used. If we fall back on the stereotype of technical services librarians as back-room technocrats with little interest in the library user, then technical services, the library, the greater interests of our profession, and most importantly, the interest of our users and our society will suffer. I doubt very much that this will happen. Instead, technical services librarians will seize the opportunity to demonstrate what we have always known to be true, that we are motivated first and foremost by a desire to serve — by acquiring, organizing, and maintaining a treasure house of knowledge, using all the tools and techniques to which we can lay claim.

NOTES

[1]Payson, Evelyn and Barbara Moore. Statistical collection management analysis of OCLC-MARC tape records. *Information technology and libraries* 4:220-232 (Sept. 1985)

[2]Potter, William Gray. Linking LCS and FBR: the library's perspective. *Information technology and libraries* 4:311-315 (Dec. 1985); Malinconico, S. Michael. Integrated online library systems — alternatives. *In* Conference on integrated library systems proceedings/ ed. by David C. Genaway. Canfield, OH: Genaway and Associates Inc., 1987. pp. 71-102

[3]Hudson, Judith. Cataloging for the local online system. *Information technology and libraries* 5:7-27 (Mar. 1986)

[4]Miller, Dan. Authority control in the retrospective conversion process. *Information technology and libraries* 3:286-292 (Sept. 1984); Logan, Susan J. The Ohio State University's Library control system: from circulation to subject access and authority control. *Library trends* 35:538-556 (Spring 1987)

[5]Cochrane, Pauline Atherton. Redesign of catalogs and indexes for improved online subject access. Phoenix, AZ: Oryx Press, 1985

[6]Cheng, Chin-Chuang. Microcomputer based user interface. *Information technology and libraries* 4:346-351 (Dec. 1985)

[7]Special Section: the IBM PC as a terminal. *Information technology and libraries* 3:47-68 (Mar. 1984); Drueke, John. LCS shelflist maintenance using an OCLC M300. *Information technology and libraries* 5:133-135 (June 1986)

[8]Davies, Roy and Brian James. Towards an expert system for cataloguing: some experiments based on AACR2. *Program* 18:283-297 (Oct. 1984)

[9]Atkinson, Hugh C. The electronic catalog. *In* The nature and future of the catalog/ ed. by Maurice J. Freedman and S. Michael Malinconico. Phoenix, AZ: Oryx Press, 1979. p. 105

[10]Potter, William Gray. Creative automation boosts interlibrary loan rates. *American libraries* 17:244-246 (Apr. 1986)

[11]Tenopir, Carol. Software for online searching. *Library journal* 110:52-53 (Oct. 15, 1985); Brunning, Dennis R. and Doug Stewart. Review of Searcher's tool kit. *Information technology and libraries* 5:363-366 (Dec. 1986)

[12]Gorman, Michael. The future of serials control and its administrative implications for libraries. *In* Serials automation for acquisition and inventory control/ ed. by William Gray Potter and Arlene Farber Sirkin. Chicago: American Library Association, 1981. pp. 120-133

[13]Hill, Janet Swan. Wanted: good catalogers. *American libraries* 16:728-731 (Nov. 1985)

Administration of Technical Services

TECHNICAL SERVICES ORGANIZATION:
Where We Have Been and Where We Are Going

JENNIFER A. YOUNGER and D. KAYE GAPEN

Technical services divisions, with their large concentrations of staff, constitute a major segment of the infrastructure of libraries. Unlike this nation's highways and bridges, however, this infrastructure is not crumbling. On the contrary, there has been a great deal of productive turmoil and change as technical services staff examine, initiate, and respond to the environmental, technological, and societal forces influencing libraries today.

As a measure of survival, review articles are at once highly selective and heuristic, or, alternatively, seemingly interminable. The intent of this chapter is modest yet complex. That is, we propose a brief review of three principles used to establish technical services divisions in libraries together with a look at contemporary use of these principles to set new organizational patterns. Further, we propose to look at how these principles might be used in the future as we look toward technical services functions in the context of a new paradigm of library services. In conclusion, we offer one view of technical services in the year 2001.

HISTORICAL BACKGROUND

Around the turn of the century, libraries were organized into departments with each department responsible for a primary function: acquisitions, cataloguing, reference, and circulation. As the number and size of departments grew, so did the need for a new structure which would reduce the number of people reporting directly to the chief librarian. The divisional structure was developed so that department heads would report to divisional directors, who in turn would report to the chief librarian.

Two basic alternatives emerged for combining departments into divisions.[1] The functional approach considered all activities as either technical services (acquisitions and cataloguing) or public services (reference and circulation) and grouped them accordingly into two divisions. Alternatively, the subject approach called for all activities to be grouped on the basis of subjects. The subject divisional plan brought together library departments by disciplinary groupings with each subject division responsible for all functions.[2] However, even when the subject-oriented plans were adopted, a trend persisted toward placing acquisitions and cataloguing functions in a separate division.[3]

Whether there was a natural affinity between acquisitions and cataloguing was questioned by some. Strong arguments were made by Swank that the organization of books for use is a single library function shared by cataloguers and bibliographers, not cataloguers and acquisition librarians.[4] However, at that time, reference services were in their infancy.[5] As a separate function, subject bibliography had little or no staff, thereby there was nothing to which cataloguers could be joined. The similarities between the acquisitions and cataloguing processing routines and the desire for closer coordination, therefore, became the basis on which those departments were linked together.[6] In 1956, when the American Library Association was reorganized, the acquisition and catalogue librarians voted to join in a single division in ALA, the Resources and Technical Services Division (beginning in 1989, the Association for Library Collections and Technical Services), thus recognizing and cementing an affiliation of their functions.

The advantages inherent in the functional approach included economies of scale with regard to use of resources, the ability to develop specialized knowledge in acquisitions and cataloguing, and the coordination of the work flow between the two departments. These three advantages were sufficiently important that, once established, technical services divisions not only survived, but flourished.

CONTEMPORARY INFLUENCES

The factors influencing technical services are numerous and diverse, ranging from the increase in numbers and complexities of published materials, computerization as seen in the growth of bibliographic networks and local systems, library standards, cycles of expansion and contraction of library funding, and the search for professionalism. That each of these has affected technical services is without question, and from that perspective, our purpose is to examine the ideas underlying the resultant changes brought about in technical services organization and staffing patterns.

Organizationally, the changes fall into one broad category, and that is the development of new departments or units to handle new formats, subjects, languages or activities (e.g., copy cataloguing). In this discussion, the organizational changes are seen to result from new approaches, considerations, and methods of implementing the ideas as they were initially used to establish technical services divisions: development and use of specialized knowledge, economies of scale, and coordination.

Specialized Knowledge and New Departments

The rapid growth in scholarly and trade publishing together with expanded library acquisitions programs resulted in a rapid increase in the quantity as well as the diversity of library acquisitions. To handle the new acquisitions, additional specialized knowledge was required. For example, government documents are published and distributed through channels different from the usual trade publication channels. Acquiring books from other countries presented a unique set of requirements, often related to language but just as often related to the manner in which the country's publishing industry functioned or the traditions of bibliographic control. Subject analysis of materials in non-Roman alphabets or complex subjects required a singular knowledge of those languages and subjects, another call for specialized expertise.

A common response was the establishment of separate technical services units to handle materials as they were distinguished by language, subject, or format characteristics (e.g., East Asian, music, or government documents units). The establishment of the new departments continued the basic functional approach of grouping acquisitions and cataloguing together while at the same time recognizing the dual knowledge base of function and subject/language/format. Based on the primary advantage of the functional approach, which is that it fosters the creation and use of specialized knowledge in acquisitions and cataloguing, this arrangement worked very well. Problem-solving activities took place easily within the boundaries of the department and the interaction of specialists led to efficient processing.

Economies of Scale and New Departments

At the same time, the establishment of new departments in technical services recognized the importance of economies of scale. Central departments were still able to share expensive resources, including order and cataloguing processing files which are expensive to create as well as to maintain. With the purchase of terminals and online access to bibliographic networks, centralized copy cataloguing departments offer, in similar fashion, efficient use of expensive equipment. The downward trend in terminal costs as well as the multi-tasking terminal of the future may shift the balance so that smaller, distributed technical services departments are more practical.

Coordination of Work Flow and New Departments

Coordination of the work flow between departments was, and is, an important issue,[7] so much so that presently the concerns about coordinating work flow are becoming the basis on which departments are organized. Work generally flowed sequentially from acquisitions to cataloguing to binding, and from there to the shelves with the coordination achieved through the department heads and the division director. Based on the knowledge that communication and mutual adjustment, which are so often the basis of coordination, are strongest within departments, new departments are formed to handle both functions.

Serials create complex work flows because the work is reciprocally interdependent, that is, the work flows back and forth between acquisitions and cataloguing as the serials change titles or other parts. The end result is a more complex coordination task. To make that task easier, serial departments were created for the purpose of integrating all operations into a single work flow. In some libraries, the serials department also manages the public services aspects (e.g., the periodicals room), with more successful service as the end result.[8]

Integrated local systems for acquisitions and cataloguing have prompted similar transformations, that is, a change from a departmental organization based solely on function to one based on work-flow integration and coordination for monographs as well.[9] Records and transactions for acquisitions and cataloguing (and, in some systems, circulation) are kept in the same online file. This opens the door to blending the operations, for example, when an item is received it is possible to record its receipt, pay for it, and complete the cataloguing as part of the same set of procedures.

Based on this idea, a fundamental reordering of technical services combined the operations for acquisitions and cataloguing into departments organized by broad disciplinary groupings (e.g., sciences and social sciences) that form the basis of the library as a whole.[10] In this arrangement, each technical services department acquires, catalogues, and processes all materials in all formats relating to the specific disciplinary grouping. Coordination is made easier on two fronts: within the department and between the "TS" departments and the libraries for which it is processing the materials. A new level of responsiveness to the needs of these libraries is achieved through better communication and a closer working relationship. Such reorganizations are not universal. Less radical reorganizations have maintained the basic functions in acquisitions and cataloguing.[11] Some reorganizations are shifting responsibilities between existing departments; for example, preorder searching and creation of the bibliographic record for ordering purposes was moved from the acquisitions department to the cataloguing department.[12] A decision to continue separate departments for acquisitions and cataloguing emphasizes the uniqueness of each function while a decision to combine the functions into one department focuses on coordinating the work flow.

Coordination, Not Direction, of Technical Services

The reorganizations mentioned above were carried out within the context of a technical services division in which the departments continue to report to a technical services director. Conventional wisdom has strongly advised that a strong, impartial division administrator was necessary for coordination.[13] However, both research and practical experimentation challenge that belief.

A landmark study carried out in the early 1950s examined the ways in which coordination between acquisitions and cataloguing had been effected with the establishment of a technical services division.[14] Coordination in broad terms was examined within technical services, between technical services and public service departments, and between cataloguing and the use of such tools as printed reference indexes. Overall, although there were slight differences in how libraries with formal technical services divisions and those without such divisions exploited various means of coordination, there was not much difference in the results. The project concluded that a technical service division was not necessary for effective coordination of acquisitions and cataloguing, an important conclusion in today's environment.

With that major exception, the literature is quiet on the advantages of coordinating, not directing, technical services. A report of one current experiment suggests that a technical services coordinator can successfully oversee the flow of work through acquisitions and cataloguing.[15] The line responsibilities of a technical services director are assigned to another director with the coordinator retaining responsibility for coordinating the work flow. A variant means of coordination is used when acquisitions and cataloguing functions are combined into one department, coordination to a greater extent through mutual adjustment. The department head is then responsible for coordinating work flows between the department and the libraries for which it is processing materials.

In the absence of a technical services director, the department head may be reporting to the same person as the heads of the smaller libraries, bringing us full circle to the situation at the beginning of the century. That is, department heads for the various functions reporting to the same person with the coordination of activities taking place in that group. In light of the criticisms that follow on the present organization of libraries, the idea of integrating technical services organizationally with other library departments offers interesting possibilities.

CRITICISMS OF THE TECHNICAL SERVICES DIVISION CONCEPT

Since the division of library operations into technical and public services, the criticisms have mounted with regard to the shortcomings of this functional bifurcation. Budget constraints and the introduction of technological innovations present only the most recent challenges to the traditional division between technical and public services.[16] A fundamental criticism concerns the organizational emphasis. The functional structure puts the focus on processing materials instead of providing service to users.[17] As previously mentioned there were advantages gained by the functional approach, efficient processing being one of them. Nevertheless, as the criticism implies, it was all too easy for processing departments to become the heart and soul of library operations with, as Hickey suggested, the library users taking a secondary role. The organization of libraries by function does not adequately direct the expert and diverse knowledge of librarians in support of the complex and sophisticated demands of users. The organization of professional expertise should be related to meeting the needs of library users rather than the size of the library or the function to be done.

There is a second aspect to the misplaced focus. Functionally oriented departments set their own goals relative to their specific activities. When an entire department is focused on creating the best possible cataloguing records, then there is correspondingly less formal emphasis on meeting users' needs. While the motivation is honorable, because cataloguing records support user services, nevertheless the overall focus has ever so slightly moved away from the users. Among library staff, the different orientations toward processing and users respectively have led to misunderstandings and poor communication between technical services and public services.[18]

Another criticism extends the concern over the misplaced organizational focus to a concern with the underuse of professional expertise. Specialization in cataloguing or reference has placed limitations on how the expertise can be used with the result being that neither category of librarians has been allowed to reach full efficiency.[19] An example illustrates that point. Subject cataloguers have extensive knowledge in particular subjects but no responsibilities for reference, therefore their knowledge is inaccessible to users.

Brief Review of Advantages and Disadvantages

The advantages and disadvantages of organizing the library by function are opposite in nature. Centralized acquisitions and cataloguing departments have led to efficient operations which, as is to be expected, reflect priorities based in part on their activities and in part on the priorities of other library departments. The criticisms suggest there is too much attention directed toward library processing activities with insufficient focus and attention on meeting users' needs. The development of specialized expertise in acquisitions and cataloguing meant high-quality work and effective problem solving in those departments, but at the same time that same professional expertise was underused because it was inaccessible to users. The separation of technical and public services has created a structure that is not as responsive as it could be to user needs or technological innovations especially under conditions of restricted budgets.

A SECOND PARADIGM SHIFT
IS ON THE WAY

While we have discussed all of the above and talked about how libraries can cope, it is still within the present paradigm — our established methods for viewing and defining and acting within the library. The context of a new paradigm — a new view of the context, assumptions, and patterns within which libraries exist — is necessary. Also, not only is it necessary for us to consider and become comfortable with a paradigm shift which we cannot control, it is equally important for us as library staff members and managers to take advantage of continuing research into the psychology of groups and corporate cultures.

Either the paradigm shift or a sense of awareness of a new psychology of social change would cause us to review the assumptions that have framed our past discussions of the organization of a major unit such as technical services. The fact that we are facing both at the same time makes it doubly important that we explore the nature of the paradigm shift we are facing and its impact on libraries and their organization.

Social Psychology and Group Dynamics

A review of current research and writing in the areas of social psychology, group dynamics, and business management reveals a different dimension within which to frame the questions that have surrounded the organization of technical services in the past. As we look to the past, we might well conclude, for example, that the discussion of the tradeoffs between function and subject of materials as an organizational focus spoke to only one layer of the many layers that make up an organizational approach. We can view the question from another dimension, asking, "Should we be efficient or should we be effective?" Such a different dimensional question enables us to extend our focus beyond the short-term questions of efficiency to the longer-term issues related to effectiveness.

Beginning to consider effectiveness opens the door to consideration of ultimate goals. The consideration of ultimate goals then leads to the consideration of the values upon which the members of the corporate culture of technical services as well as the library base their thoughts, actions, and decisions.

What a different set of issues and questions from those described in the historical part of this paper! The stream-of-consciousness linkages from efficiency to effectiveness to ultimate goals to values to decision-making processes leads us to consider the capabilities of people rather than the capabilities of processes and technologies. This is not to say that efficient processes and powerful technologies do not offer benefits to the library. Far from it, since we know today the tremendous impact of technology on all parts of society, including libraries. Nevertheless, today's research into the individual as part of a formal or informal group gives new insights into the corporate culture formed by people rather than a culture formed initially by a technology or a process.

Once we focus on people, our consideration of alternatives becomes increasingly complicated just as people are complicated. However, the potential is greater for dealing with one of the most serious challenges facing librarians today: Are we useful? Will we be useful in the future? Can we change if we must in order to be useful in the future? Being useful relates not only to process but also to the roots of process such as motivation, decision making, creativity, leadership, assumptions and values, skills, knowledge, and abilities. If we begin, thus, sorting out the people issues, such as how best to use the specialized knowledge of all library staff and the role of subject specialists as well as generalists, it will then be easier to consider questions relating to coordination and economies of scale.

Changing Paradigms of Library Services

Before discussing technical services organization and the people issues relating to technical services, it is useful to review the context in which these activities take place. New developments in electronic publishing, copyright and the protection of intellectual property, the explosion of online information sources, and the technological capabilities with which the information can be downloaded or printed for users are almost daily creating new opportunities for connecting users and information.[20]

Collections are simultaneously the bedrock of libraries and the winds of change. The paradigmatic shift summarized in the phrase *ownership to access* has been made real through the implementation of resource-sharing activities but is undeveloped in theory. New theories in collection development will expand to include the concept of temporary collections as well as permanent collections. New theories will be based on several methods of creating collections, purchasing materials, borrowing materials, or purchasing the right to on-demand access of materials. As the availability of materials increases, subject bibliography in the form of selective guides to materials on a subject — relating them not to a library collection but rather to materials accessible by specific users — assumes a new level of importance.

Information in electronic formats is leading to a library without walls, a library that has as its resources all those information sources that can be found and gotten with no regard for physical location. Negotiating the maze of available information sources, however, is not an easy process and users require assistance in this process.[21] Schlachter underscores the need for services that help users in learning of the existence of information useful to them, in devising appropriate search strategies, and in negotiating their way through the process of obtaining the desired information.[22] A new era is beginning, one in which libraries are characterized by a renewed focus on users and the provision of mediated services to meet their needs.

In this environment, technical services activities will not disappear — quite the contrary, although today it is a reasonable assumption that the technical services division will not exist as it does today. As recently as 1970, the process of acquisitions or cataloguing was still a recommended basis for departmental organization.[23] The confluence of events since then has conspired in favor of change.

TECHNICAL SERVICES IN THE YEAR 2001

The year 2001! We selected that year not only for its futuristic ring but also for a practical reason. The decade of the 1990s will set far-reaching changes into motion, that will in turn require some time for organizational adjustments to be made. With the emphasis on services to users, libraries will continue in the direction of organizing library departments around identifiable and specific groups of users. The organizational literature refers to this as the *market* approach.[24] Library services literature labels this the *client-centered* approach.[25] The organizational focus of both is on identifying the characteristics and meeting the needs of the user.

In its formal exposition, the client-centered model groups all professional activities together, including reference, online searching, collection development, and cataloguing, in a departmental organization based on specific groups of users. Examples of specific groups are children, undergraduates, and people interested in geology or music. In this way, the values and goals of the library are firmly centered on determining and meeting the needs of users.

With regard to technical services operations, the central question is how to organize these operations to support the user-oriented library departments. What balance can be reached between effectiveness and efficiency? This calls first for a consideration of the capabilities of people and their specialized knowledge, and second, matters relating to coordination and economies of scale. We foresee the following kinds of changes in technical services: (1) original cataloguing will become part of "public services"; (2) technical services departments will be organized on the same basis as the other library departments and libraries, that is, in user- or subject-based groupings; (3) technical services departments, where size permits, will be decentralized and administratively joined to other library departments; and (4) technical services will increasingly depend on the use of coordinators to provide technical expertise and to coordinate policy development in specific functions (e.g., acquisitions and cataloguing).

Original Cataloguing Becomes Part of Public Services

First, the migration of original cataloguing from a technical services environment to public services will continue a trend already begun. There are several reasons why this trend will accelerate, beginning with the truism that people are the most important resource. In libraries in which cataloguing and reference services are integrated as a dual set of responsibilities, the reports on the use of professional expertise state that not only does this arrangement allow cataloguers to use their expertise in public services[26] but also that a knowledge of collection use enhances cataloguing.[27] Many years ago, Swank made that same point. Grouping cataloguers with acquisitions isolates cataloguers from a direct knowledge of users' needs and discourages them from developing a true interlibrary approach to problems relating to the organization of books for use.[28]

A regrouping of services around specific groups of users and subject knowledge brings together the people who are collectively responsible for providing those library services. New patterns of interaction can be expected to create not simply new solutions to existing problems but also, and perhaps more importantly, to create new questions, opportunities, and services. The mutually informing aspects of collection development, reference, and cataloguing work together to produce a whole that is greater than the sum of the parts.

The last reason in support of this trend is the recognition it gives to the priorities of the knowledge bases respectively of subject areas and library functions. Although in-depth knowledge of users and subjects is widely seen as important, the formal organization by subject or users reaffirms these priorities and leads to the optimal use of professional expertise.

Technical Services in a User- or Subject-Oriented Department

In order to support user-oriented library services, technical services will be organized in departments paralleling the organization of other library departments. That is, the functions and operations of acquisitions, copy cataloguing, serials, binding, and circulation — all processes that handle material designated for the library's collections — will be integrated and carried out within the confines of a single department. If the resulting department is considered too large, further subdivision will occur on the basis of specific groups of libraries, not by library function.

Several ideas furnish the basis for this change in organization. Interdepartmental cooperation and coordination, meaning the interactions between the technical and public services departments, will be enhanced for two reasons. First, both departments aim to identify and meet the needs of the same set of users. That common ground serves to enhance their working relationship as they are working toward similar goals and objectives.

In addition, a technical services department set up to work with specific libraries and to perform all of the responsibilities will have the means within itself to be responsive to those libraries. The department can adjust priorities and assignments to meet cyclical needs (e.g., ordering at the end of the fiscal year) as well as to be responsive to unique requirements generated by that particular group of libraries and users (e.g., additional subject headings).

Within the technical services department, the coordination of the work flow will be significantly easier to integrate and to manage. Close proximity allows individuals to work out mutually satisfactory arrangements with regard to solving problems and work flow. As is often mentioned with regard to serials, acquisitions and cataloguing work are so intertwined as to be inseparable, and when both activities are handled in the same department, there is no need to spend time separating the problems.

In most libraries, order, cataloguing, volume holdings, and circulation records are or will soon be online. The optimal use of local online integrated systems rests on a knowledge of how the system fits together so that the person entering notes into ιn order record knows how that will or will not affect the subsequent check-in of new volumes. Specialized knowledge unique to each function is still required but the fact of an integrated department can easily incorporate this specialized knowledge within its boundaries.

Decentralized Technical Services

A technical services division is a useful—but not required—component of the organizational structure. Presently technical services departments have three roles: carrying out the technical services activities, coordinating the technical services work flow, and providing the technical expertise for technical service departments.

However, libraries may find it advantageous to decentralize the departments further. Just as the purpose of organizing technical services departments into user-oriented groups is designed to foster development of similar goals and cooperation between technical and public services, decentralizing further enhances this cooperation by placing the departments together under the same administrator. Acquisitions and cataloguing were initially grouped to foster coordination; the intent here is similar but in addition to work flow coordination a primary purpose is the integration of goals and objectives around user needs.

Economies of scale remain a consideration. Card files have given way to concerns about how to make the maximum use of terminals to give access to local systems as well as the bibliographic networks. Where the costs of terminals make physical centralization desirable, it may be coupled with administrative decentralization. That is, the technical services departments may be located in one physical area but administratively be a part not of a technical services division but of the other libraries with which they work.

Technical Services Coordinators

When technical services departments are integrated, the use of functional specialists to provide technical expertise and to coordinate policy development in specific functions will increase. Present acquisitions or cataloguing department heads, for example, generally serve as technical experts in addition to working with other department heads on coordination. The situation will be reversed in that department heads will work with public services to set priorities and coordinate work flows within the department. Other functional specialists (i.e., coordinators) are necessary to provide specific functional expertise for all departments. This kind of situation has been anticipated by some in considering the future of cataloguers and in suggesting that both subject and functional specialists are needed.[29]

The matrix approach provides significant flexibility in structuring the use of coordinators. Coordinators have specific assignments to provide expertise and to coordinate policies across library departments, thus taking into account distinctive conditions yet providing an overall consistent approach to creating and recording technical services transactions. Shared data and online systems in particular depend on the proper interpretation and use of library standards.

In considering the use of acquisitions, cataloguing, or circulation coordinators, parallels can be found in public services. Bibliographic instruction and online searching are two activities performed in many library departments with overall coordination provided through a coordinator position. The number of these kinds of positions suggests it works very satisfactorily.

CONCLUSION

It is our belief that the 1990s will be a decade of productive change in technical services, resulting in a new order, alternatively characterized as disorder by some. A reconceptualization of the library organization that will not only provide library services but do so with an emphasis on interactions with users, often in the form of mediated services, will produce stress, new levels of unleashed creativity, and new decisions. The functions traditionally handled by technical services staff will remain a vital part of library operations and will be organizationally integrated with the whole of library services.

NOTES

[1]Dunlap, C. R. Organizational patterns in academic libraries. *College and research libraries* 37:397 (1976)

[2]Lundy, F. A. The divisional plan library. *College and research libraries* 17:143-148 (1956)

[3]Coney, D. Administration of technical processes. *In* Current issues in library administration/ ed. by C. B. Joeckel. Chicago: University of Chicago Press, 1939. pp. 163-180

[4]Swank, R. C. The catalog department in the library organization. *Library quarterly* 18:28 (1948)

⁵Rothstein, S. The development of reference services through academic traditions, public library practice, and special librarianship. (ACRL monograph; 14) Chicago: ACRL, 1955

⁶Colburn, E. B. The value to a modern library of a technical services department. *College and research libraries* 11:47-53 (1950)

⁷Colburn. *Op. cit.*; Hershey, J. The impact of the implementation of NOTIS on the technical services workflow at ... Johns Hopkins University. *Cataloging and classification quarterly* 9:26 (1988)

⁸Collver, M. Organization of serials work for manual and automated systems. *Library resources and technical services* 24:307-316 (1980)

⁹Henn, B. and R. Sellberg. Midway to automation. *Technical services quarterly* 4:21-32 (1987)

¹⁰Gapen, D. K. Transition and change: technical services at the center. *Library resources and technical services* 33:285-296 (1989); Younger, J. A. The process of technical services reorganization at the University of Wisconsin-Madison. Speech delivered at the ALA Annual Conference, June 24, 1989, Dallas

¹¹Niles, J. Technical services reorganization for an online integrated environment. *Cataloging and classification quarterly* 9:11-17 (1988)

¹²Lambrecht, J. A case for pre-order searching in the catalog department. *Cataloging and classification quarterly* 9:27-34 (1988)

¹³Tuttle, H. W. Coordination of the technical services. *In* Advances in librarianship. Vol. 5/ ed. by M. J. Voigt. New York: Academic Press, 1974. p. 132

¹⁴Schachtman, B. E. Technical services: policy, organization, and coordination. *Cataloging and classification* 11:59-111 (1955)

¹⁵Gleason, M. L. and R. C. Miller. Technical services: direction or coordination? *Technical services quarterly* 4:17 (1987)

¹⁶Altmann, A. E. The academic library of tomorrow: who will do what? *Canadian library journal* 45:147-152 (1988); Shaughnessy, T. W. Technology and the structure of libraries. *Libri* 32:149-155 (1982)

¹⁷Hickey, D. Public and technical library services: a revised relationship. *In* Essays for Ralph Shaw/ ed. by N. Stevens. Metuchen, N.J.: Scarecrow Press, 1975

[18]Bluh, P. Truce or consequences. *Technical services quarterly* 3:25-30 (1984)

[19]Gorman, Michael. Technical services in an automated library. *In* The role of the library in an electronic society (Clinic on Library Applications of Data Processing; 1979)/ ed. by F. W. Lancaster. Urbana: University of Illinois, 1980

[20]Aveney, B. Electronic publishing and library technical services. *Library resources and technical services* 28:68-75 (1984); Brownrigg, E. *et al.* Technical services in the age of electronic publishing. *Library resources and technical services* 28:59-67 (1984)

[21]Webb, W. H. Collection development for the university and large research library. *In* Academic libraries by the year 2000/ ed. by H. Poole. New York: R. R. Bowker, 1977. pp. 139-151

[22]Schlachter, G. The service imperative for libraries. Littleton, CO: Libraries Unlimited, 1982

[23]Auld, L. Functional organization plan for technical services. *Library resources and technical services* 14:458-462 (1970)

[24]Mintzberg, H. The structuring of organizations. Englewood Cliffs, N.J.: Prentice-Hall, 1979

[25]Martell, C. The client-centered academic library. Westport, CT: Greenwood, 1983

[26]McBride, R. The past, present, and future of a cataloguer. *Technical services quarterly* 1:138-141 (1983)

[27]Thompson, A. F. Music cataloging in academic libraries and the case for physical decentralization. *Journal of academic librarianship* 12:79-83 (1986)

[28]Swank. *Op. cit.*

[29]Holley, R. P. The future of catalogers and cataloging. *Journal of academic librarianship* 7:90-93 (1981); Abell, M. D. and J. M. Coolman. Professionalism and productivity. *In* Priorities for academic libraries/ ed. by T. J. Galvin. San Francisco: Jossey-Bass, 1982. pp. 71-87

TECHNICAL SERVICES
BUDGETING AND FINANCE

SUSAN F. RHEE

Most libraries, like their parent institutions, whether those be cities, universities, other types of nonprofit agencies, or private corporations, are faced with the dual dilemmas of constrained funding and increasing demands for service. The relative scarcity of resources with which to accomplish desired goals and carry out high-priority service programs requires that libraries plan effectively and use the resources available to them as efficiently as possible. Because funds are short, decisions about their allocation have become at once more important and more difficult. The budget itself and the process used to formulate it are among the library administrator's most valuable management tools because they can be used to establish, document, and communicate the library's service priorities, plan its programs, fund them, and monitor or evaluate the extent to which each program and the library as a whole have met their planned goals.

This chapter will discuss basic budgeting and finance concepts and techniques that pertain to technical services as well as in the library as a whole. It will focus on operational budgeting, or how to allocate and spend a budget appropriation. It will not address the processes by which a library might seek appropriations (or increased appropriations) from its parent body or other funding source, such as a legislature; nor will it provide detailed managerial or financial accounting concepts necessary to the budgetary process. It will summarize some of the trends in the budgeting and finance of libraries and technical service functions in libraries.

THE PURPOSE OF, AND NEED FOR, A BUDGET

The budget of the library represents a financial plan designed to carry out an operational plan. Therefore, before the budget can be formulated and implemented, the library must establish its overall goals and objectives, and decide how it will measure its success in meeting those goals. For technical service departments, these performance measures might include such things as expenditure of materials budgets within a given period of time, acquisition of a given number of new titles and/or volumes per year, cataloguing of new acquisitions within the year acquired, or checking in of new serial issues within a certain period after receipt. Formulation of an operating plan for the library as a whole and for the technical service programs within it guides the technical services administrator in suballocating the budget to the appropriate operations, functions, or departments. The operational budget should support the performance expectations of the operating plan. It expresses financially how technical services will reach its goals, and indicates which departments or other organizational units will be responsible for the particular operations which will lead to success.

Not only does the budget allocation express organizational goals formulated at the beginning of the budget year, it also serves as a benchmark of success during the year. For example, the actual performance of the individual units responsible for executing parts of the program, and of technical services as a whole, should be measured regularly and monitored to ensure that both the operational plan and the budget plan are being implemented smoothly and synchronized with one another. The budget may need to be modified or reallocated periodically to ensure that the performance goals it supports are being met, or to accommodate changes to the operational plan.

Most managers understand the usefulness of a budget during times of fiscal crisis or straitened resources, because it helps them to reduce funding to programs in an orderly way, congruent with the desire to maintain the library's most important programs. In general, when budgets are declining, across-the-board percentage cuts in department or units are not the most effective course of action for an administrator. Instead, each operation and program as well as the programs of the library as a whole should be reviewed and have priorities assigned so that funds can be reallocated internally to maximize the number and quality of services provided, minimize the retrenchments in the programs of highest priority, and maintain a reasonable balance among all service programs. In technical services this strategy might mean, for example, protecting funding for development of an automated system during its formative years even if that protection were to occur at the expense of current cataloguing. The rationale for such a strategy might be that automation, in the long run, would increase productivity among technical services staff so that backlogs of cataloguing that accumulated during lean budget years could be eradicated, and resources eventually reallocated to other programs (e.g., public service or preservation) once the funding and automation programs are stabilized.

Effective budgeting is equally important during times of funding growth to ensure that new programs or expansions to existing programs are carried out as efficiently as possible and that a full range of expansionary programs is considered. During eras of steady-state funding, the budget can be used gradually to redirect the library's priorities in order to build up new programs, or to maintain a steady course. In any case, a carefully prepared budget ensures that well-defined performance goals are met as cost-effectively as possible, and that adequate consideration is given to alternative programs and expenditure patterns.

The budget can provide an objective basis for program development, for assessing alternative uses of available funds, and for predicting the effects of reductions or augmentations to funds. It can indicate areas of under- or over-funding of particular programs, serve as a managerial tool to guide service priorities and programs, and enable the manager to demonstrate accountability to higher-level administrators or to funding agencies. When the planning and budgeting processes involve a wide spectrum of managers and staff, they also assist the development of a common understanding of library-wide goals and problems.

Most operations in a library are interrelated, and the budget of one function or program cannot be reduced significantly without affecting the workload or effectiveness of other operations. There are relatively fixed costs essential to the library's mission, and it is difficult to reduce these below a certain basic level, even when budgets are cut severely. For example, acquisition staffing levels must be adequate to catalogue materials received, and binding funds must be adequate to keep serials in usable condition. Almost all library costs can be placed in one of four categories: personnel, collections, other operating expenses incurred to support the staff's operations and the library's programs, and capital costs of buildings and equipment. The library manager should know how much funding is absolutely required in each category in each functional area in order for the library to operate at a minimal level and how much of the given budget is discretionary and therefore available for redirection to new programs or expansion of existing programs.

TYPES OF BUDGETS AND BUDGETING SYSTEMS

The *legislative budget* is used to acquire resources, that is, to request funds from administrators or other funding sources. It may entail either justification of the existing budget levels or substantiation of requests for new funding.

The *operating budget* is prepared after the library's appropriation is known. The operating budget suballocates the library's total appropriation to the various departments and programs and represents a plan for the budget year.

The *cash budget* describes the cash receipts and disbursements that are expected to occur as a result of the planned operations. It identifies the cash flow needs over the period of the budget.

The *capital budget* enumerates capital expenditures that will be needed over and above the operating budget.

Traditionally budgets are divided into *line items*, or specific types of expenses such as salaries and benefits, supplies and equipment, subcontracting, and so on, for the library as a whole. Line-item budgets are easy to prepare and understand, and it is easy to account for expenditures within categories. However, simple line-item budgets do not represent the programs or goals of the library in budgetary terms, nor do they allow for easy monitoring of the performance of individual units. Since the entire budget is allocated to the entire library, there is little or no ability to assure the cost-effectiveness or efficiency of individual units or functions, and it is difficult to provide incremental strengthening of the budget of any particular program.

Because of the deficiencies of line-item budgets, various types of *program budgets* have been developed over the past quarter of a century. Program budgets of all types focus on the major programs or objectives of an organization and allocate funds to these programs at a level commensurate with the service objectives to be accomplished. In a program budget, the budget of each program can be suballocated by types of expense, similar to a line-item budget in monitoring expenditures, and also provide the advantages of focusing on individual programs and priorities, monitoring their budget performance and goal attainment, and demonstrating the balance between various programs in budgetary terms. Because the program budget explicitly requires goal setting, performance planning, and financial planning, it communicates much more about the library than does a line-item budget. The program budget clearly expresses the library's goals and objectives and the budgetary plans for attaining them.

The *performance budget* carries program budgeting to the next logical step by also addressing in concrete, measurable terms the output results to be achieved through the implementation of the programs funded by the budget. The performance budget describes the efficiency and effectiveness of the various categories of program expenditures. When the budget is planned, measures of work must also be adopted so that costs standards can be applied to each unit and to each activity or program. In technical services, output measures might be the number of orders prepared, the number of titles catalogued, the number of serial issues checked in, or the number of serial volumes bound. Performance budgets help establish specific, often numerical, performance goals and efficiency standards for each program, department, or unit. A performance budget also makes the controlling and accountability processes easier by making them explicitly measurable.

A *planning-programming budgeting system* (PPBS) combines many of the techniques used in program and performance budgets. Although this technique of budgeting is not now used as often as in recent decades, many of the concepts and techniques are valuable to managers using other types of budgeting systems. The intent of PPBS is to integrate organizational planning and goal setting, determination of specific objectives to meet the goals established, and budgeting of the resources to achieve the objectives. Goals for various programs and departments are set, priorities assigned, and performance measures established. Alternative programs and objectives are identified and their costs thoroughly developed; these various alternatives are then weighed in various combinations in order to identify the most cost-beneficial set of alternatives. Results of the planning and budget are then monitored to ensure that the planned objectives are accomplished. The primary benefits of PPBS result from setting goals and objectives and analyzing alternative courses of action.

Zero-based budgeting is seldom used in libraries. The zero-based budget begins with the assumption that the library's budget for the next year is zero. Each program, and each expenditure within each program, must be thoroughly justified by anticipated results. Therefore, any program, whether new or continuing, must be fully analyzed and justified each year. An advantage of zero-based budgeting is that it requires the library to redefine its goals regularly and to evaluate the success of each program. However, because of the work involved in justifying the entire budget each year, and because of the need for some assurance of the continuation of funding for basic programs, this type of budgeting has fallen out of favor in recent years.

THE BUDGET CYCLE

Certain tasks must be accomplished no matter which type of budgeting system a library uses. Usually, a library manager is dealing with several planning and budgeting time frames at once. The long-range plan for the library and its programs is always on the back of his or her mind. For example, does a particular program have a definite or an indefinite life? Will the need to acquire electronic data resources for the library's collection be a continuing program? Is the online catalogue a new program that will continue indefinitely? Second is an intermediate planning span. Will retrospective conversion be completed within the next five years? Can a particular cataloguing backlog be eliminated within the next seven years? Third is a short-range planning horizon, within the range of one to three budget years. Finally, the annual budget covers a one-year period, and establishes allocations for programs in all three planning horizons.

The budget should not be seen as a single document, fixed in time, but rather as a continuing process. The library administration must establish a timetable which allows all managers to participate in formulating, allocating, and monitoring the budget. In general, the budget process for a given year begins more than six months before the start of the year. At that time, decisions are made regarding the rest of the timetable, the format to be used for requests and documentation, and guidelines for planning. At the outset of the budget process, the upper levels of the library administration should explain to managers the constraint and opportunities they foresee and the general goals for achievement during the budget year. The upper-level library administrators may choose to impose budgets from above, essentially as directives to the departments, or they may adopt a participatory process involving managers and staff at lower levels in budget planning and preparation.

The participatory approach offers many advantages to the library. Through their participation, middle- and lower-level managers become more aware of the library's overall goals and the resource limitations with which it must deal. They are more likely to understand fully their own roles within the larger programs of the library, to share the values of the upper-level administrators, and to agree with the priorities of the library. Involving department heads in the budget process enables them to set departmental goals that are congruent with library-wide goals and to participate as team members with other department heads rather than as competitors. A participatory approach makes explicit the interrelationships between the work of various departments and the need to balance resource allocations among the departments in order to achieve the library's overall goals more efficiently and effectively. For example, the acquisition department's budget allocation must be related to the library materials budget, the catalogue department's budget related to the number of new titles to be acquired, the binding budget synchronized with the number of unbound serial issues and monographs received, and the automation budget adequate to pay for bibliographic records derived by the acquisition and catalogue departments from the bibliographic networks and loaded into the local online catalogue.

Once upper management has established its timetables and guidelines, and has articulated its budgeting assumptions, the department heads can proceed to prepare their budget requests for the next fiscal year. Depending on local policies and practice, this request may be incremental, building on previous budget allocations in light of anticipated changes in expenditure rates or program priorities; developed from a formula given known or anticipated activity levels in the program; or a zero-based-budget request. Agreement between the department heads and the upper library administration on the programmatic goals of each department should precede formulation of the individual departmental budget requests.

After the departmental budget requests have been completed, they may be presented to the other department heads in formal or informal hearings. This process enables each department head to become familiar with the programmatic goals and needs of each of the other departments and to understand better the library-wide context of his or her own department.

Next, upper management, possibly with representation from the departments, reviews the departmental budget requests. Their review results in an assessment of the total budgetary needs of the library, given existing programmatic goals. They scrutinize the individual requests in light of expected revenues, the cost-effectiveness of each program, and the desired programmatic balance for the library. When anticipated revenues fall short of the aggregate requests, programmatic goals may be revised, or additional revenue sources identified to bring the budget into balance.

After upper management has completed its allocation process, the results are communicated to other managers and the library staff. The communication of the library's goals as reflected in the budget plan is important in building a common understanding of the directions management at all levels of the library are expected to take during the upcoming year. Unless the staff fully understand the budgetary constraints under which the administration is working and the library-wide goals it hopes to achieve, they will view the participatory budgetary process with cynicism and will not consent to the priorities established.

At least once during the budget year, the initial allocations to departments and programs should be reviewed in light of revised revenue projections, other changes in environmental conditions, or desired modifications to programs. The mid-year budget review cycle although less time-consuming than the initial budget process should also be participatory. It requires that department heads and top management review the performance of the individual units formally in terms both of output and expenditures. It also allows them to learn how well the library as a whole is meeting its goals and to contribute to modifications in the program or budget that will lead to improved performance of the whole. It also provides a final, formal library-wide opportunity to ensure that budgetary targets and programmatic goals for the next year are met.

IMPLEMENTING A PARTICIPATORY BUDGETARY PROCESS

To be most effective, a participatory budgetary process must give department heads responsibility for, and control over, their individual budgets commensurate with the programmatic control given to them. They should be expected to monitor expenditures and productivity at least monthly to see that they are on target. When actual output measures or expenditure levels differ from those expected, the department head should take action to bring them into line. Actions to be taken might include such measures as improving productivity, reducing expenditures, and expanding or contracting programmatic goals.

The department head and upper administration should be able to distinguish between two types of deviation from the budget plan. One cause of a variation from the plan is an inaccurate expenditure projection. This type of error can usually be corrected in the subsequent year's budget process, but can wreak havoc during the year in which it occurs. The second type of deviation is caused by a lack of control over expenditures or performance of objectives. When this latter type of variation from the budget and/or performance plan occurs, the department head should take action to bring expenditures and productivity into accordance with the plan. Department heads should be evaluated on their ability to project accurate budget needs to achieve the agreed-upon programmatic plan and to take corrective action regularly during the budget year to ensure that the plan is executed within the budget available. Reward systems for managers should take into account their success in budgeting for their departments.

TRENDS IN TECHNICAL SERVICES BUDGETING

Until recently, technical service budgets in libraries were incorporated into the library's whole budget, and not managed separately. While there was a great deal in the literature about the *costs* of technical services, and interest in *controlling* those costs, delegation of direct budgetary responsibility and authority to directors of technical services was rare. Even rarer still was delegation to department heads. The failure to delegate budgetary responsibility and authority was due in part to a traditional, hierarchical management belief that budgetary control was the prerogative of the director of the library only, and in part to the lack of internal budgeting and reporting systems that could be used to delegate budget management to lower levels of the organization in an efficient manner. More modern concepts of organizational management coupled with automated internal budgeting systems are gradually resulting in delegation of major responsibility for budgeting to ever lower levels of the library hierarchy. The delegation of this responsibility and authority has had the effect of making library managers more accountable for the results produced by their units and of ensuring that those results are produced as cost-effectively as possible. It also leads to greater common understanding among department heads and staff of the goals and objectives of the library programs and generates more widespread appreciation for the constraints faced by upper management when presented with budgetary allocations that are insufficient to fulfill all desirable service goals.

As library technical service managers become more cognizant of the costs of their operations, and of the costs of alternative ways of producing the desired work, several budgeting trends gradually emerge. These include movement from the funding of labor-intensive methods of production to automated modes, increased use of subcontractors for certain types of operations, and heightened reliance on cooperative programs. In addition, preservation has begun to receive a higher budgeting priority than in the past, and libraries have begun intensive efforts to raise external funds. These trends are summarized below.

The implementation of automation results in a shift of budgets from operational categories such as the personnel and supply lines to capital, equipment, and subscription lines. For example, libraries that have implemented OCLC have frequently paid for the online services of that network and for the tape records of local cataloguing derived from its resource base by leaving open certain technical services staff lines and recovering those budgetary allocations originally made to the personnel budget. Other shifts in the budget are required to pay for the initial purchase of the equipment and for equipment replacement. Since capital budgets are frequently inadequate to pay for purchase and installation of local library systems in a single year, many libraries have resorted to financing of the capital and equipment costs over several years, thereby effectively converting these costs into operating costs instead of capital costs. Modern computer equipment has an expected life span of three to five years, and, although many libraries keep equipment in service for much longer periods of time, the library must provide an organized and systematic method for regular equipment replacement in its budget. If an equipment replacement program is not funded and implemented, the library runs the risk of eventually having a technically obsolete system which could be prohibitively expensive to replace.

As personnel budgets rise, and as the costs of managing operations within the library rise, vendors have entered the marketplace, providing on a contract, or fee-for-service basis services that libraries once carried out internally. Examples include vendors that provide approval plans for acquisitions, eliminating the need for the library to select items from publishers' lists and bibliographies, place individual direct orders, claim unreceived materials, and pay invoices for each title received; serial jobbers that place and maintain subscriptions, issue claims, and provide consolidated invoices; cataloguing agencies that provide machine-readable records for new acquisitions or from old card catalog records; and many other types of contractors.

The use of bibliographic networks has also had a major impact on technical service budgets. The use of online shared cataloguing has reduced the need for original cataloguers in many libraries and engendered both a rise in the numbers of clerical support staff and development of new paraprofessional staff series. The personnel budgets of technical services have, therefore, seen movement from the professional staff lines to other staff lines, and this shift in budget has occurred in concert with rising staff productivity attributable to the use of the resource databases of the networks.

Another trend has been toward increased funding of preservation programs, at least in large or specialized libraries. Not only are libraries more attuned to the needs to preserve their own collections (collections that represent huge capital resources accumulated over decades or even centuries), but also to cooperate with one another in preserving the nation's information resources in the aggregate. The focus on preservation has meant that new sources of funding have to be found: to train and hire conservators of circulating as well as rare materials; to renovate the physical plant to provide for conservation laboratory space; and to fund equipment for microfilming, photocopy replacement, or contract services. When incremental funding cannot be found from the library's institutional funding source, internal library budgets must be reprogrammed to carry out this new function, or external sources for revenue found and tapped.

Finally, libraries are recognizing increasingly that institutional funds will never be sufficient to carry out the entire range of continuing and one-time programs necessary to provide excellent service to the clientele. To fill the gap between the service needs identified and the funding available, libraries are engaging in various types of fund-raising. For example, the federal government has provided funds through such programs as the Department of Education's Title II-C program; the National Endowment for the Humanities' Challenge Grant, Access, and Preservation programs; and the Library Services and Construction Act (LSCA). Most of these programs require that the library contribute institutional funds as a condition for receiving federal funds, but they can be used to provide the margin of excellence that cannot be supported through the regular budget.

In addition, many libraries have established fund-raising, or development programs that tap the resources of the community, corporate philanthropy, or foundations. These programs require a commitment of start-up funds and may not pay off for some years. In the long run, however, they can provide annual supplements to the operating budget, as well as steady continuing support through the establishment of endowments.

CONCLUSION

A sophisticated understanding of budgeting principles and practices is important to any technical services librarian, but especially to the manager, because the budget reflects the library's service priorities, is used to define and fund its programs, and is a tool to judge individual departmental, and library-wide effectiveness in carrying out its mission. Understanding the budget allows one to redirect resources to establish new programs, strengthen existing programs, and use external funds most effectively.

FURTHER READINGS

Conners, Tracy D. and Christopher T. Callaghan. Financial management for nonprofit organizations. New York: American Management Association, 1982

Cummings, Martin M. Economics of research libraries. Washington, DC: Council on Library Resources, 1986

Getz, Malcolm and Doug Phelps. Labor costs in the technical operation of three research libraries. *Journal of academic librarianship* 10:209-219 (Sept. 1984)

Hayes, Robert M. The management of library resources: the balance between capital and staff in providing services. *Library research* 1, no. 2: 119-142 (1979)

Lancaster, F. W. The measurement and evaluation of library services. Washington, DC: Information Resources Press, 1977

Leimkuhler, Ferdinand F. and Michael D. Cooper. Cost accounting and analysis for university libraries. *College and research libraries* 32, no. 6:449-464 (Nov. 1971)

Martin, Murray S. Budgetary control in academic libraries. Greenwich, CT: JAI Press, 1978

Martin, Murray S. Budgetary strategies: coping with a changing fiscal environment. *Journal of academic librarianship* 2:297-302 (Jan. 1977)

Martin, Murray S. Cost benefit analysis for austerity. *In* Austerity management in academic libraries/ ed. by John F. Harvey and Peter Spyers-Duran. Metuchen, NJ: Scarecrow Press, 1984

Shirk, Gary M. Financing new technologies, equipment/furniture replacement and building renovation: a survey report. *College and research libraries* 45:462-470 (Nov. 1984)

Young, Harold Chester. Planning, programming, budgeting systems in academic libraries. Detroit, MI: Gale Research, 1974

Zaltman, Gerald, *ed.* Management principles for nonprofit agencies and organizations. New York: American Management Association, 1979

Postscriptum

TECHNICAL SERVICES TOMORROW

MICHAEL GORMAN

The essays in this volume have demonstrated that the activities that make up technical services are alive and thriving. There is little or no doubt that those activities will be pursued in libraries for the foreseeable future. Some writers on the topic have confused questions about how technical services functions are organized with questions about the viability of those functions themselves. To take an obvious example, cataloguing is still cataloguing whether it is carried out in a traditional cataloguing department, a decentralized "holistic" library, or at home as part of a computerized cottage industry. Unless one is a proponent of the dream or nightmare of the totally electronic library, can it be doubted that the acquiring and cataloguing of the range of library materials will go on for, at least, decades? Can it be doubted that those materials will need to be stored and preserved, or that we will need to provide access to them?

The future of librarianship as a whole lies in the application of enduring principles of service to changing circumstances. We must rediscover and reaffirm those principles and devise ways in which they can be applied with efficiency and effectiveness. The mission of the technical services librarian is to make sure that carriers of knowledge and information of all kinds are acquired, organized, made accessible, preserved, and circulated with minimal time and expense. Underlying our mission is a basic assumption that the connection between library users and the knowledge and information that they seek is of great benefit to the individuals and to society. Therefore, anything that makes that connection cost-effectively is good and anything that hinders cost-effectiveness is bad.

We live in times that are neither completely utilitarian nor conducive to idealism. The utilitarian spirit is one that seeks the greatest good of the greatest number. It does not bother with idealism or romance but neither is it interested in humbug. Its robust practicality and single-minded pursuit of the greater good would be of great benefit to the intensely practical world of technical services. That practicality, though, if not based on ideals, becomes sterile. One has to have a sense of the greater good before one can pursue it by practical means. The idealism that lies in the heart of every true librarian is passionate in its commitment to freedom of enquiry, to the belief that a knowledgeable and informed society would be a transcendent good, to the equality of humankind, and to the central role of the library in the progress of humanity. It seems to me that we could evolve a new librarianship based on an ethic that is utilitarian without being mean-spirited or crass, and that is idealistic without being foolish or weak. The technical processes in libraries can be an important part of that new librarianship, but only if they are perceived as being important means to a lofty end. Libraries are not *about* computers, information services, the processing of materials — these things are tools and methods that we use to achieve important results. It is quite possible to become so entranced with the tools and methods that we forget the purposes for which we use them.

The future of technical services, and of librarianship as a whole, lies in keeping our eyes on the mission of libraries and adapting our tools and methods in the light of modern technology. We should not be afraid to abandon established methods and procedures simply because they are established. Nor should we be afraid to adapt old methods to new circumstances. Electronic online bibliographic systems are better than card catalogues and all the other paper files not because computers are inherently better than cards but because they have much greater potential for service than the card files could ever offer. Technomania and technophobia are equally foolish; someone besotted with computers is just as dangerous to the future of libraries as any Luddite. The first key to successful services in the future, then, lies in the judicious use of modern technology to advance our continuing purpose.

Technical services (under that or any other name) will change as the kinds of material with which libraries are concerned change. In the library of today and tomorrow with books, microforms, maps, manuscripts, sound recordings, CD-ROM machines, computer terminals of all kinds, collections of videodiscs, computer software, holograms, and optical archives, there will still be a need for speedy and efficient acquisition, organization for access, preservation, and circulation control. The methods may well change. Who knows, for example, what the bibliographic network of 2001 will look like and what its services will be? Who knows exactly how the scholar, student, or casual library user will use the libraries of the next millennium? Absent a cultural cataclysm, however, we know that there will be libraries, that they will contain all the things listed above and more, and that the role of the librarian will include some version, changed in details but not in essence, of work in what we now call technical services.

The future lies, as ever, with those who seize it. This is not a time for the technical services librarian to be fearful or self-deprecating. The skills that we have in acquisitions, serials control, cataloguing, preservation, circulation, and special collections will stand us in good stead if we are conscious of their value. For a librarian to acquire or catalogue or preserve a carrier of knowledge and information is a good thing whether that carrier is a book or a piece of computer software. To enable the users of the library to have access to, and benefit from, that carrier of knowledge and information is to advance the cause of culture and civilization. We should not be afraid of acquiring new skills or extending old skills, we should not be afraid of adapting our methods to match new realities, and we should certainly not be afraid that our professional skills will ever be found wanting, no matter what marvels or horrors technology may wreak.

The intricate structures of bibliographic control are the intellectual playgrounds of the technical services librarian. They will continue to be so — to our benefit and to the benefit of library users—if we allow them to be adapted and modified as times and methods change. Technical services librarians are pragmatic idealists or they are nothing. We have to know the price *and* the value of everything in the library and strive, somehow, to reconcile the two. In the process we must never let our pragmatism sour our idealism or our idealism divorce us from reality.

Index

AAASS. *See* American Association for the Advancement of Slavic Studies
AACR. *See Anglo-American Cataloguing Rules*
AACR2. *See Anglo-American Cataloguing Rules, Second Edition*
Abbey Newsletter, 107
Abel, Richard, 15
Academic and research libraries, 26, 31, 99, 144-45, 151
  acquisitions, 11, 16, 18-19
  exchange and gift operations, 23-27
  online cataloguing, 157-69
  preservation of materials, 105-29
Access points, 63-64, 66, 86, 96. *See also* Authority files
  automated keyword searching, 77, 88-89, 157, 162
  copy cataloguing, 99
  form of entry, 69-70
  LC NAF standardization, 87-88
  names, 67-68
  online cataloguing, 90-91, 162-63
  subject cataloguing, 74-77
  titles, 68
Accounting. *See* Budgeting and finance
Acid-free paper. *See* Paper deterioration
ACLIS. *See* American Council of Learned Societies
Acquisition of Library Materials, 8, 9
Acquisitions, 173
  automated systems, 12-13, 157-59
  bibliographic searching, 8
  book gathering plans, 15-22
  book review services, 21
  budgeting and finance, 9-10, 12, 16-17, 20, 50-62
  future trends, 12-13
  gifts and exchanges, 23-37
  ordering, claiming, and receipt of materials, 7-14
  organization, 10-11
  serial publications, 38-49
  Slavic and East European language collections, 131-34
  staffing, 11-12
Acquisitions Librarian, 12
Adams, Randolph G., 105
Administration, 4
  budgeting and finance, 184-93
  client-centered approach, 178
  coordination of work flow, 173-75
  decentralization, 180-81
  efficiency or effectiveness, 176-77
  exchange partnerships, 25-26
  format-based approach, 10-11
  functional approach, 10, 171-73, 175-76
  future trends, 176-81
  gifts, 28
  subject approach, 172
ADONIS, 44
Africana microfilming project, 109
ALA. *See* American Library Association

Alley, Brian, 51
American Association for the Advance-
    ment of Slavic Studies (AAASS), 140
American Council of Learned Societies
    (ACLIS), 138
American Institute for Conservation, 106
American Library Association (ALA), 21,
    34, 40, 106, 109, 140, 172
American Library Association Midwinter
    Conference, 30-31
American Library Association Slavic and
    East European Section, 136
American Philological Association, 109
American Theological Library Associa-
    tion, 109
Anderson, Paul M., 143
Andrew W. Mellon Foundation, 106
Anglo-American Cataloguing Rules
    (AACR), 65, 68
Anglo-American Cataloguing Rules,
    Second Edition (AACR2), 64, 66,
    68-70, 77, 89, 98, 119, 137, 139, 160
Approval book gathering plan, 15-18
ARL. See Association of Research
    Libraries
ARL SPEC-kit survey, 29
Armenian script, 133
Ash, Lee, 117
Association for Library Collections and
    Technical Services, 172
Association of Research Libraries (ARL),
    29, 31, 43, 106-7, 109, 114-15, 121
Astle, Deana, 40
Auld, Lawrence W. S., 51
Authority control, 86-87, 98-99, 157, 162
Authority files, 69-70, 81, 88-89, 92-94,
    96-97, 101, 159-62. See also Access
    points
Authority records, 70, 86, 90, 92-94,
    138-39. See also References
Authority work, 87, 93-94, 98-99, 157,
    159, 162
    defined, 86, 89
    online catalogs, 88-92
"Authority Work, Authority Records, and
    Authority Files," 64
Authorship, 68
Automated systems, 3. See also Integrated
    library systems (ILS); Microcompu-
    ters (PCs); Online cataloguing sys-
    tems; Online circulation systems;
    Online information retrieval systems
    acquisitions, 12-13, 157-59
    authority work, 88-92
    bibliographic networks, 96-99

Boolean operations, 78
    budgeting for, 191
    call number searching, 82
    cataloguing systems, 76-79, 97-98, 157-69
    circulation systems, 143-56
    classification, 80-83
    collection development, 158
    gifts and exchanges, 30-31
    information resources budget, 57-58
    keyword searching, 77, 88-91
    serial publications, 38-39, 42-47, 97
    staff training and adjustment, 151-54
    standardization, 88-92
Automatic switching, 78

Backlogs, 138-39
Baker & Taylor, 96
BALLOTS, 97
Banks, Paul, 107
Bar-codes, 46, 150
Barker, Joseph W., 23
Barr, Pelham, 105
Barrow, William J., 108
Barter exchange. See Exchange partner-
    ships, barter
Bibliographic control, 63-104
Bibliographic description, 64
    defined, 63
    standardization, 65-67
Bibliographic networks, 96-97, 101-3
    authority control, 86-87, 98-99
    defined, 95
    economics, 99-100
Bibliographic searching, 8
Bibliographic utilities. See Bibliographic
    networks
Bibliography, Information Retrieval, and
    Documentation Committee (BIRD),
    138
Bibliography of Co-operative Cataloguing
    and Printing of Catalogue Cards
    with Incidental References to Inter-
    national Bibliography and the Uni-
    versal Catalogue (1850-1902), 96
Biblioteka Narodowa, 133
Binding and maintenance of materials.
    See Preservation
Binding Institute, 118
BIRD. See Bibliography, Information
    Retrieval, and Documentation Com-
    mittee
BISAC. See Book Industry Systems
    Advisory Committee
Blackwell North America, 162

Blanket order book gathering plan, 15, 18-19
Bleil, Leslie A., 95
BNA, 96
Bonk, Sharon C., 43
Book gathering plans, 22
  approval plan, 15-18
  blanket order plan, 15, 18-19
  book review services, 21
  and collection development, 20-21
  economics, 20
  new proposal, 19-21
  role of vendors, 20-21
Book Industry Systems Advisory Committee (BISAC), 12
Book review services, 21
Book vendors. *See* Vendors
Bookkeeper Process, 110-11, 120
Books in Print, 8, 132, 144
Booksellers. *See* Vendors
Boolean operators, 157
Boss, Richard W., 13, 148
British Museum, 67
Brittle Books, 113
Brittle books program, 113-14. *See also* Preservation
Brodart, 96
Brodart's Sysdac Mark III, 145
Brown, Norman B., 105
Budgeting and finance, 184, 193. *See also* Economic considerations;
  acquisitions, 9-10, 12, 16-17, 20
  fund-raising, 192
  future trends, 190-92
  for materials, 50-62
  participatory approach, 188-90
  purpose of, 185-86
  types of budgets, 50, 186-88
Burger, Robert H. 139
Business Index, 76

Call number searching, 82
Camp, John, 148
Cancellation of book orders, 9-10
Capital budget, 186
Cargill, Jennifer, 43, 50
CARL system, 166
Cash budget, 186
Catalogue card headings. *See* Access points
Catalogue maintenance. *See* File maintenance
Cataloguing, 12, 86-94, 119. *See also* Copy cataloguing; Descriptive cataloguing; Online cataloguing systems; Subject cataloguing and classification

coordination with acquisitions, 173-75
levels, 95
NACO program, 138-39
NCCP program, 139
and public services, 179
Slavic and East European language collections, 135-39
Cataloguing codes, 64-65, 67-68
Cataloguing in Publication (CIP), 101
Cataloguing Service Bulletin 6, 138
CD-ROM, 51, 159, 165
Chan, Lois Mai, 5, 74
Charbonneau, Gary, 102
CIP. *See* Cataloguing in Publication
Circulation services, 156-57
  automated systems, 146-55
  keypunch cards, 146
  manual files, 145-46
  nonreturn materials, 143-44
  not-on-shelf materials, 143-44
CL Systems, Inc., 146
Classification systems, 74-75, 83-85. *See also* Dewey Decimal classification (DDC); Library of Congress classification (LCC)
  enhanced vocabulary, 80-81
  online subject browsing, 81-82
  Slavic and East European language collections, 136
Client-centered approach to library administration, 178
Cline, Hugh F., 154
CLR. *See* Council on Library Resources
CLSI, 146
Cochrane, Pauline Atherton, 80
Collection Analysis Project, 107
Collection development, 7, 12, 15
  book gathering plans, 20-21
  copy cataloguing, 102
  gifts and exchanges, 26, 28
  online catalogues, 158
Collections of record, 117
Columbia's Rare Book School, 107
Commission on Preservation and Access, 113
Committee on the Preservation of Research Library Materials, 106
Computers. *See* Automated systems; Microcomputers
Conference on Access to Slavic Materials in North American Libraries, 138
CONSER. *See* Cooperative Online Serials
Conservation Administration News, 107
Consumer Price Index, 41
Converting to automated systems, 161-62

Cooperative cataloguing. *See* Copy cataloguing
Cooperative Online Serials (CONSER), 97
Cooperative Preservation Microfilming Project (CPMP), 109-10
Copy cataloguing, 159
  and bibliographic networks, 95-103
  economics, 99-100
  Library of Congress, 100-101
  quality control, 98-99
Copyright Clearance Center, 46
Council on Library Resources (CLR), 76
Coyle, Kevin, 15
CPMP. *See* Cooperative Preservation Microfilming Project
CRL Foreign Newspaper Microfilming Project, 109
Cross-catalog consistency, 87
Cross-references. *See* References
Cummings' survey, 113
Cumulative Book Index, 76
Cunha, George M., 111, 120
Cutter, Charles Ammi, 64, 68, 72, 75, 86, 92
Cyrillic script, 130-31, 133
Czech language collections. *See* Slavic and East European language collections

DataPhase, 147
DDC. *See* Dewey Decimal classification
DDC Online Project, 80-82
De Gennaro, Richard, 39
Deacidification, 108, 134
  Bookkeeper Process, 110-11, 120
  Diethylzinc Process, 110-11, 120
  Wei T'o System, 110-11, 120
Department of Education's Title II-C program, 192
Derthick, Jan, 43
Descriptive cataloguing, 73
  access points, 63-64, 67-69
  authority files, 69-70
  bibliographic description, 63-67
  defined, 63
  MARC formats, 70-72
  nonbook material, 65-67
  Slavic and East European language collections, 137-39
  standardization, 65-67
  superimposition, 138
Dewey Decimal classification (DDC), 74-75, 80-82
DEZ. *See* Library of Congress's Diethylzinc Process

DIALOG, 76
Documents, 44
Donations. *See* Gifts
Donor files, 27

Eastern Washington University, 152
EBSCO, 43, 46
EBSCONET, 43
Economic considerations. *See also* Budgeting and finance
  copy cataloguing, 99-100
  exchange partnerships, 33-35
  serial publications, 39-41
  Slavic and East European language collections, 134
Education Index, 76
Educational Resources Information Center (ERIC), 79
Ekonomika, 139
Electronic publishing, 166-67
Enhance program, 97
Epstein, Susan Baerg, 143
ERIC. *See* Educational Resources Information Center
"Escalating Journal Prices," 39
Exchange partnerships, 23, 36-37
  automated systems, 30-31, 33
  barter, 25
  blanket exchanges, 24
  economics, 26, 33-35
  future trends, 29-31
  monographs, 24
  organization and staffing, 25-26
  policies, 31-33
  serial publications, 24

Fast cataloguing. *See* Copy cataloguing
Faxon company, 39, 41-44, 46
Fayen, Emily Gallup, 147
File maintenance, 9, 91-92, 160-61
Finance. *See* Budgeting and finance; Economic considerations
Finansy i statistika, 139
Fine, Sara, 154
Ford, Stephen, 8-9
Foreign publishers, 40-41, 139
Forest Press, 80
Format-based approach to library organization, 10-11
Freedman, Maurice, J., 146
Freeman, Robert R., 80
Functional approach to library organization, 10, 171-73, 175-76
Futas, Elizabeth, 31

Future trends, 195-97
  acquisitions, 12-13, 19-21
  administration, 176-81
  budgeting and finance, 190-92
  cataloguing, 70-72, 101-3, 161-67
  gifts and exchanges, 29-35
  preservation, 114-22
  serial publications, 39-41, 44-47
  Slavic and East European language
    collections, 139-40

Gapen, D. Kaye, 171
Gaylord, 96
Gaylord's Model C Book Charger, 145
GEAC, 46, 147
General ISBD, 66
Georgian script, 133
Gifts, 26, 36-37
  automated systems, 31-32
  donor management, 27
  economics, 34-35
  future trends, 29-31
  organization, 28-29
  policies, 31-32
  tax laws, 27-28, 34
Gifts and exchanges. *See* Exchange partner-
    ships; Gifts
Glogoff, Stuart, 153
Gorman, Michael, 1, 45, 66, 195
Government Printing Office (GPO), 88
GPO. *See* Government Printing Office

H. W. Wilson Foundation, 113
Hamaker, Charles, 40
Harvard University, 139-40, 145
Hayes' study, 113
Haykin, David Judson, 75
Headings. *See* Access points
Hickey, D., 175
Historical Price Analysis Report, 43
Hodges, Theodora, 74
Hollerith cards, 146
Horney, Karen L., 152
Houbeck, Robert L., 41

IFLA, 66
ILS. *See* Integrated library systems
IMCE. *See* International Meeting of Cata-
    loguing Experts
Immroth, John Philip, 81
Indiana University, 102, 139
Information on Demand, Inc., 44

Information resources budget, 50, 55,
    60-62
  accountability, 51-54
  automated systems, 51, 57
  staffing, 56-57
  statistics, reports and audits, 58-59
Information Systems Consultants, Inc., 44
Innovacq, 159
Innovative Interfaces, 46, 159
Integrated library systems (ILS), 148-49,
    151, 153, 174
Interfacing. *See* Library/vendor interfaces
International exchanges. *See* Exchange
    partnerships
International Meeting of Cataloguing
    Experts (IMCE), 66
*International Standard Bibliographic
    Description (ISBD)*, 64, 66, 71-72,
    98, 137
International Standard Serial Numbers
    (ISSNs), 101
International Standards Organisation
    (ISO), 64
ISBD. *See* International Standard Bib-
    liographic Description
ISO. *See* International Standards Organi-
    sation
ISSNs. *See* International Standard Serial
    Numbers
IUrid. lit., 139

Jamieson, Alexis, 90
Jewett, Charles C., 64
Journal publishing and pricing, 39-41

Kantor, Paul B., 113
Keypunch cards, 146
Keyword searching, 77, 88-91, 157, 162
Kilgour, Fred, 45
Kirtland, Monika, 77
Kniga, 139
Koppers Chemical Company, 110-11
Kovacic, Mark, 29, 31
Kruger, Betsy, 38
Kubon & Sagner, 132
Kultura, 132

Latin American microfilming project, 109
Laughrey, Edna, 15
Laws of Library Science, 1
LC NAF. *See* Library of Congress name
    authority file

LCC. *See* Library of Congress classification
LCSH. *See Library of Congress Subject
    Headings*
Leavis, Dr., 64
Legislative budget, 186
Leich, Harold, 136
Lennie, Michael, 43
Lenzini, Rebecca T., 42
Les Livres Étrangers, 132
Librarian's Guide to Serials, 42
Librarianship, 1, 4, 195-97
Library Acquisitions, 12
Library Binding Institute, 106
Library education and practice, 4-5
Library of Congress, 64-65, 70, 76, 95-96,
    100, 106-8, 138-39
  authority control, 98-99
  microfilming project, 109-10
  preservation, 110-12
Library of Congress authority files, 81,
    97, 159-62
Library of Congress classification (LCC),
    74-75, 80-82, 136
Library of Congress name authority file
    (LC NAF), 87-88, 90-91
*Library of Congress Subject Headings
    (LCSH)*, 74-83, 136-37
Library of Congress's Diethylzinc Process
    (DEZ), 110-11, 120
Library Services and Construction Act
    (LSCA), 192
Library Trends, 106
Library/vendor interfaces, 46
LIBRIS, 8
LIBS 100 automated circulation system,
    146
Line-item budgets, 50, 186-87
Linked Systems Project (LSP), 88, 95
LINX, 43-44
Lockman, Edward J., 15
Lotus 1-2-3, 57
Lowry, Charles B., 153
LSCA. *See* Library Services and Construc-
    tion Act
LSP. *See* Linked Systems Project
Lump-sum budgets, 50

Machine Readable Cataloguing (MARC),
    63-64, 68, 70-72, 76, 78-79, 88-89,
    91-92, 95-98, 101, 138-39, 159,
    162-63
Magazine Index, 76
Main entry. *See* Access points
MAPS. *See* Mid-Atlantic Preservation
    Service

Manual files, 145-46
MARC. *See* Machine Readable Cataloguing
MARC Cataloguing Distribution Service,
    110
Market approach to library administration.
    See Client-centered approach to
    library administration
Markey, Karen, 80
Materials budget. *See* Information
    resources budget
McBee Key-Sort System, 145
McDonald, Thomas, F., 154
McQueen, Judy, 148
Melcher, Daniel, 8
Melcher on Acquisition, 8
MELVYL, 88-91
MeSH. *See* National Library of Medi-
    cine's medical subject headings
Mezh. otosheniia, 139
Microcomputers (PCs), 30-32, 92, 140,
    163-65
  information resources budget, 51
  serial publications, 45-46
Microfilming, 109-10, 112-13, 117-20, 134,
    145
Microlinx, 46
Mid-Atlantic Preservation Service (MAPS),
    110, 114, 118
Monographs, 10-11, 24
Moran, Barbara B., 43
Mysl', 139

NACO. *See* Name Authority Coopera-
    tive project
Name Authority Cooperative project
    (NACO), 88, 138-39
Name Authority Records (NARs), 138-39
NARs. *See* Name Authority Records
National Advisory Council on Preserva-
    tion, 113
National Coordinated Cataloguing Opera-
    tions (NCCO), 101
National Coordinated Cataloging Program
    (NCCP), 101, 137-39
National Endowment for the Humanities'
    Challenge Grant, Access, and Pre-
    servation programs, 192
National Endowment of the Humanities
    (NEH), 106, 109, 113, 121
National Institute for Occupational Safety
    and Health (NIOSH), 152
National Institute for the Conservation of
    Cultural Property, 106
National Library and Public Archives of
    Canada, 110

National Library of Medicine's medical subject headings (MeSH), 79
National Newspaper Index, 76
National Preservation News, 107
National Register of Microform Masters (NRMM), 110, 119
National Serials Data Program (NSDP), 101
National Union Catalog, 96, 100, 108, 112
NCCO. *See* National Coordinated Cataloging Operations
NCCP. *See* National Coordinated Cataloging Program
NEDCC. *See* Northeast Document Conservation Center
NEH. *See* National Endowment of the Humanities
New Serials Titles (NST), 101
New York Public Library, 107, 109
Newberry Library, 107
Nijhoff, 43
NIOSH. *See* National Institute for Occupational Safety and Health
Nonlibrary jobs, 4
Nonreturn materials, 143-44
Nonturnkey library systems, 147
Northeast Document Conservation Center (NEDCC), 110, 118
Northwestern University, 90
NOTIS, 46, 90, 147, 159
Not-on-shelf materials, 143-44
NRMM. *See National Register of Microform Masters*
NDSP. *See* National Serials Data Program
NST. *See New Serials Titles.*

OCLC. *See* Online Cooperative Library Center
Office of Management Services (OMS), 106-7
Office of Technology Assessment (OTA), 111
Ohio College Library Center, 96
OMS. *See* Office of Management Services
OMS SPEC kits, 107, 115
Online cataloguing systems. *See also* Automated systems
   academic and research libraries, 157-69
   access points, 90-91, 162-63
   acquisitions, 158-59
   collections development, 158
   converting to, 161-62
   copy cataloguing, 96-98
   electronic publishing, 166-67
   file maintenance, 91-92
   full text possibilities, 166

remote access, 163-65
transaction monitoring, 163
Online circulation systems, 146-49, 155-56. *See also* Automated systems
   bar codes, 46, 150
   staff training, 151-55
Online Cooperative Library Center (OCLC), 8, 21, 45, 71, 76, 80, 86-87, 96-97, 101, 110, 158-60, 191
Online information retrieval systems, 75, 80-82. *See also* Automated systems
Operating budget, 186
ORBIT, 76
Ordering, claiming and receipt of library materials, 7-14. *See also* Acquisitions
Organization. *See* Administration
OTA. *See* Office of Technology Assessment
Out-of-print materials, 26, 32

Panizzi, Anthony, 64, 67
Paper deterioration, 108-09. *See also* Preservation
Paris Principles, 66
Partnerships. *See* Exchange partnerships
Paul, Huibert, 10
PCs. *See* Microcomputers
Performance budgets, 187
Pergamon, 43
Peter Principle, 4
Policy for gifts and exchanges, 31-33
Polish language collections. *See* Slavic and East European language collections
Politizdat, 139
Potter, William Gray, 10, 157
PPBS. *See* Program Planning Budget Systems
Preorder searching. *See* Bibliographic searching
Preservation, 106, 123-29
   binding, 105, 118
   brittle books program, 113-14
   costs, 115, 191
   deacidification systems, 110-12, 120-22
   education, 107
   institutional programs, 114-16
   microfilming, 109-10, 112-13, 117-20, 134
   national strategy, 112-14
   paper deterioration, 108-12
   prevention, 117-18
   priorities, 116-17, 120-22
Preservation Manual, 110, 119
Preservation Microfilming, 119
Preservation Microfilming Committee, 106
Preservation Planning Program, 107, 115

Primary research material, 26
Princeton University, 110
Program Planning Budget Systems (PPBS), 50, 187
Public Services, 2, 175-76, 178-79, 181
PUBLINX, 43
Publishing. *See* Electronic publishing; Foreign publishers

R. R. Bowker, 42
Ramsey, Inez L., 51
Ramsey, Jackson E., 51
Ranganathan, S. R., 1
RDC. *See* Rules for Descriptive Cataloguing
References, 69-70, 74, 78, 89-91. *See also* Authority records
Reformatting. *See* Microfilming
Relative Index, 80
Renner, Charlene, 95
Research Libraries Group (RLG), 21, 97, 102, 106, 109-10, 117, 119
Research Libraries Information Network (RLIN), 76, 86, 96-97, 110, 158-60
Resources and Technical Services Committee, 12
Resources and Technical Services Division, 102, 172
Resources and Technical Services Division's Preservation of Library Materials and Reproduction of Library Materials Sections (ALA), 106
Resources Notebook, 107
Richmond, Phyllis A., 81
RIs. *See* Rules Interpretations
RLG. *See* Research Libraries Group
RLIN. *See* Research Libraries Information Network
Rose, Michael, 154-55
RTSD RS Gift and Exchange Discussion Group, 30, 32
Rules for Descriptive Cataloguing (RDC), 65
Rules Interpretations (RIs), 87
Runkle, Martin, 87
Russian language collections. *See* Slavic and East European language collections

SC350, 45
Schlachter, G., 178
Schmidt, Karen A., 7
SCOPE Report, 43
SCS. *See* Serials Control System

SDI. *See* Selective Dissemination of Information
Sears' List of Subject Headings, 74-75, 82
Selective Dissemination of Information (SDI), 82
Serbo-Croatian language collections. *See* Slavic and East European language collections
Serial publications, 10-11, 174
  acquisitions, 38-47
  automated systems, 38-39, 43, 45-46
  CONSER project, 97, 101
  copy cataloguing, 101
  economics, 34, 39-41
  exchange partnerships, 24-26
  journals, 39-41
  role of vendors, 38-39, 41-44
  Slavic and East European language collections, 131
Serials Control System (SCS), 30, 45
Serials Industry Systems Advisory Committee (SISAC), 12, 43
Shared cataloguing. *See* Copy cataloguing
Simpson, Charles W., 101
SISAC. *See* Serials Industry Systems Advisory Committee
SISAC machine-scannable bar-code format, 46
SISAC Test Report (1987), 46
Slavic and East European language collections, 130, 140-41
  acquisitions, 131-34
  cataloguing, 135-39
  classification, 136
  costs, 134
  preservation, 134
  recordkeeping, 133
Slavic and East European Section (ALA), 140
Slavic Librarians' Seminar, 140
Slavic Reference Service and Slavic Exchange Program, 140
"Slow Fires," 113, 121
Smith, G. Stevenson, 51
Social Sciences Index, 76
Society of American Archivists, 106
South Asian microfilming project, 109
Southeast Asian microfilming project, 109
Soviet and East European Studies conference, 140
Soviet publishers, 139
Spatz, Richard, 111
SPEC kits, 29, 31, 107, 115
Special collections, 26, 34
Staffing
  acquisitions, 11-12, 56-57

budgeting for, 191
training for automation, 151-54
Standardization
cataloguing, 65-67, 86-88, 97-98
serial publications, 46
Standing order book gathering plan. *See* Blanket order book gathering plan
Stanford University, 97
Stevenson, Marsha J., 143
Subject approach to library organization, 172
Subject Authority File, 76
Subject cataloguing and classification, 5 75-75, 84-85
automated systems, 76-83
Boolean operations, 78
call number searching, 82
keyword searching, 77
Subject Collections, 117
Subscription agencies. *See* Vendors
Swank, R. C., 172, 179
Swersey, Patricia, 51
Synonym operation. *See* Automatic switching

Tantalus, Inc., 139
Tauber, Maurice, xv-xvi
Tax laws and gifts, 27-28, 32, 34
Tax Reform Act (1984), 27, 31-32
Tax Reform Act (1986), 29, 34
Taylor, Arlene G., 89-90, 101
Taylor, David C., 39
Technical services, 1-5
Third World collections, 34
Thomas, Catharine M., 89-90
Thyden, Wayne, 42
Title II-C program, 192
Trinity College (Texas), 135
Turchyn, Andrew, 136
Turkic language collections. *See* Slavic and East European language collections
Turnkey library systems, 147

UBC. *See* Universal Bibliographic Control
UIUC. *See* University of Illinois at Urbana-Champaign
Ukrainian language collections. *See* Slavic and East European language collections
UNIMARC, 71
Union Catalog, 96
U.S. Newspaper Project, 109
Universal Bibliographic Control (UBC), 67

University Microfilms, 166
University Microfilms International, 134
University of California, 88-89, 139-40
University of Chicago, 106, 139
University of Illinois at Urbana-Champaign (UIUC), 88, 91, 133, 135, 139
University of Michigan, 41, 139
University of Texas, 139, 146
University of Toronto Library Automated Systems (UTLAS), 86, 96, 98, 159, 162
University of Washington, 135
User-oriented library services, 178-81
USMARC, 95
USMARC Format for Holdings and Location, 46-47
UTLAS. *See* University of Toronto Library Automated Systems

VDT. *See* Video display terminal
Vendors, 9-10, 13, 46, 96, 146-47, 162
book gathering plans, 15-21, 132
domestic vs. foreign, 42-43, 132-34
selection and evaluation, 41-44
serial publications, 38-39, 41-44
Victor Kamkin, Inc., 132
Video display terminal (VDT), 151-52
VisiCalc, 57

Wajenberg, Arnold S., 5, 64, 86
Washington State University, 100
Watson, M. R. 89
Wei T'o Nonaqueous Book Deacidification System, 110-11, 120
Wells, James H., 153
Western Library Network (WLN), 86, 89, 91, 96, 98, 159-60
Western Michigan University, 100
Western Ontario University, 90
Williams, Edwin, 108
Williams, Gordon R., 112
WILSONLINE, 76, 78
WLN. *See* Western Library Network

Yale collection condition survey, 108
Yale University, 139
Younger, Jennifer A., 171

ZBB. *See* Zero-based budgeting
Zero-based budgeting (ZBB), 50, 187-88
Zuboff, Shoshana, 154